Programming for System 7

Programming for System 7

Gary Little
Tim Swihart

Addison-Wesley Publishing Company, Inc.

Reading, Massachusetts   Menlo Park, California   New York
Don Mills, Ontario   Wokingham, England   Amsterdam   Bonn
Sydney   Singapore   Tokyo   Madrid   San Juan
Paris   Seoul   Milan   Mexico City   Taipei

Many of the designations used by manufacturers and sellers to distinguish their products are claimed as trademarks. Where those designations appear in this book, and Addison-Wesley was aware of a trademark claim, the designations have been printed in initial capital letters or all capital letters.

The authors and publishers have taken care in preparation of this book, but make no expressed or implied warranty of any kind and assume no responsibility for errors or omissions. No liability is assumed for incidental or consequential damages in connection with or arising out of the use of the information or programs contained herein.

Library of Congress Cataloging-in-Publication Data

Little, Gary B., 1954-
    Programming for System 7 / Gary Little, Tim Swihart.
      p. cm. -- (Macintosh inside out)
    Includes bibliographical references and index.
    ISBN 0-201-56770-9
    1. Macintosh (Computer)--Programming. 2. Operating systems
(Computers) 3. System 7. I. Swihart, Tim. II. Title.
III. Series.
QA76.8.M3L583 1991
005.265--dc20   91-18050
                                                      CIP

Cover design by Ronn Campisi
Set in 10-pt Palatino by Scot Graphics
Sponsoring Editor: Carole McClendon
Project Editors: Debbie McKenna and Joanne Clapp Fullagar
Technical Reviewer: Jim Luther

1 2 3 4 5 6 7 8 9-MW-9594939291
First printing, September 1991

For my two favorite Little people: my wife Pamela, and daughter Adrienne (GL)

To my wife Avery, for putting up with my very late nights and preoccupation with System 7 while I worked on this book (TS)

▶ Contents

Foreword by Scott Knaster

On May 13, 1991, Apple introduced Macintosh System 7, the culmination of the greatest software effort in Apple's history. There was so much stuff in System 7 that it took Apple three Worldwide Developers' Conferences to get it out the door. So far, it looks like all the hard work was worth it (this is especially easy for me to say, since I didn't have to do any of the work).

I'm running System 7, and you probably are, too. In fact, I started running a pre-release version of System 7 several months before it shipped, and I was the proverbial first one on my block to have it. Although I had to be very considerate of my System 6 neighbors when I printed (there was no way to avoid laser printer wars at that time, so every time I printed, the next unlucky System 6 user had to reset the printer), I really didn't want to think about going back to System 6.

System 7 provided Apple with a chance to give its users a bunch of great new stuff, and there's something in there for everyone. I love the way I'm in control of the Apple menu, and I can now really file things the way I want to, thanks to aliases. File Sharing is wonderful, especially at home, where I share a LocalTalk network with my wife (no more eye injuries from misplaced floppies tossed my way). There are a bunch of neat new things in the Finder, including a real live Find command!

I know that there have been third-party utilities available for years that do many of these things. I've used some of them, and I've even known some of the fine programmers who created them. When Apple builds these features into the official System and Finder, though, it's good for everyone, because all users get better goodies, while the hip developers can dream up even better new treasures.

I also know that Apple has published 70 or 80 or 1600 pages of programmer documentation on System 7, the well-known *Inside Macintosh*, Volume 6. This book is not that book. While Volume 6 is absolutely indispensible for doing real Macintosh programming, this book provides a friendly, spirited guide through many of the new features in System 7. From their well-placed cubicles hard by the mean streets of Cupertino, Gary and Tim give you incredibly valuable information, such as telling you fun new stuff about files, showing how to take advantage of balloon help, and pointing out why Apple events will change your life.

I hope you enjoy this guide to the secrets of System 7, and that your aliases always remain unbroken.

Scott Knaster
Macintosh Inside Out Series Editor

Preface

System 7 adds many new features to Macintosh system software, thereby justifying Apple's internal code name for the project—Big Bang. Many of these new features appear as improvements to the Finder that make it much easier for users to handle files, folders, and volumes. Digging into the underlying system, however, you will find several new software managers and many improvements to older managers; programmers can exploit these new managers to create more interesting and powerful applications than were possible with earlier versions of system software.

This book presents many of the important new System 7 features. Some of the more interesting topics we will cover are

- using **Gestalt** to check for system features
- using new routines in the File Manager
- using new routines in the Standard File Package
- cooperative multitasking and the Process Manager
- using Apple events to communicate between applications
- using the Communications Toolbox to quickly add advanced communications capabilities to your applications
- adding balloon help to your applications
- making applications and documents support new System Finder features

The book explains why new toolbox routines are important, when you're most likely to use them, and exactly how to call them. In many cases, sample code shows how to use the routines in the context of a real application.

Keep in mind, however, that this analysis is certainly not exhaustive—we do not cover every new toolbox routine and every new feature of System 7. For that, refer to Apple's definitive reference, *Inside Macintosh*, Volume VI. Instead, this book focuses on those routines you are apt to use most often.

This book is not for novice programmers. We expect that you already have some programming experience on the Macintosh and are reasonably familiar with how to construct simple applications. We will extend your core knowledge so that you become comfortable with implementing new System 7 functionality. If you need to develop your basic Macintosh programming skills, we recommend *Macintosh C Programming Primer*: Volume I by Dave Mark and Cartwright Reed.

The sample code in this book is in the THINK C language. THINK C is a very popular C development environment sold by Symantec Corporation. It is a particularly powerful environment to use when you're experimenting with new system features because it compiles and links very quickly and has an integrated symbolic debugger. If you're using Apple's MPW C, fear not—it should be easy to convert the THINK C code to the MPW C dialect.

We hope that by the time you finish reading this book you'll have a much better appreciation of System 7 and how to exploit it. You should then be well prepared to dive into your next project and create an application that captures the System 7 spirit.

In closing, we would both like to thank C.K. Haun and Jim Luther for taking the time to review early drafts of this manuscript. We especially appreciated C.K.'s insights into the operation of the Edition Manager.

Gary Little
Tim Swihart
August 1991

1 ▶ Preparing for System 7

System 7 introduces important new functionality to all members of the Macintosh family of computers having at least 2 Mb of RAM. This extra functionality results from the addition of new toolbox routines and managers, enhancements to existing toolbox routines, a powerful new Finder, and changes in the way files are organized and managed. In this book you will learn how to harness the power of System 7 to create applications that are much more versatile than anything you could write under System 6.x.

The System 7 advantage becomes obvious as soon as you boot up for the first time and start discovering the new features of the Finder. The presence of some of these features will influence the way you develop new applications for the Macintosh. Here are some examples:

Balloon Help—You can turn on balloon help by selecting the Show Balloons item in the Help menu on the right side of the menu bar. Once on, small balloons—like the ones you see in comic books—appear when you move the mouse over areas where menu names and items, window parts, icons, and other interesting objects appear. These balloons contain helpful information about the object below the mouse pointer. As you'll see in Chapter 8, you can use the Balloon Manager to add help balloons to objects unique to your own applications.

Director alias **Aliases**—You can create an alias file by clicking on a file (or folder) name, then selecting the Make Alias item in the File menu. The Finder creates an alias file using the same name as the original file with an 'alias' suffix, and the name is italicized. The alias file contains only the information the system needs to locate the original file, not the contents of the original file itself. When you open an alias file from the Finder, the Finder *resolves* the alias by locating the original file (the system can do this even if the file has been renamed, moved, or is located on a network file server), then opens the original file instead. By using alias files, you no longer have to remember the locations of your favorite documents or applications—simply create alias files for them, then put the aliases in a convenient location such as on the Finder desktop or in the Apple Menu folder in the System folder (so that they will appear in the Apple menu). Most applications you write won't have to resolve aliases because they will use the Standard File routines for opening files, which automatically resolve aliases. If your application does need to resolve an alias (perhaps because it saved an alias record in the resource fork of a document), it can do so using Alias Manager and File Manager routines that you will learn about in Chapter 2.

Color Icons —The Finder displays standard black-and-white icons, 4-bit color icons, or 8-bit color icons—both regular size (32x32) and small (16x16)—depending on the bit-depth of your video monitor. Like any good application developer, you should design your suite of icons first (with the ResEdit icon editor, for example) before writing a single line of code! (In reality, the T-shirts usually come first.)

Stationery Pads—If you click on the name of a document, then choose the Get Info item from the File menu, a window appears containing information about the document. In the lower right corner is a *Stationery Pad* check box. If you check this box, the document becomes a stationery pad and its icon changes to look like a pad of paper with a curled-up corner. A stationery pad resembles a regular document file but, by convention, an untitled copy of the pad must be made when the file is opened; that way, there is little danger of overwriting the pad or destroying the blank template it contains when the document is saved back to disk. If your application doesn't understand the concept of stationery pads, the user will see annoying warning dialogs when trying to open stationery pads. If your application knows how to handle stationery pads properly, its isStationeryAware flag in the 'SIZE' resource will be set and the aforementioned dialogs won't appear. (See Appendix B for a detailed description of the 'SIZE' resource of an application.)

Program Linking—If you click on the name of an application, then select the Sharing . . . item in the File menu, you will see a window with a check box called *Allow remote program linking*. If your application does not support high-level events, events that can be sent from program to program locally or across a network, this box will be dimmed and will not toggle. All System 7-compatible applications you write will be high-level event aware, and you'll learn how to satisfy the requirements in Chapter 4 when you learn about Apple events. (An Apple event is a high-level event that adheres to a well-defined data-exchange protocol.) If your application does know how to handle high-level events, its isHighLevelEventAware flag in the 'SIZE' resource will be set.

Of course, you can add to applications more System 7 features than the Finder indicates. As usual, *Inside Macintosh*, Volume VI is the definitive source for in-depth information on all System 7 topics.

Several other new system features of interest to programmers are the following:

- **Edition Manager**—lets applications share data dynamically, based on a publisher/subscriber data-sharing model. In brief, one application—the publisher (originator of data such as text or graphics)—can save information in an edition file. Another application—the subscriber (recipient)—can copy the information from that file into its own document. When the publisher changes the edition, the changes are reflected in the subscriber's document, either automatically or upon request. This "live pasting" is invaluable in situations where you want documents to reflect the current state of a standard set of data maintained elsewhere, such as a corporate organizational chart or a pie chart showing sales by region. The Edition Manager is discussed in detail in Chapter 5.

- **File Manager**—supports a new data structure for uniquely identifying files—FSSpec, the file system specification record. New routines are available that use an FSSpec instead of a working directory reference number or directory ID. One powerful new routine **(PBCatSearch)** provides a searching function you can use to quickly scan a volume for a particular file or for a group of files with specified characteristics. The new File Manager routines are examined in Chapter 2.

- **Standard File Package**—procedures in this package bring up standard Open File and Save File dialog boxes. Four routines are now available that work with the new FSSpec record. In addition, it is now easier to create your own custom Open and Save dialog boxes, as you will see in Chapter 2.

- **Resource Manager**—lets you open or create a file without having to specify a full pathname or setting up a working directory, making it the default directory, and providing a partial pathname. Instead, you can specify the file using the new FSSpec record. New routines for reading or writing a portion of a resource are particularly handy for dealing with very large resources. You will become familiar with some of the new Resource Manager routines in Chapter 2.

- **Process Manager**—is responsible for launching applications and managing information about applications that are running. You will use it if you want to launch another application directly from your application or if you want to determine quickly if there's an active application in memory to which you can send an Apple event. You will see how to use the Process Manager in Chapter 3.

- **Communications Toolbox**—you can easily add standard communications capabilities to your applications with the Communications Toolbox. It provides a standard programming interface for terminal emulation, connection, and file transfer tools you can acquire to use with System 7. You will see how to use the Communications Toolbox in Chapter 6.

- **TrueType fonts**—System 7 understands new types of fonts, TrueType fonts, as well as the more familiar bit-mapped fonts. TrueType fonts can be rendered very well at any arbitrary size because they are defined by mathematical equations—thus, you don't see the jaggies that appear when you try to scale bit-mapped fonts to unusual sizes. In Chapter 7, you will learn about TrueType fonts and the minor impact they have on application development.

- **Color QuickDraw**—is the color equivalent of the classic black-and-white QuickDraw imaging system. It supports multiple gray-scale and color monitors, both indexed (where each pixel is associated with an index into a color table) and direct (each pixel is associated with an explicit color value). The System 7 version of Color QuickDraw incorporates the 32-bit QuickDraw routines introduced with System 6.0.5 and are described in *Inside Macintosh*, Volume VI.

- **Data Access Manager**—provides a group of routines that make it possible to communicate effectively with remote (or local) databases without understanding the intricacies of the query language the database understands. This is made possible by using standard query documents created by someone who *is* a database guru. The Data Access Manager is not covered in this book—instead, refer to *Inside Macintosh*, Volume VI.

- **Virtual Memory**—the ability of the Macintosh to operate as if it has more RAM than it actually does. This illusion is carried out by a relatively complex scheme involving the swapping of data between real RAM and a special storage area on a hard disk. Most applications you will write won't need to know if virtual memory is being used. If you need to understand the intricacies of Virtual Memory, refer to *Inside Macintosh*, Volume VI.

    Virtual memory is only available on Macintoshes using a MC68030 microprocessor, or an MC68020 with an MC68851 PMMU.

▶ System 7 or Bust!

Although this book, of course, focuses on system software features unique to System 7, it also covers recent enhancements to System 6.x that have migrated to System 7. The sample code is designed to run under System 7. As a result, you will not see code cluttered with conditional statements that would permit it to run without traumatic incident under earlier versions of system software. (The only exception will be a one-time check that System 7 is actually present.) Less powerful, but System 6.x- and System 7-compatible, toolbox routines are not used where more appealing System 7-specific routines are available for the same general operation.

By adopting a similar strategy, you will find that your code will be much easier to develop, giving you more time to concentrate on adding functionality made possible by the new features provided in System 7. You will also avoid having to design an application that uses System 7-specific features but which is still useful for System 6.x users.

Of course, you could avoid System 7 altogether and simply develop System 6.x applications so you can maximize your potential customer base. After all, the Macintosh Plus, and all models introduced after it, run System 6.x right out of the box, but System 7 requires users with 1 Mb systems to upgrade to at least 2 Mb of RAM. This is true, of course, but many customers add more memory to their 1 Mb systems shortly after purchase. Also keep in mind that the street price of memory has plummeted below $50 per megabyte, so it's unlikely customers would snub your software because it requires System 7.

▶ # Hello! Hello! System 7, Are You There?

Since you'll be writing System 7-specific applications, you obviously need some code to determine whether System 7 (or higher) is the active operating system. This code will make it possible to exit gracefully from the program if a user tries to launch it under an earlier system. Having a bomb alert appear when you call a routine that's available only under System 7 is not considered graceful!

For System 6.x applications, you would use either the **SysEnvirons** routine or, for System 6.0.4 or higher, the **Gestalt** routine to determine the version of system software. You have access to both these routines under System 7, but **Gestalt** is more powerful and convenient, so it is clearly the preferred routine for determining not only the system software version number, but all sorts of other information about your software and hardware operating environment. In fact, System 7-specific applications should never have to use **SysEnvirons** or its predecessor, **Environs**.

Here's the function prototype for **Gestalt**:

```
pascal OSErr Gestalt( OSType selector, long *response );
```

To use **Gestalt**, pass it a selector that specifies the kind of information you want returned in the response variable. System 7 supports a variety of selectors that are briefly summarized in Listing 1-1. Refer to *Inside Macintosh*, Volume VI for a detailed description of the information that each selector returns.

Listing 1-1. Selectors for Gestalt

```
/* environmental selectors: */

#define  gestaltVersion              'vers' /* Gestalt version number */
#define  gestaltAddressingModeAttr   'addr' /* Addressing mode attr */
#define  gestaltAliasMgrAttr         'alis' /* Alias Manager attr */
#define  gestaltAppleTalkVersion     'atlk' /* AppleTalk version number */
#define  gestaltAUXVersion           'a/ux' /* A/UX version number */
#define  gestaltConnMgrAttr          'conn' /* Connection Manager attr */
#define  gestaltCRMAttr              'crm ' /* Communications Rsrc Mgr attr */
#define  gestaltCTBVersion           'ctbv' /* Communications Toolbox version */
#define  gestaltDBAccessMgrAttr      'dbac' /* Data Access Manager attr */
#define  gestaltDITLExtAttr          'ditl' /* Dialog Manager attr */
#define  gestaltEasyAccessAttr       'easy' /* Easy Access attr */
#define  gestaltEditionMgrAttr       'edtn' /* Edition Manager attr */
#define  gestaltAppleEventsAttr      'evnt' /* Apple Events Manager attr */
#define  gestaltFindFolderAttr       'fold' /* FindFolder attr */
#define  gestaltFontMgrAttr          'font' /* Font Manager attr */
#define  gestaltFPUType              'fpu ' /* floating point unit type code */
#define  gestaltFSAttr               'fs  ' /* File Manager attr */
#define  gestaltFXfrMgrAttr          'fxfr' /* File Transfer Manager attr */
```

Listing 1-1. Selectors for Gestalt (continued)

```
#define gestaltHardwareAttr          'hdwr' /* System hardware attr */
#define gestaltHelpMgrAttr           'help' /* Help Manager attr */
#define gestaltKeyboardType          'kbd ' /* Keyboard type code /*
#define gestaltLowMemorySize         'lmem' /* Size of low-memory global area */
#define gestaltLogicalRAMSize        'lram' /* Size of logical RAM space */
#define gestaltMiscAttr              'misc' /* Miscellaneous system attr */
#define gestaltMMUType               'mmu ' /* Memory management unit type */
#define gestaltStdNBPAttr            'nlup' /* Standard NBP attr */
#define gestaltNotificationMgrAttr   'nmgr' /* Notification Manager attr */
#define gestaltOSAttr                'os  ' /* Operating system attr */
#define gestaltOSTable               'ostt' /* Addr of OS trap table */
#define gestaltLogicalPageSize       'pgsz' /* Size of logical page * */
#define gestaltPopupAttr             'pop!' /* Popup menu attr */
#define gestaltPowerMgrAttr          'powr' /* Power Manager attr */
#define gestaltPPCToolboxAttr        'ppc ' /* PPC Toolbox attr */
#define gestaltProcessorType         'proc' /* Microprocessor type code */
#define gestaltParityAttr            'prty' /* Parity attr */
#define gestaltQuickdrawVersion      'qd  ' /* QuickDraw version */
#define gestaltQuickdrawFeatures     'qdrw' /* QuickDraw features */
#define gestaltPhysicalRAMSize       'ram ' /* Physical RAM size */
#define gestaltResourceMgrAttr       'rsrc' /* Resource Manager attr */
#define gestaltScriptCount           'scr#' /* Number of scripts available */
#define gestaltScriptMgrVersion      'scri' /* Script Manager version */
#define gestaltSerialAttr            'ser ' /* Serial attr */
#define gestaltNuBusConnectors       'sltc' /* NuBus connector bitmap */
#define gestaltSoundAttr             'snd ' /* Sound Manager attr */
#define gestaltStandardFileAttr      'stdf' /* Standard File attr */
#define gestaltTextEditVersion       'te  ' /* TextEdit version number */
#define gestaltToolboxTable          'tbtt' /* Addr of toolbox trap table */
#define gestaltTermMgrAttr           'term' /* Terminal Manager attr */
#define gestaltTimeMgrVersion        'tmgr' /* Time Manager version */
#define gestaltVMAttr                'vm  ' /* Virtual Memory attr */
#define gestaltExtToolboxTable       'xttt' /* Addr of extended trap table */

/* Informational selectors: */

#define gestaltMachineType           'mach' /* Macintosh system type code */
#define gestaltMachineIcon           'micn' /* ID of ICON/sicn for system */
#define gestaltROMSize               'rom ' /* size of ROM */
#define gestaltROMVersion            'romv' /* ROM version */
#define gestaltSystemVersion         'sysv' /* system software version */
```

The Gestalt.h interface file that comes with THINK C or MPW C includes the definitions in Listing 1-1. It also includes symbolic constants for the **Gestalt** responses to some of the selectors. Note that most of these constants do not represent *response values; rather they refer to bit numbers in the long word that `response` points to. (The symbolic constants associated with all the selectors that have an `Attr` suffix are like this.) To determine if the feature associated with the bit is available, check to see whether the expression

```
(*response) & ( 1<<bitnumberConstant )
```

is true.

For example, suppose you've called **Gestalt** with the `gestaltHardwareAttr` selector to determine if the Macintosh has an Apple Sound Chip installed. The sound chip is installed if the expression `(*response)` & (`1<<gestaltHasASC`) is true. The constant `gestaltHasASC` (from Gestalt.h) specifies the bit number for the attribute in which you're interested.

The selector we need for determining the system software version number is `gestaltSystemVersion`. The version is returned in the low-order word of the `response` variable as four BCD digits with implicit decimal points between the digits. The low-order word is 0x0700 for System 7, for example. (**Gestalt** uses the same format for the version word it returns in response to other selectors whose symbolic names have a `Version` suffix.) Here's how to make the call for the version number:

```
OSErr myError;
long  sysVersion;
myError = Gestalt( gestaltSystemVersion, &sysVersion );
```

But you're a little bit ahead of yourself. Before you actually try to use **Gestalt** in a program, you had better make sure the routine is available. To do this, check to see if the toolbox trap for **_GestaltDispatch** is present. The Apple-approved way for doing this is illustrated in Listing 1-2: By calling the `TrapAvailable` function (which uses the `GetTrapType` function) with the trap number you're seeking.

Listing 1-2. Source code for System7Available and related functions

```
Boolean System7Available( void )
{
    long  sysVersion;

    if ( !TrapAvailable( _GestaltDispatch ) ) return( false );

    if ( !Gestalt( gestaltSystemVersion, &sysVersion ) ) {

            if ( sysVersion >= 0x0700 ) return( true );
```

Listing 1-2. Source code for System7Available and related functions (continued)

```
    }
    return( false );
}

Boolean TrapAvailable( short theTrap )
{
    TrapType      tType;

    tType = GetTrapType( theTrap );

    if ( tType == ToolTrap ) {

        theTrap = ( theTrap & 0x07FF );

        if ( theTrap >= NumToolboxTraps() ) theTrap =_Unimplemented;
    }
    return ( NGetTrapAddress( theTrap, tType ) !=
                    NGetTrapAddress( _Unimplemented, ToolTrap ) );
}

TrapType GetTrapType( short theTrap )
{
    if ( ( theTrap & 0x0800 ) > 0 ) {

        return ( ToolTrap );

    } else {

        return ( OSTrap );
    }
}

short NumToolboxTraps( void )
{
    if ( NGetTrapAddress( _InitGraf, ToolTrap ) ==
                NGetTrapAddress( 0xAA6E, ToolTrap ) ) {

        return ( 0x0200 );

    } else {

        return ( 0x0400 );
    }
}
```

Listing 1-2 also includes the `System7Available` routine that you'll call to check that System 7 is present. It returns a Boolean true if System 7 is present.

For now, it's safe to check simply for system software version 7.0 before using the software features described in this book and *Inside Macintosh*, Volume VI. System 7 always includes all these features. As Apple releases versions of system software beyond 7.0, however, it will become more difficult to remember the specific features introduced with each new release. It's also conceivable that capability could be added without the system software version changing. The best strategy, therefore, is to check for specific features you need using the selectors in Listing 1-1.

▶ A Skeleton in the Closet

When the Macintosh first appeared in 1984 it quickly gained a reputation as being very difficult to program. And it really was—not only were few development tools available, but programmers also had to learn new programming concepts such as event loops, resources, and the desktop interface.

Now several excellent development environments and tools are available, notably Apple's Macintosh Programmer's Workshop (MPW) and Symantec's THINK environments for C and Pascal. But it's still hard to grind out that first "Hello World!" application without a little help.

The THINK C source code in Listing 1-3 is for the Skeleton application, an application you can use as the core of your own full-blown System 7 application. It implements many of the functions you would expect in any application, including a menu bar with standard Apple, File, and Edit menus, an event loop, and an event-handling mechanism. When you select the New item from the File menu, Skeleton brings up an Untitled window you can draw in using QuickDraw routines. Skeleton always displays a Message window you can use to facilitate debugging using the procedures described at the end of this section. Listings 1-4 and 1-5 contain source code for Skeleton resources (in Apple's Rez format) and the header file, respectively.

| Note ▶ | Apple's Rez tool for creating resources is now available for the THINK C environment, but it has been shipping with THINK Pascal and Macintosh Programmer's Workshop for some time. See Appendix A for a brief introduction to Rez and how you can use it to simplify resource creation and editing. You should also study the reference materials that come with THINK C (or MPW) for a complete description of the Rez tool. |

Skeleton also provides a Special menu with a Test item that, when selected, is handled by the DoStuff procedure. You can easily experiment with toolbox features by writing a complete DoStuff procedure, recompiling, and choosing Test from the Special menu.

Note ▶

Skeleton does not yet support all the core functions that any application that runs under System 7 should. Skeleton will become more robust as you cover new topics in later chapters.

Since Skeleton will be using System 7-specific toolbox routines, it calls the System7Available routine described in the previous section when it first starts up. If you run Skeleton under an older version of system software, you get a friendly stop dialog and the program quits.

Skeleton should look reasonably familiar to anyone who's ever written a Macintosh application. Note the following features (or missing features) made possible because the application is designed for System 7 and not earlier versions:

- No explicit check exists for the presence of the **WaitNextEvent** trap. This trap is always available under System 7 and, in fact, you *must* use it (instead of **GetNextEvent**) to allow other open applications to run in the background. With some older system software releases, **WaitNextEvent** may be unavailable if MultiFinder is not active; hence the need for a check if you're writing a pre-System 7 application that is to run under Finder. System 7's Finder is roughly equivalent to MultiFinder in that it permits multiple applications to cooperatively multitask. More on this in Chapter 3.

- DoEvent, the Skeleton routine that handles incoming events returned by **WaitNextEvent**, includes a check for high-level events (kHighLevelEvent) and deals with them by calling **AEProcessAppleEvent**. The Apple event handlers to which **AEProcessAppleEvent** dispatches control are installed using **AEInstallEventHandler** (see Skeleton's DoAEInstallation routine). Handlers for the four required Apple events—open application, open document, print document, and quit—are included and will be described in more detail in Chapter 4.

- A file whose stationery pad attribute bit is set is assigned to an untitled window, per the guidelines for handling this new class of file. Stationery files are examined in more detail in Chapter 2.

- **CountAppFiles** and **GetAppFiles** are not used to process the list of files that the Finder passes to the application for opening or printing. In Chapter 4, you'll see that under System 7 the Finder passes similar information using high-level Apple events, if the application is high-level event aware (set the isHighLevelEventAware flag in the application's 'SIZE' resource to indicate that it is). The code needed to handle these events will be explained in that chapter.

- The window type (application or system) is not checked before closing a window with **CloseWindow** or **DisposeWindow.** The only windows an application running under System 7 knows about are its own. System windows (used by desk accessories) do not appear in the same plane as the active application, as they do in the pre-System 7 Finder, so you do not need to check for them and close them with **CloseDeskAcc**.

- Two new Standard File package routines, **StandardPutFile** and **StandardGetFile**, are used instead of **SFPutFile** and **SFGetFile** to present standard Save File and Open File dialog boxes. As you will see in Chapter 2, these routines are more convenient to use because they work with the file system specification (FSSpec) records introduced by the System 7 File Manager.

Skeleton also includes several useful routines that will assist you in testing and debugging your applications:

void ShowError(Str255 errorMessage, long errorNumber **);**

This routine displays errorMessage (a Pascal string) and errorNumber in the Message window.

void PrintOSType(OSType theType **);**

This routine converts theType to a text string and displays it in the Message window.

void PrintString(Str255 s **);**

This routine displays s (a Pascal string) in the Message window.

void PrintHex(long theNumber **);**

This routine converts theNumber to a string of hexadecimal digits and displays the string in the Message window.

void CRLF(void **);**

This routine moves the active drawing position for the front window to the left margin of the next line. The left margin is given by the LEFT_MARGIN constant.

```
void pStringCopy( Str255 srcString, Str255 destString );
```

This routine copies the `srcString` Pascal string to the space reserved for the `destString` Pascal string.

```
void ConcatString( Str255 s1, Str255 s2 );
```

This routine concatenates two Pascal strings and assigns the result to the `s1` string. The concatenation does not take place if the resultant string would be greater than 255 characters long.

Listing 1-3. Skeleton.c. The THINK C source code for the Skeleton application

```
/*
    Skeleton.c

    This is the skeleton of a 7.0-dependent application.
    Written in THINK C.

    Copyright © 1991 Gary Little
*/

#include "Skeleton.h"

/* Constants */

#define kDITop      0x0050   /* top coord for disk init dialog */
#define kDILeft     0x0070   /* left coord for disk init dialog */
#define LEFT_MARGIN 10       /* left margin for window drawing */

/* Function prototypes: */

void main( void );
void Initialize( void );
void EventLoop( void );
void DoIdle( EventRecord *event );
void DoEvent( EventRecord *event );
void DoMenuCommand( long menuResult );
void CleanUp( void );
void DoActivate( WindowPtr window, Boolean becomingActive );
Boolean DoCloseWindow( WindowPtr wp );
void DoUpdate( WindowPtr wp );
void AdjustMenus( void );

OSErr CreateUntitledWindow( void );
OSErr CreateFileWindow( FSSpecPtr opFSSpec, Boolean isStationery );
OSErr NewDocWindow( long winPrivateSize );
```

Listing 1-3. Skeleton.c. The THINK C source code for the Skeleton application (continued)

```
void GetOpenName( StandardFileReply *toReply );
void GetSaveName( StandardFileReply *toReply, Str255 defaultName,
                  Boolean *isStationery );

Boolean System7Available( void );
Boolean TrapAvailable( short theTrap );
TrapType GetTrapType( short theTrap );
short NumToolboxTraps( void );

void ShowError( Str255 errorMessage, long errorNumber );
void PrintHex( long theNumber );
void PrintString( Str255 s );
void PrintOSType( OSType theType );
void CRLF( void );
void pStringCopy( Str255 srcString, Str255 destString );
void ConcatString( Str255 s1, Str255 s2 );

void DoAEInstallation( void );
pascal OSErr HandleOAPP( AppleEvent *theAppleEvent, AppleEvent *reply,
                  long myRefCon );
pascal OSErr HandleODOC( AppleEvent *theAppleEvent, AppleEvent *reply,
                  long myRefCon );
pascal OSErr HandlePDOC( AppleEvent *theAppleEvent, AppleEvent *reply,
                  long myRefCon );
pascal OSErr HandleQUIT( AppleEvent *theAppleEvent, AppleEvent *reply,
                  long myRefCon );
OSErr RequiredCheck( AppleEvent *theAppleEvent );

/* You'll have to add code for these: */

void DrawWindowContents( WindowPtr wp );
void DoContentClick( WindowPtr wp, Point where);
void DoTest( WindowPtr wp );

/* Special types */

/* The 'winPrivate' struct describes the data that is
   attached to each document window via the window's refCon */
typedef struct {
   short data1; /* etc. */
   /* define other data elements here that you
      want associated with a window */
} winPrivate, *winPrivatePtr, **winPrivateHndl;

/* Global variables: */
```

Listing 1-3. Skeleton.c. The THINK C source code for the Skeleton application (continued)

```c
Boolean    gQuitting;
Boolean    gInBackground;
WindowPtr  gMessageWindow;
RgnHandle  gCursorRgn;

/* Procedures and functions: */

void main( void )
{
    Initialize();

    EventLoop();

    ZeroScrap();
    TEToScrap();
}


void Initialize( void )
{
    short i;
    Handle    menuBar;

    MaxApplZone();
    for ( i=1; i<=4; i++ ) MoreMasters();

    FlushEvents ( everyEvent, 0 );

    InitGraf( &thePort );
    InitFonts();
    InitWindows();
    InitMenus();
    TEInit();
    InitDialogs( 0L );
    InitCursor();

    gInBackground = false;
    gQuitting = false;
    gCursorRgn = NewRgn();  /* (forces cursor-move event right away) */

    TEFromScrap();

    menuBar = GetNewMBar( rMenuBar );  /* Create the menu bar */
    if ( menuBar ) {
```

Listing 1-3. Skeleton.c. The THINK C source code for the Skeleton application (continued)

```
        SetMenuBar( menuBar );
        DisposHandle( menuBar );
        AddResMenu( GetMHandle( mApple ), 'DRVR' ); /* add Apple Menu items */
        DrawMenuBar();

    } else {

        gQuitting = true;
        return;
    }

    if ( !System7Available() ) {

      Alert( rNotSystem7, 0L );
      gQuitting = true;
      return;
    }

    InitEdition Pack();   /* initialize Edition Manager */
    DoAEInstallation();   /* install AppleEvent handlers */

/* this window is for debugging purposes only: */
    gMessageWindow = GetNewWindow( rDebugWindow, (Ptr)0L, (WindowPtr)-1 );
}


void EventLoop()
{
    Boolean      gotEvent;
    EventRecord     event;
    long         sleepTime;

    while ( !gQuitting ) {

        sleepTime = GetDblTime(); /* if front window has TE record */
/*      if ( gInBackground ) sleepTime = -1L; */ /* set approp. bkgnd value */

        gotEvent = WaitNextEvent( everyEvent, &event, sleepTime, gCursorRgn );

        if ( gotEvent ) {

            DoEvent( &event );

        } else {

            DoIdle( &event );
```

Listing 1-3. Skeleton.c. The THINK C source code for the Skeleton application (continued)

```c
        }
};
}

void DoIdle( EventRecord *event )
{
    /* do idle stuff */
}

void DoEvent( EventRecord *event )
{
    short       myError;
    short       windowPart;
    WindowPtr   window;
    char        key;
    Point       mountPoint;

    switch ( event->what ) {
        case mouseDown:
            windowPart = FindWindow( event->where, &window );
            switch ( windowPart ) {
                case inMenuBar:
                    AdjustMenus();     /* prepare menu items first */
                    DoMenuCommand( MenuSelect( event->where ) );
                    break;
                case inContent:
                    if ( window != FrontWindow() ) {
                        SelectWindow( window );
                    } else {
                        DoContentClick( window, event->where );
                    }
                    break;
                case inDrag:
                    DragWindow( window, event->where, &screenBits.bounds );
                    break;
                case inGrow:
                    break;
                case inGoAway:
                    if ( TrackGoAway( window, event->where ) ) {
                        DoCloseWindow( window );
                    }
                    break;
                case inZoomIn:
                case inZoomOut:
                    if ( TrackBox( window, event->where, windowPart ) ) {
                        SetPort( window );
                        EraseRect( &window->portRect );
```

Listing 1-3. Skeleton.c. The THINK C source code for the Skeleton application (continued)

```
                        ZoomWindow( window, windowPart, true );
                        InvalRect( &window->portRect );
                }
                break;
    }
    break;
case keyDown:
case autoKey:
    key = event->message & charCodeMask;
    if ( event->modifiers & cmdKey ) {    /* is command key down? */
        if ( event->what == keyDown ) {
            AdjustMenus();   /* prepare menu items first */
            DoMenuCommand( MenuKey( key ) );
        break;
        }
case activateEvt:
    DoActivate( (WindowPtr) event->message,
                (event->modifiers & activeFlag) != 0 );
    break;
case updateEvt:
    DoUpdate( (WindowPtr) event->message );
    break;
case diskEvt:
    if ( (event->message >> 16) != noErr ) {
        mountPoint.h = kDILeft;
        mountPoint.v = kDITop;
        myError = DIBadMount( mountPoint, event->message );
    }
    break;
case osEvt:
    switch ( (event->message >> 24) & 0x0ff ) {
        case suspendResumeMessage:

            if ( ( event->message & resumeFlag ) == 0 ) { /* suspend */

                gInBackground = true;
                ZeroScrap();
                TEToScrap();

                DoActivate( FrontWindow(), false );   /* deactivate */

            } else { /* resuming */

                gInBackground = false;

                if ( event->message & convertClipboardFlag )
```

Listing 1-3. Skeleton.c. The THINK C source code for the Skeleton application (continued)

```
                            TEFromScrap();

                    DoActivate( FrontWindow(), true );  /* activate */
            }
        break;
    case mouseMovedMessage:
            DisposeRgn( gCursorRgn ); /* get rid of old region */
            gCursorRgn = NewRgn();
            SetRectRgn(gCursorRgn, -32768, -32768, 32766, 32766);
            break;
    }
    break;

/* brand new for System 7.0: */
    case kHighLevelEvent:
        AEProcessAppleEvent( event );
        break;
    }
}


void DoMenuCommand( long menuResult )
{
    short           menuID;         /* ID of selected menu */
    short           menuItem;       /* item number in selected menu */
    short           itemHit;
    Str255          daName;
    StandardFileReply   reply;
    WindowPtr       wp;
    Str255          defaultName;
    Boolean         isStationery;

    menuID = menuResult >> 16;
    menuItem = menuResult & 0x0000ffff;

    switch ( menuID ) {
        case mApple:
            switch ( menuItem ) {
                case iAbout:  /* display the About box */
                    itemHit = Alert( rAboutBox, 0L );
                    break;
                default:      /* handle DA selection */
                    GetItem( GetMHandle( mApple ), menuItem, daName );
                    OpenDeskAcc( daName );
                    break;
            }
            break;
```

Listing 1-3. Skeleton.c. The THINK C source code for the Skeleton application (continued)

```
case mFile:
    switch ( menuItem ) {
        case iNew:
                CreateUntitledWindow( );
                break;
        case iOpen:
            GetOpenName( &reply );
                    if ( reply.sfGood ) {

                            isStationery = ( (reply.sfFlags & 0x0800) != 0 );
                            CreateFileWindow( (FSSpecPtr)&reply.sfFile,
                                        isStationery );

                    }

                break;
        case iClose:
                DoCloseWindow( FrontWindow() );
                break;
        case iSave:

                /* save the file to disk with current name */

                break;
        case iSaveAs:
                wp = FrontWindow();
                GetWTitle( wp, defaultName );
                GetSaveName( &reply, defaultName, &isStationery );
                    if ( reply.sfGood ) {

                            /* save the file to disk with new name */

                            SetWTitle( wp, reply.sfFile.name );
                    }
                    break;
        case iQuit:
                CleanUp();
                gQuitting = true;
                break;
    }
        break;
case mEdit:
    break;
case mSpecial:
        switch ( menuItem ) {
```

Listing 1-3. Skeleton.c. The THINK C source code for the Skeleton application (continued)

```
                    case iTest:
                        DoTest( FrontWindow() );
                        break;
                }
                break;
        }
    HiliteMenu(0);
} /*DoMenuCommand*/


/*  Close the specified window and dispose of
    the private data handle in the refCon.
    Returns true if the operation was not
    cancelled.
*/
Boolean DoCloseWindow( WindowPtr wp )
{
    winPrivateHndl myPrivate;

    if ( wp ) {

        SetPort( wp );
        myPrivate = (winPrivateHndl)GetWRefCon( wp );

/* put code here to ask user to verify the close if the window is "dirty" */   /*  return(
false ) if user cancels */

        if ( myPrivate ) {
            /* warning: dispose of any handles in the private data first! */
            DisposHandle( (Handle)myPrivate );
        }
        DisposeWindow( wp );
    }
    return( true );
}

void CleanUp( void )
{
    WindowPtr      wp;
    Boolean        closed;

    closed = true;
    do {
        wp = FrontWindow();
        if ( wp )
```

Listing 1-3. Skeleton.c. The THINK C source code for the Skeleton application (continued)

```
            closed = DoCloseWindow( wp );
    } while ( closed && wp );

    if ( closed )
        gQuitting = true;       /* exit if no cancellation */
}

void DoActivate( WindowPtr wp, Boolean becomingActive )
{
    if ( becomingActive ) {

        /* do activation stuff */

    } else {

        /* do deactivation stuff */

    }
}

void DoUpdate( WindowPtr wp )
{
        SetPort( wp );
        BeginUpdate( wp );
        if ( !EmptyRgn( wp->visRgn ) )
            DrawWindowContents( wp );
        EndUpdate( wp );
}

void DrawWindowContents( WindowPtr wp )
{
    /* insert your code here for redrawing window */
}

/*  Enable and disable menu items
    as required by the context.
*/
void AdjustMenus( void )
{
    WindowPtr       wp;
    MenuHandle      fileMenu, editMenu, specialMenu;

    wp = FrontWindow();

    fileMenu = GetMHandle( mFile );
    editMenu = GetMHandle( mEdit );
```

Listing 1-3. Skeleton.c. The THINK C source code for the Skeleton application (continued)

```
    specialMenu = GetMHandle( mSpecial );

    DisableItem( editMenu, iUndo );
    DisableItem( editMenu, iCut );
    DisableItem( editMenu, iCopy );
    DisableItem( editMenu, iClear );
    DisableItem( editMenu, iPaste );

    EnableItem( fileMenu, iOpen );
    EnableItem( fileMenu, iNew );

    if ( !wp ) {
        DisableItem( fileMenu, iClose );
        DisableItem( fileMenu, iSave );
        DisableItem( fileMenu, iSaveAs );
        DisableItem( specialMenu, iTest );
    } else {

        if ( wp == gMessageWindow ) {
            DisableItem( fileMenu, iClose );
            DisableItem( fileMenu, iSave );
            DisableItem( fileMenu, iSaveAs );
            DisableItem( specialMenu, iTest );
        } else {
            EnableItem( fileMenu, iClose );
            EnableItem( fileMenu, iSave );
            EnableItem( fileMenu, iSaveAs );
            EnableItem( specialMenu, iTest );
        }
    }
}


void DoTest( WindowPtr wp )
{
    SetPort( wp );
    EraseRect( &wp->portRect );
    MoveTo( 10, 20 );
    DrawString( (StringPtr)"\pInsert your test code here." );
}


/* Handle clicks inside a window */
void DoContentClick( WindowPtr wp, Point where)
```

Listing 1-3. Skeleton.c. The THINK C source code for the Skeleton application (continued)

```c
{
    /* insert your code here to handle clicks in a window */
}


/* Install AppleEvent handlers */
void DoAEInstallation( void )
{
    AEInstallEventHandler( kCoreEventClass,
                           kAEOpenDocuments,
                           (EventHandlerProcPtr)HandleODOC,
                           0,
                           false );

    AEInstallEventHandler( kCoreEventClass,
                           kAEQuitApplication,
                           (EventHandlerProcPtr)HandleQUIT,
                           0,
                           false );

    AEInstallEventHandler( kCoreEventClass,
                           kAEPrintDocuments,
                           (EventHandlerProcPtr)HandlePDOC,
                           0,
                           false );

    AEInstallEventHandler( kCoreEventClass,
                           kAEOpenApplication,
                           (EventHandlerProcPtr)HandleOAPP,
                           0,
                           false );
}


OSErr CreateUntitledWindow( void )
{
    OSErr       myErr;
    WindowPtr   wp;

    myErr = NewDocWindow( sizeof( winPrivate ) );
    if ( myErr ) return( myErr );

    wp = FrontWindow();
    SetWTitle( wp, (StringPtr)"\pUntitled" );
    return( noErr );
}
```

Listing 1-3. Skeleton.c. The THINK C source code for the Skeleton application (continued)

```c
OSErr CreateFileWindow( FSSpecPtr opFSSpec, Boolean isStationery )
{
    OSErr           fileError;
    WindowPtr           wp;

    /* Insert code here to open and read in file's data. */

    fileError = NewDocWindow( sizeof( winPrivate ) );
    if ( fileError ) return( fileError );

    wp = FrontWindow();

    /*  Insert code here to attach data to window, perhaps
        by storing a handle to it in the winPrivate structure. */

    if ( isStationery ) { /* it's a stationery file */

        SetWTitle( wp, (StringPtr)"\pUntitled" );

    } else { /* it's a regular file */

        SetWTitle( wp, opFSSpec->name );
    }
    return( noErr );
}

/* Create the new window and attach (via the RefCon)
    a handle to your private data for the window.
*/
OSErr NewDocWindow( long winPrivateSize )
{
    WindowPtr           wp;
    Handle          myPrivate;

    wp = GetNewWindow( rMainWindow, (Ptr)0L, (WindowPtr)-1 );
    if ( !wp ) return( memFullErr );

    SetPort( wp );

    myPrivate = NewHandleClear( winPrivateSize );
    if ( !myPrivate ) return ( memFullErr );

    SetWRefCon( wp, (long)myPrivate );

    return( noErr );
}
```

Listing 1-3. Skeleton.c. The THINK C source code for the Skeleton application (continued)

```
void GetOpenName( StandardFileReply *toReply )
{
    StandardGetFile( 0L, -1, 0L, toReply );
}


void GetSaveName( StandardFileReply *toReply, Str255 defaultName, Boolean *isStationery )
{
    *isStationery = false;
    StandardPutFile( (StringPtr)"\pSave file as:", defaultName, toReply );
}


/*  A P P L E   E V E N T   H A N D L E R S
    -------------------------------------
    for required Apple events
*/
pascal OSErr HandleODOC( AppleEvent *theAppleEvent, AppleEvent *reply, long myRefCon )
{
    OSErr       myErr;
    AEDescList  docList;
    FSSpec      myFSS;
    long        itemsInList;
    AEKeyword   theKeyword;
    DescType    typeCode;
    Size        actualSize;
    long        i;
    Handle      winDataHndl;
    FInfo       theFInfo;
    Boolean     isStationery;

    myErr = AEGetParamDesc( theAppleEvent, keyDirectObject, typeAEList,
                    &docList );
    if ( myErr ) return( myErr );

    myErr = RequiredCheck( theAppleEvent );
    if ( myErr ) return( myErr );

    myErr = AECountItems( &docList, &itemsInList );
    if ( myErr ) return( myErr );

    for (i = 1; i <= itemsInList; i++ ) {

        myErr = AEGetNthPtr( &docList, i, typeFSS, &theKeyword, &typeCode,
                        (Ptr)&myFSS, sizeof( FSSpec ), &actualSize );
```

Listing 1-3. Skeleton.c. The THINK C source code for the Skeleton application (continued)

```
        if ( myErr ) return( myErr );

        FSpGetFInfo( &myFSS, &theFInfo ); /* check for stationery */
        isStationery = ( (theFInfo.fdFlags & 0x0800) != 0 );
        CreateFileWindow( &myFSS, isStationery );
    }
    return( noErr );
}

pascal OSErr HandleQUIT( AppleEvent *theAppleEvent, AppleEvent *reply,
    long myRefCon )
{
    OSErr   myErr;

    myErr = RequiredCheck( theAppleEvent );
    if ( myErr ) return( myErr );

    gQuitting = true;
    return( noErr );
}

pascal OSErr HandleOAPP( AppleEvent *theAppleEvent,
    AppleEvent *reply, long myRefCon )
{
    OSErr       myErr;

    myErr = RequiredCheck( theAppleEvent );
    if ( myErr ) return( myErr );

    myErr = CreateUntitledWindow();
    return( myErr );
}

pascal OSErr HandlePDOC( AppleEvent *theAppleEvent, AppleEvent *reply, long myRefCon )
{
    return( errAEEventNotHandled );
}


OSErr RequiredCheck( AppleEvent *theAppleEvent )
{
    OSErr       myErr;
    DescType    typeCode;
    Size        actualSize;

    myErr = AEGetAttributePtr( theAppleEvent, keyMissedKeywordAttr,
                               typeWildCard, &typeCode, 0L, 0, &actualSize );
```

Listing 1-3. Skeleton.c. The THINK C source code for the Skeleton application (continued)

```
    if ( myErr == errAEDescNotFound ) return( noErr );
    if ( myErr == noErr ) return( errAEEventNotHandled );
    return( myErr );
}


/*  C H E C K I N G   F O R   7 . 0
    -----------------------------
    Call System7Available to determine whether
    the system software version is 7 or higher.
*/
Boolean System7Available( void )
{
    long    sysVersion;

    if ( !TrapAvailable( _GestaltDispatch ) ) return( false );

    if ( !Gestalt( gestaltSystemVersion, &sysVersion ) ) {

            if ( sysVersion >= 0x0700 ) return( true );
    }
    return( false );
}

Boolean TrapAvailable( short theTrap )
{
    TrapType    tType;

    tType = GetTrapType( theTrap );

    if ( tType == ToolTrap ) {

        theTrap = ( theTrap & 0x07FF );

        if ( theTrap >= NumToolboxTraps() ) theTrap = _Unimplemented;
    }
    return ( NGetTrapAddress( theTrap, tType ) !=
                NGetTrapAddress( _Unimplemented, ToolTrap ) );
}

TrapType GetTrapType( short theTrap )
{
    if ( ( theTrap & 0x0800 ) > 0 ) {

        return ( ToolTrap );

    } else {
```

Listing 1-3. Skeleton.c. The THINK C source code for the Skeleton application (continued)

```c
        return ( OSTrap );
    }
}

short NumToolboxTraps( void )
{
    if ( NGetTrapAddress( _InitGraf, ToolTrap ) ==
            NGetTrapAddress( 0xAA6E, ToolTrap ) ) {

        return ( 0x0200 );

    } else {

        return ( 0x0400 );
    }
}


/*
    U T I L I T Y   F U N C T I O N S
    ---------------------------------
    · ShowError
    · PrintOSType
    · PrintString
    · PrintHex
    · CRLF
    · pStringCopy
    · ConcatString
*/

/* ShowError: display error message and error number in Message window */
void ShowError( Str255 errorMessage, long errorNumber )
{
    WindowPtr       wp;
    Str255          numberString;

    NumToString( errorNumber, numberString );

    GetPort( &wp );

    SetPort( gMessageWindow );
    EraseRect( &gMessageWindow->portRect );
    MoveTo( 10, 20 );

    DrawString( errorMessage );
    DrawString( numberString );

    SetPort( wp );
```

Listing 1-3. Skeleton.c. The THINK C source code for the Skeleton application (continued)

```c
}

/* PrintOSType: display an OSType string in the Message window */
void PrintOSType( OSType theType )
{
    Str255      typeString;
    WindowPtr   wp;
    short       i;

    typeString[0] = 4;

    for ( i = 0; i <= 3 ; i++ ) {

        typeString[4-i] = (char)(theType & 0x000000FF);
        theType = theType >> 8;
    }

    GetPort( &wp );

    SetPort( gMessageWindow );
    EraseRect( &gMessageWindow->portRect );
    MoveTo( 10, 20 );

    DrawString( typeString );

    SetPort( wp );
}

/* PrintString: display string in Message window */
void PrintString( Str255 s )
{
    WindowPtr   wp;

    if ( !s ) return;

    GetPort( &wp );

    SetPort( gMessageWindow );
    EraseRect( &gMessageWindow->portRect );
    MoveTo( 10, 20 );

    DrawString( s );

    SetPort( wp );
}

/* PrintHex: convert number to a hex string and display in Message window */
void PrintHex( long theNumber )
{
```

Listing 1-3. Skeleton.c. The THINK C source code for the Skeleton application
(continued)

```
    char        theString[10];
    long        digit;
    short       i;
    WindowPtr       wp;

    GetPort( &wp );

    SetPort( gMessageWindow );
    EraseRect( &gMessageWindow->portRect );
    MoveTo( 10, 20 );

    theString[0] = 9;
    theString[1] = '$';

    for ( i = 0; i <= 7 ; i++ ) {

        digit = theNumber & 0x0000000F;
        if ( digit < 10 ) {
           digit += (long)('0');
        } else {
           digit += (long)('A' - 10);
        }

        theString[9-i] = (char)digit;
        theNumber = theNumber >> 4;
    }
    DrawString( (StringPtr)theString );

    SetPort( wp );
}

/* CRLF: advance drawing position in front window to left side of next line */
void CRLF( void )
{
    Point       currentPosition;
    FontInfo    theFontInfo;
    register short lineHeight;

    GetPen( &currentPosition );

    GetFontInfo( &theFontInfo );
    lineHeight = theFontInfo.ascent + theFontInfo.descent + theFontInfo.leading;

    MoveTo( LEFT_MARGIN, currentPosition.v + lineHeight );
}

/* pStringCopy: copy one Pascal string to another */
```

Listing 1-3. Skeleton.c. The THINK C source code for the Skeleton application (continued)

```
void pStringCopy( Str255 srcString, Str255 destString )
{
    register short index;

    index = srcString[0] + 1;

    while ( index— ) {

        *destString++ = *srcString++;
    }
}


/* ConcatString: concatenate two Pascal strings */
void ConcatString( Str255 s1, Str255 s2 )
{
    Byte    index1, index2;

    if ( s2[0] == 0 ) return;
    if ( ( (short)s1[0] + (short)s2[0] )  > 255 ) return;

    for ( index1 = s1[0]+1, index2 = 1; index2 <= s2[0]; index1++, index2++ ) {

        s1[index1] = s2[index2];
    }
    s1[0] += s2[0];
}
```

Listing 1-4. Skeleton.r. The Rez source code for the resources used by Skeleton

```
/*---------------------------------
#
#       Skeleton.r
#
#       Rez Source
#
#       Copyright © 1991 Gary Little
#       All rights reserved.
#
-----------------------------------*/

#define SystemSevenOrLater 1

#include "Types.r"
```

Listing 1-4. Skeleton.r. The Rez source code for the resources used by Skeleton (continued)

```
#include "SysTypes.r"

#include "Skeleton.h"

/* MBAR defines our menu bar */
resource 'MBAR' (rMenuBar, "Menu bar", preload) {
    { mApple, mFile, mEdit, mSpecial }
};

resource 'MENU' (mApple, "Apple menu", preload) {
    mApple, textMenuProc,
    AllItems & ~MenuItem2,
    enabled, apple,
    {
        "About " AppName "…",
            noicon, nokey, nomark, plain;
        "-",
            noicon, nokey, nomark, plain;
    }
};

resource 'MENU' (mFile, "File menu", preload) {
    mFile, textMenuProc,
    MenuItem11,
    enabled, "File",
    {
        "New",
            noicon, "N", nomark, plain;
        "Open…",
            noicon, "O", nomark, plain;
        "-",
            noicon, nokey, nomark, plain;
        "Close",
            noicon, "W", nomark, plain;
        "Save",
            noicon, "S", nomark, plain;
        "Save As…",
            noicon, nokey, nomark, plain;
        "-",
            noicon, nokey, nomark, plain;
        "Page Setup…",
            noicon, nokey, nomark, plain;
        "Print…",
            noicon, nokey, nomark, plain;
        "-",
            noicon, nokey, nomark, plain;
```

Listing 1-4. Skeleton.r. The Rez source code for the resources used by Skeleton (continued)

```
            "Quit",
                noicon, "Q", nomark, plain;
        }
};

resource 'MENU' (mEdit, "Edit menu", preload) {
    mEdit, textMenuProc,
    NoItems,
    enabled, "Edit",
      {
        "Undo",
            noicon, "Z", nomark, plain;
        "-",
            noicon, nokey, nomark, plain;
        "Cut",
            noicon, "X", nomark, plain;
        "Copy",
            noicon, "C", nomark, plain;
        "Paste",
            noicon, "V", nomark, plain;
        "Clear",
            noicon, nokey, nomark, plain;
    }
};

resource 'MENU' (mSpecial, "Special menu", preload) {
    mSpecial, textMenuProc,
    NoItems,
    enabled, "Special",
    {
        "Test",
            noicon, nokey, nomark, plain;
    }
};


/* About box */
resource 'ALRT' (rAboutBox, "About box", purgeable) {
    {0, 0, 120, 270},
    rAboutBox,
    silentStages,
    alertPositionMainScreen
};

resource 'DITL' (rAboutBox, "About box items", purgeable) {
    {

        {88, 180, 108, 260},
```

Listing 1-4. Skeleton.r. The Rez source code for the resources used by Skeleton (continued)

```
        Button {
            enabled,
            "OK"
        };

        {8, 8, 24, 214},
        StaticText {
            disabled,
            AppName " " AppVers
        };

        {32, 8, 48, 237},
        StaticText {
            disabled,
            CopyrightNotice
        };
    }
};


/* "Wrong System" alert box */
resource 'ALRT' (rNotSystem7, "Not System 7", purgeable) {
    {40, 20, 140, 260},
    rNotSystem7,
    beepStages,
    noAutoCenter
};

resource 'DITL' (rNotSystem7, "Not System 7 items", purgeable) {
    {
        {70, 150, 90, 230},
        Button {
            enabled,
            "OK"
        };

        {10, 55, 50, 230},
        StaticText {
            disabled,
            AppName " runs under System 7.0 only."
        };

        {8, 8, 40, 40},
        Icon {
            disabled,
            StopIconID
```

Listing 1-4. Skeleton.r. The Rez source code for the resources used by Skeleton (continued)

```
        };
    }
};


/* Main document window */
resource 'WIND' (rMainWindow, "Untitled", preload, purgeable) {
    {0, 0, 230, 460},
    zoomDocProc, visible, GoAway, 0x0, "",
    centerMainScreen
};


/* Debugging window */
resource 'WIND' (rDebugWindow, "Message window", preload, purgeable)
{
    {400, 85, 430, 560},
    noGrowDocProc, visible, noGoAway, 0x0, "Message",
    noAutoCenter
};


resource 'BNDL' (rBundle, "Finder bundle") {
    ApplCreator,
    rSignature,
    {
        'FREF',
        {
            0, rRefAPPL,
            1, rRefTEXT,
        },
        'ICN#',
        {
            0, rIconAPPL,
            1, rIconTEXT,
        }
    }
};

resource 'FREF' (rRefAPPL, "Application") {
    'APPL', 0, ""
};

resource 'FREF' (rRefTEXT, "TEXT Document") {
    'TEXT', 1, ""
};

type ApplCreator as 'STR ';
```

Listing 1-4. Skeleton.r. The Rez source code for the resources used by Skeleton (continued)

```
resource ApplCreator (rSignature, "Signature") {
     AppName " " AppVers ", " CopyrightNotice
};


resource 'vers' (1, purgeable) {
     0x1,
     0x00,
     final,
     0x0,
     verUS,
     AppVers,
     AppVers ", " CopyrightNotice
};

resource 'vers' (2, purgeable) {
     0x1,
     0x00,
     final,
     0x0,
     verUS,
     AppVers,
     AppName " " AppVers
};

resource 'ICN#' (rIconAPPL, "Application") {
     {
        /* image */
        $"0001 0000 0002 8000 0004 4000 000B A000"
        $"0014 5000 002A A800 0048 2400 008A A200"
        $"0105 4100 0202 8080 0401 0040 0807 C020"
        $"1018 3010 202E E808 40D8 3604 80AE EA02"
        $"40C8 2601 200F E002 1009 2004 0809 2008"
        $"0409 2010 0209 2020 0119 3840 00A1 0480"
        $"007F FD00 0020 0200 0010 0400 0008 0800"
        $"0004 1000 0002 2000 0001 4000 0000 8000",
        /* mask */
        $"0001 0000 0003 8000 0007 C000 000F E000"
        $"001F F000 003F F800 007F FC00 00FF FE00"
        $"01FF FF00 03FF FF80 07FF FFC0 0FFF FFE0"
        $"1FFF FFF0 3FFF FFF8 7FFF FFFC FFFF FFFE"
        $"7FFF FFFF 3FFF FFFE 1FFF FFFC 0FFF FFF8"
        $"07FF FFF0 03FF FFE0 01FF FFC0 00FF FF80"
        $"007F FF00 003F FE00 001F FC00 000F F800"
        $"0007 F000 0003 E000 0001 C000 0000 8000"
     }
};
```

Listing 1-4. Skeleton.r. The Rez source code for the resources used by Skeleton (continued)

```
resource 'ICN#' (rIconTEXT, "TEXT Document") {
    {
        /* image */
        $"0000 0000 0000 0000 0FFF FF00 0800 0180"
        $"0803 8140 0804 4120 080A A1F0 0808 2010"
        $"080A A010 0805 4010 0802 8010 0801 0010"
        $"0807 C010 0818 3010 082E E810 08D8 3610"
        $"08AE EA10 08C8 2610 080F E010 0809 2010"
        $"0809 2010 0809 2010 0809 2010 0819 3810"
        $"0821 0410 083F FC10 0800 0010 0800 0010"
        $"0FFF FFF0 0000 0000 0000 0000 0000 0000",
        /* mask */
        $"0000 0000 0000 0000 0FFF FF00 0FFF FF80"
        $"0FFF FFC0 0FFF FFE0 0FFF FFF0 0FFF FFF0"
        $"0FFF FFF0 0FFF FFF0 0FFF FFF0 0FFF FFF0"
        $"0FFF FFF0 0FFF FFF0 0FFF FFF0 0FFF FFF0"
        $"0FFF FFF0 0FFF FFF0 0FFF FFF0 0FFF FFF0"
        $"0FFF FFF0 0FFF FFF0 0FFF FFF0 0FFF FFF0"
        $"0FFF FFF0 0FFF FFF0 0FFF FFF0 0FFF FFF0"
        $"0FFF FFF0 0000 0000 0000 0000 0000 0000"
    }
};

/* See Appendix B for a complete description
    of all the items in the 'SIZE' resource
*/
resource 'SIZE' (-1, "Application attributes") {
    reserved,
    acceptSuspendResumeEvents,
    reserved,
    canBackground,
    doesActivateOnFGSwitch,

    backgroundAndForeground,
    dontGetFrontClicks,
    acceptAppDiedEvents,
    is32BitCompatible,
    isHighLevelEventAware,
    localAndRemoteHLEvents,
    isStationeryAware,
    useTextEditServices,
    reserved,
    reserved,
    reserved,
    kPrefSize * 1024,
    kMinSize * 1024
};
```

Listing 1-5. Skeleton.h. The interface file used by Skeleton.c

```
/*-------------------------------------------------------------------
#
#        Skeleton.h - Rez and C Include Source
#
#        Copyright © 1991 Gary Little
#        All rights reserved.
#
-------------------------------------------------------------------*/

#define AppName          "Skeleton"
#define AppVers          "1.0"
#define CopyrightNotice  "© 1991 Gary Little"
#define ApplCreator      'SKel'                  /* Application signature */

/* Resource IDs: */

#define StopIconID       0      /* Stop sign icon */

#define rBundle          128    /* Application bundle */
#define rSignature       0      /* Signature resource */
#define rRefAPPL         128    /* APPL file reference */
#define rRefTEXT         129    /* TEXT file reference */
#define rRefsEXT         130    /* sEXT file reference */
#define rIconAPPL        128    /* Application ICN# */
#define rIconTEXT        129    /* Document ICN# */
#define rIconsEXT        130    /* Stationery ICN# */

#define rAboutBox        128    /* About box */
#define rNotSystem7      129    /* Alert box */

#define rMainWindow      128    /* main application window */
#define rDebugWindow     129    /* Message window (for debugging) */

#define rHelpString      128    /* Finder help string */


/* Menu and Menu Item IDs: */
/* (Note: we use Menu resource IDs that are the same as Menu IDs) */

#define rMenuBar             128   /* application's menu bar */

#define mApple           128   /* Apple menu */
#define iAbout           1

#define mFile            129   /* File menu */
#define iNew             1
#define iOpen            2
#define iClose           4
```

Listing 1-5. Skeleton.h. The interface file used by Skeleton.c (continued)

```
#define  iSave                5
#define  iSaveAs              6
#define  iQuit                11

#define  mEdit                130  /* Edit menu */
#define  iUndo                1
#define  iCut                 3
#define  iCopy                4
#define  iPaste               5
#define  iClear               6

#define  mSpecial             131  /* Special menu */
#define  iTest                1


/* Miscellaneous: */

#define  kMinSize         23   /* minimum partition size (in K) */
#define  kPrefSize        35   /* preferred partition size (in K) */

/* Use these to set the enable/disable flags of a menu: */

#define  AllItems      0b1111111111111111111111111111111  /* 31 flags */
#define  NoItems       0b0000000000000000000000000000000
#define  MenuItem1     0b0000000000000000000000000000001
#define  MenuItem2     0b0000000000000000000000000000010
#define  MenuItem3     0b0000000000000000000000000000100
#define  MenuItem4     0b0000000000000000000000000001000
#define  MenuItem5     0b0000000000000000000000000010000
#define  MenuItem6     0b0000000000000000000000000100000
#define  MenuItem7     0b0000000000000000000000001000000
#define  MenuItem8     0b0000000000000000000000010000000
#define  MenuItem9     0b0000000000000000000000100000000
#define  MenuItem10    0b0000000000000000000001000000000
#define  MenuItem11    0b0000000000000000000010000000000
#define  MenuItem12    0b0000000000000000000100000000000
#define  MenuItem13    0b0000000000000000001000000000000
#define  MenuItem14    0b0000000000000000010000000000000
```

▶ Summary

In this chapter, we summarized the major new features of System 7 that provide interesting new opportunities for application developers. We also covered the **Gestalt** routine that applications should use to determine which features are present in the system at runtime. Finally, we presented the 7.0-specific Skeleton application, which you can use as the foundation for your own applications.

In the next chapter we begin our detailed exploration of System 7 by examining new features of the File Manager, Resource Manager, and the Standard File Package. We also cover the new Alias Manager.

2 ▶ Dealing with Files

The File Manager in System 7 introduces many new features that make it much more convenient to perform standard—and not so standard—file I/O operations. The File Manager also provides applications with easy access to special folders the system maintains, including the Temporary Folder and the Preferences Folder for storage of temporary work files and configuration files.

The Resource Manager also offers new routines. For the first time, you can open and create a resource fork without having to specify a full pathname or to set up a working directory and specify a partial pathname.

The Alias Manager is a completely new System 7 manager that applications can use to create and resolve alias records. An alias record is the electronic fingerprint of a target file that may reside on a local hard disk, a removable floppy disk, or an AppleShare volume. Identifying a file with an alias record enables the system to find the file even if it has been moved or renamed.

Here are some of the interesting topics in this chapter:

- the file system specification record (FSSpec)
- high-level file I/O routines that use FSSpec records
- Resource Manager routines that use FSSpec records
- Standard File Package Save and Open routines that use FSSpec records
- alias records for files and resolving alias records
- special folders on the boot volume

▶ Identifying Files

System 7 introduces yet another data structure for identifying a particular file on disk: the *file system specification record* (FSSpec). In case you've lost count, the other techniques involve the use of drive numbers, volume reference numbers, directory IDs, working directory reference numbers, full pathnames, partial pathnames, and various combinations thereof. By the time you finish reading this chapter, you will understand that using a file system specification record is now the preferred technique, primarily because the FSSpec is more convenient to deal with and is supported throughout the toolbox.

Here is the structure of an FSSpec record:

```
typedef struct FSSpec {
      short vRefNum;
      long parID;
      unsigned char name[64];
} FSSpec, *FSSpecPtr, **FSSpecHandle;
```

As is apparent, an FSSpec is made up of three components: a volume reference number (vRefNum) which identifies the disk volume, a directory ID (parID) which identifies the parent folder, and the name of the file itself (name[64]).

Later in this chapter you will see that the File Manager, Resource Manager, and Standard File Package provide new FSSpec-aware routines that perform most of the file-related operations you're likely to need. The only time you might need to use another technique to specify a file is if you call the low-level file I/O routines that use parameter blocks (described in *Inside Macintosh*, Volume IV). Most of these routines, however, simply need the three components inside an FSSpec, so you can pass the components separately and you'll be in fine shape.

▶ File I/O Operations

A number of new File Manager and Resource Manager routines work with FSSpec records instead of the file names and volume reference numbers that the older high-level File Manager routines (described in *Inside Macintosh*, Volume IV) use.

Here are descriptions of each of the new FSSpec-aware routines:

FSpCatMove(FSSpecPtr source, FSSpecPtr dest);

This routine moves the file or folder given by source to the folder (on the same volume) given by dest. The file or folder is also renamed if the name field of the destination FSSpec is different than the name field of the source FSSpec.

| Note ▶ | This routine just *moves* the source file, it does not copy it. |

FSpCreate(FSSpecPtr spec, OSType creator, OSType fileType,
        ScriptCode scriptTag);

This routine creates a file with the given spec and sets its creator and file type to the specified values. The scriptTag code tells the Finder which script system to use when displaying the file name (the permitted values are enumerated in the ScriptMgr.h header file). Pass the value returned by **StandardPutFile** or **CustomPutFile** (both described at the end of this chapter) in the sfScript field of the StandardFileReply record. If you aren't using these Standard File Package routines to get a file name, pass the value smSystemScript (the system script) instead.

FSpCreateResFile(FSSpecPtr spec, OSType creator, OSType fileType,
            ScriptCode scriptTag);

This routine adds a resource fork to the file given by spec. If the file does not already exist, one with the specified creator, fileType, and scriptTag is created first.

FSpDelete(FSSpecPtr spec);

This routine deletes the file given by spec. Only unlocked files on unlocked volumes may be deleted.

FSpDirCreate(FSSpecPtr spec, ScriptCode scriptTag,
            long *createdDirID);

This routine creates the folder given by spec. The scriptTag code has the same meaning as described above for **FSpCreate**. The directory ID of the created folder is returned in the createdDirID variable.

FSpGetFInfo(FSSpecPtr spec, FInfo *fndrInfo);

This routine returns the Finder information (FInfo) record for the file given by spec. See Listing 2-1 for a detailed description of the structure of this record. This is the routine you will use, for example, to determine the file type and creator of a file and to determine whether a document file is a stationery pad or an alias.

Listing 2-1. The structure of the FInfo (Finder information) record

```
typedef struct {
    OSType    fdType;        /* file type */
    OSType    fdCreator;     /* creator type */
    short     fdFlags;       /* Finder flags */
    Point     fdLocation;    /* location in folder */
    short     fdFldr;        /* folder containing file */
} FInfo ;
```

This is the format of the fdFlags word:

Bit Number	Meaning
isAlias (15)	The file is an alias file.
isInvisible (14)	The file is invisible. (Neither the Finder nor the Standard File routine displays its name.)
hasBundle (13)	The file has a 'BNDL' resource tying icons to file types. (See Chapter 9.)
nameLocked (12)	The file cannot be renamed from the Finder. In addition, you cannot change its icon by pasting a new one into the file's Get Info window in the Finder.
isStationery (11)	The file is a stationery pad.
hasCustomIcon (10)	The file has a custom icon family in its resource fork. (See Chapter 9.)
reserved (9)	Unused and reserved—set to 0.
hasBeenInited (8)	The Finder has already processed the file's 'BNDL' information.
hasNoINITs (7)	The file contains no 'INIT' resources.
isShared (6)	The file may be used by more than one user at once.
reserved (5)	Unused and reserved—set to 0.

Bit Number	Meaning
reserved (4)	Unused and reserved—set to 0.
color (1-3)	The label code for the file, as set by the items in the Finder's Label menu.
reserved (0)	Unused and reserved—set to 0.

FSpOpenDF(FSSpecPtr spec, char permission, short *refnum);

This routine opens the data fork of the file given by spec with the read/write permission given by permission. (Read/write permission values are enumerated in FileMgr.h.) The file reference number, needed by high-level routines that act on open files, is returned in the refnum variable.

FSpOpenResFile(FSSpecPtr spec, char permission);

This routine opens the resource fork of the file given by spec with the read/write permission given by permission. (Read/write permission values are enumerated in FileMgr.h.) Once you've opened the resource fork in this way, you may access individual resources with Resource Manager routines.

FSpOpenRF(FSSpecPtr spec, char permission, short *refnum);

This routine opens the resource fork of the file given by spec with the read/write permission given by permission. (Read/write permission values are enumerated in FileMgr.h.) The file reference number, needed by high-level routines that act on open files, is returned in the refnum variable. Don't use this routine to open a resource fork so that it can be accessed by Resource Manager routines; for that, use **FSpOpenResFile** instead. **FSpOpenRF** is for the benefit of utilities—such as file copiers—that need to access directly the data in the resource fork.

FSpRename(FSSpecPtr spec, StringPtr newName);

This routine changes the name of the file given by spec. The new name is given by the newName string.

FSpRstFLock(FSSpecPtr spec);

This routine unlocks the file given by spec. This makes it possible to delete the file with the **FSpDelete** routine.

```
FSpSetFInfo( FSSpecPtr spec,  FInfo *fndrInfo );
```

This routine sets the Finder information (FInfo) record for the file given by spec. See Listing 2-1 for a detailed description of the structure of this record. The preferred technique for changing Finder information, such as the value of the isStationery bit, is to use **FSpGetFInfo** to get the file's current FInfo record, insert the new values for the attributes you want to change, then write the same record back to disk with **FSpSetFInfo**.

```
FSpSetFLock( FSSpecPtr spec );
```

This routine locks the file given by spec. A locked file cannot be deleted with the **FSpDelete** routine unless it is first unlocked with the **FSpRstFLock** routine.

The high-level routines that accept file reference numbers have not changed, and you will still use them to deal with open files. This group includes **FSRead**, **FSWrite**, **GetFPos**, **SetFPos**, **GetEOF**, **SetEOF**, **Allocate**, and **FSClose**—all of which are described in *Inside Macintosh*, Volume IV.

The OpenDoc routine in Listing 2-2 shows how to use the new File Manager routines to open a file and load the contents of its data fork into memory. Notice that you use the new **FSpOpenDF** routine (instead of **FSOpen**) to open the file with the read/write permission granted by the file's attributes (fsCurPerm). Apart from that, OpenDoc is remarkably similar to what you'd write to open files in a System 6.x application.

Listing 2-2. OpenDoc, a routine for opening a file and loading the contents of its data fork into memory

```
/*    OpenDoc loads the entire contents of the data fork of the
      file specified by opFSSpec into memory. The handle to
      the loaded data is returned at *toDataHndl.
*/
OSErr OpenDoc( FSSpecPtr opFSSpec, Handle *toDataHndl )
{
    OSErr         fileError;
    short         fileRef;
    long          dataCount;
    Handle  fileDataH;

    fileError = FSpOpenDF( opFSSpec, fsCurPerm, &fileRef );
    if ( fileError ) return( fileError );

    fileError = GetEOF( fileRef, &dataCount );
    if ( fileError ) return( fileError );
```

Listing 2-2. OpenDoc, a routine for opening a file and loading the contents of its data fork into memory (continued)

```
        fileDataH = NewHandle( dataCount );
        if ( !fileDataH ) { FSClose( fileRef ); return( memFullErr ); }

        HLock( fileDataH );
        fileError = FSRead( fileRef, &dataCount, *fileDataH );
        HUnlock( fileDataH );

        /* We'll close now; in a real app, you would leave the file open
            until you close its window (this prevents others from editing
            a document on a network volume until you're through with it). */
        FSClose( fileRef );
        if ( fileError ) return( fileError );

        *toDataHndl = fileDataH;
        return( noErr );
}
```

The SaveDoc routine in Listing 2-3 is for saving a file to disk. The parameters you pass to it indicate the name of the file (svFSSpec), a handle to the location of the file's data (fileDataH), the file type and creator type (fileType and creator), whether the file is to be saved as a stationery pad (isStationery), and the script system identification number (scriptTag).

Listing 2-3. SaveDoc, a routine for saving a file to disk

```
/*   SaveDoc saves the contents of the fileDataH handle to the
     file specified by svFSSpec. The file type and creator are
     given by the fileType and creator parameters. If isStationery
     is true, the document is saved as a stationery pad file.
     scriptTag is the script system identification number.
*/
OSErr SaveDoc( FSSpecPtr svFSSpec, Handle fileDataH,
                 ResType fileType, ResType creator,
                 Boolean isStationery, ScriptCode scriptTag )
{
    OSErr   fileError;
    long    dataCount;
    short   fileRef;
    FInfo   theFInfo;

/* unlock and delete existing file: */

    fileError = FSpRstFLock( svFSSpec );
    if ( !(( fileError == fnfErr ) || ( fileError == noErr )) )
            return( fileError );
```

Listing 2-3. SaveDoc, a routine for saving a file to disk (continued)

```
        if ( fileError == noErr ) {

                fileError = FSpDelete( svFSSpec );
                if ( fileError ) return( fileError );
        }

        fileError = FSpCreate( svFSSpec, creator, fileType, scriptTag );
        if ( fileError ) return( fileError );

        if ( isStationery ) {

            FSpGetFInfo( svFSSpec, &theFInfo );
            theFInfo.fdFlags = theFInfo.fdFlags | 0x0800; /* set stationery bit */
            FSpSetFInfo( svFSSpec, &theFInfo );
        }

        fileError = FSpOpenDF( svFSSpec, fsCurPerm, &fileRef );
        if ( fileError ) return( fileError );

        dataCount = GetHandleSize( fileDataH );

        HLock( fileDataH );
        fileError = FSWrite( fileRef, &dataCount, *fileDataH );
        HUnlock( fileDataH );

        FSClose( fileRef );
        if ( fileError ) return( fileError );

        return( noErr );
}
```

SaveDoc illustrates the standard techniques to use when saving a file to disk. The routine begins by deleting any file that may already exist with the same name. It does this by first calling **FSpRstFLock** to unlock the file. If the file already exists, **FSpRstFLock** returns noErr and the file is deleted with **FSpDelete**; if the file doesn't exist, **FSpRstFLock** returns fnfErr (file not found) and no deletion is necessary. SaveDoc then calls **FSpCreate** to create the file.

Next, SaveDoc checks to see whether the file is to be saved as a stationery pad. If it is, it sets the isStationery bit in the file's Finder information record (see Listing 2-1). To do this, SaveDoc calls **FSpGetFInfo** for the current Finder information, sets the isStationery bit of the fdFlags field, then writes the Finder information back to disk with **FSpSetFInfo**.

Finally, SaveDoc opens the newly created file with **FSpOpenDF**, writes the data to disk with **FSWrite**, then closes the file with **FSClose**.

You can add these two routines to the Skeleton application to extend its capabilities. First, place a call to `OpenDoc` at the beginning of the `CreateFileWindow` function. Place calls to `SaveDoc` in the handlers for the `iSave` and `iSaveAs` menu items (part of the `DoMenuCommand` routine).

▶ Searching Volumes

There is one completely new File Manager routine that you may find useful from time to time—**PBCatSearch**. This rather powerful routine quickly scans a volume for files that satisfy criteria that you specify. For example, with **PBCatSearch** you could search a volume for all files that haven't been backed up since November 30, 1986 (hopefully you don't have too many of these), all files whose names begin with "Test" (most programmers have lots of these), or all files with a file type of `'APPL'`.

Here is the function prototype for **PBCatSearch**:

```
pascal OSErr PBCatSearch( CSParamPtr paramblock,
                          Boolean async );
```

Notice that **PBCatSearch**, as its `PB` prefix suggests, uses a parameter block (of type `CSParam`) to accept data from and return data to your application. File Manager routines like this are called *low-level* routines. As described in *Inside Macintosh*, Volume IV, you can call such routines either asynchronously (where the routine returns immediately, before the operation completes) or synchronously (where the routine waits until the operation is complete before returning a result). To make an asynchronous call, you must put the address of a completion procedure in the `ioCompletion` field of the parameter block before calling the File Manager routine with the `async` parameter set to true.

Listing 2-4 shows the structure of the `CSParam` parameter block that **PBCatSearch** uses. It also shows the structure of the `CInfoPBRec` to which the `ioSearchInfo1` and `ioSearchInfo2` fields of `CSParam` point. Notice that `CInfoPBRec` is a union record which contains either a `DirInfo` record or a `HFileInfo` record, depending on whether you're dealing with a folder or with a regular file.

Listing 2-4. The CSParam and CInfoPBRec structures used by PBCatSearch

```
typedef struct  {
    struct QElem *qLink;        /* beginning of STANDARD_PBHEADER */
    short       qType;          /* queue type */
    short       ioTrap;         /* routine trap */
    Ptr         ioCmdAddr;      /* routine address */
    ProcPtr     ioCompletion;   /* needed for async calls */
```

Listing 2-4. The CSParam and CInfoPBRec structures used by PBCatSearch (continued)

```
    OsErr          ioResult;        /* result code */
    StringPtr      ioNamePtr;       /* pathname */
    short          ioVRefNum;       /* end of STANDARD_PBHEADER */
    FSSpecPtr      ioMatchPtr;      /* pointer match list space */
    long           ioReqMatchCount;/* maximum match count */
    long           ioActMatchCount;/* actual match count */
    long           ioSearchBits;    /* enabling flags for search */
    CInfoPBPtr     ioSearchInfo1;   /* values and lower bounds */
    CInfoPBPtr     ioSearchInfo2;   /* enabling flags and upper bounds */
    long           ioSearchTime;    /* maximum search time (milliseconds) */
    CatPositionRec ioCatPosition;  /* current catalog position */
    Ptr            ioOptBuffer;     /* pointer to optional read buffer */
    long           ioOptBufSize;    /* size of optional read buffer */

} CSParam, *CSParamPtr;

typedef union {
  HFileInfo      hFileInfo;
  DirInfo        dirInfo;
} CInfoPBRec, *CInfoPBPtr;

typedef struct {
  STANDARD_PBHEADER
  short          ioFRefNum;
  SignedByte     ioFVersNum;
  SignedByte     filler1;
  short          ioFDirIndex;
  SignedByte     ioFlAttrib;       /* file attributes */
  SignedByte     ioACUser;
  FInfo          ioFlFndrInfo;     /* Finder information */
  long           ioDirID;
  short          ioFlStBlk;
  long           ioFlLgLen;        /* logical size of data fork */
  long           ioFlPyLen;        /* physical size of data fork */
  short          ioFlRStBlk;
  long           ioFlRLgLen;       /* logical size of resource fork */
  long           ioFlRPyLen;       /* physical size of resource fork */
  long           ioFlCrDat;        /* creation date of file */
  long           ioFlMdDat;        /* modification date of file */
  long           ioFlBkDat;        /* backup date of file */
  FXInfo         ioFlXFndrInfo;    /* extended Finder information */
  long           ioFlParID;        /* parent directory ID for the file */
  long           ioFlClpSiz;
} HFileInfo;

typedef struct {
  STANDARD_PBHEADER
```

Listing 2-4. The CSParam and CInfoPBRec structures used by PBCatSearch (continued)

```
    short           ioFRefNum;
    SignedByte      ioFVersNum;
    SignedByte      filler1;
    short           ioFDirIndex;
    SignedByte      ioFlAttrib;         /* folder attributes */
    SignedByte      ioACUser;
    DInfo           ioDrUsrWds;         /* Finder information */
    long            ioDrDirID;
    short           ioDrNmFls;          /* number of files in folder */
    short           filler3[9];
    long            ioDrCrDat;          /* creation date of folder */
    long            ioDrMdDat;          /* modification date of folder */
    long            ioDrBkDat;          /* backup date of folder */
    DXInfo          ioDrFndrInfo;       /* extended Finder information */
    long            ioDrParID;          /* parent directory ID for the folder */
} DirInfo;
```

Before calling **PBCatSearch**, you must fill in CSParam properly. Begin by putting the reference number of the volume you want to search at ioVRefNum (this will be -1 for the boot volume, for example). Then store at ioMatchPtr a pointer to the data space you've reserved for the array of FSSpec records that **PBCatSearch** returns, and store the number of FSSpec records in the array at ioReqMatchCount.

Next, tell **PBCatSearch** to start the search from the first file on the volume by setting ioCatPosition.initialize to zero. If you don't want to provide **PBCatSearch** with an extra read buffer, also zero the ioOptBuffer and ioOptBufSize fields; otherwise pass a pointer to the buffer and the size of the buffer. (Using a read buffer will speed up file search operations.)

Next, store a timeout value, in milliseconds, in the ioSearchTime field. If **PBCatSearch** doesn't find the requested number of files within this time period, it stops searching and returns control to the application. The application can then check to see if the user wants to cancel the operation, and continue the search, if appropriate, by calling **PBCatSearch** again. Breaking a complete search into pieces like this is advisable when searching very large volumes because the search will take a long time to complete.

The fields ioSearchInfo1 and ioSearchInfo2 together define the search criteria. **PBCatSearch** examines the values in these two fields to determine whether a particular file is a "hit" or a "miss." Here are the values you place in the CInfoPBRec structures pointed to by ioSearchInfo1 and ioSearchInfo2:

Field	*ioSearchInfo1 value	*ioSearchInfo2 value
`ioNamePtr`	file name	must be zero
`ioFlAttrib`	file attributes (bit 0: file is locked) (bit 4: file is a folder)	file attributes mask
`ioFlFndrInfo`	Finder information	Finder information mask
`ioFlLgLen`	smallest logical size (data)	largest logical size (data)
`ioFlPyLen`	smallest physical size (data)	largest physical size (data)
`ioFlRLgLen`	smallest logical size (rsrc)	largest logical size (rsrc)
`ioFlRPyLen`	smallest physical size (rsrc)	largest physical size (rsrc)
`ioFlCrDat`	earliest creation date	latest creation date
`ioFlMDat`	earliest modification date	latest modification date
`ioFlBakDat`	earliest backup date	latest backup date
`ioFlXFndrInfo`	extended Finder information	extended Finder information mask

Key Point ▶

Notice how you specify ranges of sizes or dates—you put the smallest size (or earliest date) in the appropriate `*ioSearchInfo1` field and the largest size (or latest date) in the corresponding field of `*ioSearchInfo2`.

For the `ioFlAttrib`, `ioFlFndrInfo`, and `ioFlXFndrInfo` fields, the corresponding field of `*ioSearchInfo2` holds masks that indicate which bits are relevant to the search. For example, if you're searching for files only, you clear bit 4 of `ioFlAttrib` in `*ioSearchInfo1` ("no folder files") and then set bit 4 of `ioFlAttrib` in `*ioSearchInfo2` ("the file/folder bit is relevant").

If a particular field of `*ioSearchInfo1` is not relevant to the search, don't bother filling in a value. You specify a mask in the `ioSearchBits` field to indicate which of the `*ioSearchInfo1` fields are relevant to the search. To determine the value to pass in `ioSearchBits`, sum the weights of the masks (shown in Listing 2-5) for the fields relevant to the search operation. For example, if you're looking for an exact name match and the date of creation is relevant, set `ioSearchBits` to `fsSBFullName+fsSBFlCrDat`. By including the value of the `fsSBNegate` mask, you can tell **PBCatSearch** to invert the search operation—in other words, to return files that do *not* satisfy the search criteria rather than those that do.

Listing 2-5. The values of the masks used with the ioSearchBits field of CSParam

```
enum {
        fsSBPartialName = 1,        /* want names that include the specified name */
        fsSBFullName    = 2,        /* full name match */
        fsSBFlAttrib    = 4,        /* ioFlAttrib field is relevant */
        fsSBNegate      = 16384,    /* invert the search */
/* the following are for regular files only: */
        fsSBFlFndrInfo  = 8,        /* ioFlFndrInfo field is relevant */
        fsSBFlLgLen     = 32,       /* ioFlLgLen field is relevant */
        fsSBFlPyLen     = 64,       /* ioFlPyLen field is relevant */
        fsSBFlRLgLen    = 128,      /* ioFlRLgLen field is relevant */
        fsSBFlRPyLen    = 256,      /* ioFlRPyLen field is relevant */
        fsSBFlCrDat     = 512,      /* ioFlCrDat field is relevant */
        fsSBFlMdDat     = 1024,     /* ioFlMdDat field is relevant */
        fsSBFlBkDat     = 2048,     /* ioFlBkDat field is relevant */
        fsSBFlXFndrInfo = 4096,     /* ioFlXFndrInfo field is relevant */
        fsSBFlParID     = 8192,     /* ioFlParID field is relevant */
/* the following are for folders only: */
        fsSBDrUsrWds    = 8,        /* ioDrUsrWds field is relevant */
        fsSBDrNmFls     = 16,       /* ioDrNmFls field is relevant */
        fsSBDrCrDat     = 512,      /* ioDrCrDat field is relevant */
        fsSBDrMdDat     = 1024,     /* ioDrMdDat field is relevant */
        fsSBDrBkDat     = 2048,     /* ioDrBkDat field is relevant */
        fsSBDrFndrInfo  = 4096,     /* ioDrFndrInfo field is relevant */
        fsSBDrParID     = 8192      /* ioDrParID field is relevant */
};
```

PBCatSearch returns control to you as soon as one of the following conditions becomes true:

- the time specified by ioSearchTime expires
- the maximum number of files (ioReqMatchCount) is found
- the entire volume has been searched (**PBCatSearch** returns eofErr)

When **PBCatSearch** returns, check the value of ioActMatchCount to determine the actual number of files, if any, that were found.

If the search ends because of a time-out or because the maximum number of files was found, **PBCatSearch** saves the current search position in the ioCatPosition field of CSParam. You can continue the search from this position by calling **PBCatSearch** once again and specifying that value of ioCatPosition.

The routine in Listing 2-6, GetAPPLNames, shows how you can use **PBCatSearch** to obtain a list of application programs on the boot volume. For such a search, the only criteria are that the file is not a folder and that the file type is 'APPL'. Since the file/folder bit is part of the ioFlAttrib field of CInfoPBRec and the file type is part of the ioFlFndrInfo field, GetAPPLNames sets `ioSearchBits` to `fsSBFlAttrib+fsSBFlFndrInfo` to indicate that these two fields are the only ones that **PBCatSearch** should examine when testing for a match.

Listing 2-6. GetAPPLNames, a routine for returning a list of applications on the boot volume

```
/* GetAPPLNames returns the FSSpecs of up to *groupSize application
     files (creator: 'APPL') on the volume given by theVRefNum. The
     FSSpecs are stored in the foundSpecs array. The actual number
     of FSSpecs found is returned in *groupSize.
*/
OSErr GetAPPLNames( long theVRefNum, FSSpec foundSpecs[], long *groupSize )
{
     OSErr          fileError;
     CSParam        SearchPB;
     HFileInfo      search1, search2;
     long           foundCount = 0;

     SearchPB.ioReqMatchCount = *groupSize;

     SearchPB.ioCompletion = 0L;
     SearchPB.ioNamePtr = 0L;
     SearchPB.ioVRefNum = theVRefNum;
     SearchPB.ioMatchPtr = foundSpecs;
     SearchPB.ioSearchBits = fsSBFlAttrib+fsSBFlFndrInfo;
     SearchPB.ioSearchInfo1 = (CInfoPBPtr)&search1;
     SearchPB.ioSearchInfo2 = (CInfoPBPtr)&search2;
     SearchPB.ioSearchTime = 5000L; /* 5 seconds */
     SearchPB.ioCatPosition.initialize = 0L;
     SearchPB.ioOptBuffer = 0L;
     SearchPB.ioOptBufSize = 0L;

     search1.ioNamePtr = 0L;                         /* name not important */
     search1.ioFlAttrib = 0x00;                      /* files only - no folders */
     search1.ioFlFndrInfo.fdType = 'APPL';           /* 'APPL' only */

     search2.ioNamePtr = 0L;                         /* (not used) */
     search2.ioFlAttrib = 0x10;                      /* file/folder bit is hot */
     search2.ioFlFndrInfo.fdType = -1L;              /* type is hot */
     search2.ioFlFndrInfo.fdFlags = 0;               /* not relevant */
     search2.ioFlFndrInfo.fdCreator = 0L;            /* not relevant */
     search2.ioFlFndrInfo.fdLocation.v = 0;          /* not relevant */
     search2.ioFlFndrInfo.fdLocation.h = 0;          /* not relevant */
     search2.ioFlFndrInfo.fdFldr = 0L;               /* not relevant */

     do {
           fileError = PBCatSearch( &SearchPB, false );
           if ( !(fileError == 0 || fileError == eofErr) )
                return( fileError );

           foundCount += SearchPB.ioActMatchCount;
           SearchPB.ioReqMatchCount -= SearchPB.ioActMatchCount;
```

Listing 2-6. GetAPPLNames, a routine for returning a list of applications on the boot volume (continued)

```
        /* put code here to see if user cancels operation */

    } while ( (fileError != eofErr) & (SearchPB.ioReqMatchCount != 0) );

    *groupSize = foundCount;
    return( fileError );
}
```

GetAPPLNames then clears the file/folder bit in search1.ioFlAttrib to indicate that folder files are not acceptable and sets the search1.ioFlFndrInfo.fdType field to 'APPL'. To tell **PBCatSearch** that only the file/folder bit of search1.ioFlAttrib is relevant, the corresponding bit in the search2.ioFlAttrib field is set to 1. Finally, the search2.ioFlFndrInfo.fdType field is set to -1 (all bits set) to indicate that the file type field is relevant. (All the other fields of ioFlFndrInfo are zeroed because they are not relevant.)

Notice that GetAPPLNames keeps calling **PBCatSearch** until it returns eofErr ("the entire volume has been searched") or until the file name array fills up. (**PBCatSearch** might return before searching the entire volume if a time-out occurs or if it finds ioReqMatchCount matches.) GetAPPLNames returns in the groupSize variable the actual number of files it finds.

▶ Special Folders

A System 7 boot volume contains several special folders used to organize groups of related system files, or files with certain special attributes. With a few exceptions noted below, most applications will never need to access these folders directly—they are for system or Finder use only.

Table 2-1 is a complete list of the special folders that System 7 maintains.

Table 2-1. Special folders maintained by System 7

Names on U.S. System Disk	*folderType identifier*
System Folder	kSystemFolderType
Extensions	kExtensionFolderType
Startup Items	kStartupFolderType
Control Panels	kControlPanelFolderType

Table 2-1. Special folders maintained by System 7 (continued)

Names on U.S. System Disk		*folderType identifier*
	Apple Menu Items	kAppleMenuFolderType
	PrintMonitor Documents	kPrintMonitorDocsFolderType
	Trash	kTrashFolderType
	(shared, network trash folder)	kWhereToEmptyTrashFolderType
	Desktop Folder	kDesktopFolderType
	Preferences	kPreferencesFolderType
	Temporary Folder	kTemporaryFolderType

Here are descriptions of what each of these folders generally contain:

System Folder—Located at the root of the volume, this folder is where the system software keeps the files it needs to operate, including the System file itself. Some of these files are stored in special folders inside the System Folder.

Extensions Folder—This folder, inside the System Folder, contains 'INIT' type files which have code resources the system loads and executes at boot time. It also contains files that extend the general functionality of the system, such as printer drivers and networking control software.

Startup Items—This folder, inside the System Folder, contains application files that the system automatically starts up when it boots.

Control Panels —This folder, inside the System Folder, contains control panel applications that the user can run to change system settings or the system configuration.

Apple Menu Items—This folder, inside the System Folder, contains files that appear in the standard Apple menu. Any type of file can appear in the Apple menu, not just desk accessories.

PrintMonitor Documents—Located inside the System Folder, this folder contains spooled document files that the Print Manager has not yet printed.

Trash—This invisible folder, in the root of the volume, is represented by a trash can icon on the desktop. It contains files that the user moves to the

Trash from the Finder; the files are deleted when the user chooses Empty Trash from the Finder's Special menu.

Shared Trash —Inside the Trash Folder are invisible trash folders for each user who has logged on to the system to access a shared folder. The Shared Trash folders have unique names assigned by the system at run time.

Desktop Folder—This invisible folder is in the root of every volume, not just the boot volume. The files here show up as icons on the Finder desktop.

Preferences—This folder is inside the System Folder. This is where applications should store configuration files.

Temporary Folder—This invisible folder is in the root of every volume, not just the boot volume. This is where an application should store scratch files that it will delete before it quits. On boot, the system checks this folder and moves any files it finds to a folder called "Rescued Items for <volume name>" inside the Trash Folder. Files might be in the Temporary Folder at boot time if an application crashed before deleting its temporary files— moving them to the Trash Folder makes it easier for the user to remove them and ensures that the disk won't become cluttered with unwanted temporary files.

System —The System file, located inside the System Folder, is not really a folder, but it behaves like one when you access it from the Finder. When you double-click the System file, it opens up to reveal the names of all the sound and font resources it contains. To install new fonts and sounds, you simply drag them to the System file or the System Folder.

To locate a particular folder (that is, to find its volume reference number and directory ID), use the **FindFolder** routine:

```
pascal OSErr FindFolder( short vRefNum,
                         OSType folderType,
                         Boolean createFolder,
                         short* foundVRefNum,
                         long* foundDirID );
```

The parameters you supply to **FindFolder** are vRefNum (the volume reference number; use the kOnSystemDisk constant for the boot volume), folderType (the identifier for the special folder you want; see Table 2-1), and createFolder (true if you want the folder to be created if it doesn't already exist).

FindFolder returns the volume reference number and directory ID of the appropriate folder. You can store this information in an FSSpec record, along with a file name, to create the FSSpec for a file to be read from, or saved in, the folder. In the next section on alias records and alias files, for example, you'll see how to save a file in the Desktop Folder so that it shows up on the Finder desktop.

Key Point ▶

In summary, most applications will use only four special folders:

- Temporary Folder
- Preferences Folder
- Apple Menu Items
- Desktop Folder

In general, you should avoid accessing the other folders directly.

▶ Alias Records and Alias Files

As you now know, using an FSSpec record to identify a file has many advantages, but you cannot use it to locate the same file the next time your application runs. That's because the FSSpec is "hard-wired" to a particular volume reference number, directory ID, and name. It becomes invalid if the file is moved or renamed, or the file is on an AppleShare volume or a floppy disk.

System 7 introduces the *alias record* to overcome this limitation. An alias record contains enough information to allow the system, in most cases, to find the file it describes, even if the file has been renamed, moved to another folder, or located on an AppleShare volume or an unmounted disk. The Alias Manager has routines for creating an alias record from an FSSpec record and for creating an FSSpec record from an alias record (the latter conversion process is called *resolving* an alias).

Key Point ▶

If your application needs to save the location of a file so that the file can be found in subsequent sessions, save the alias record of the file, not the FSSpec.

To create an alias record for a file, use **NewAlias**:

```
pascal OSErr NewAlias( FSSpec *fromFile,
                       FSSpec *target,
                       AliasHandle *alias );
```

The first parameter, `fromFile`, is generally not used and is set to zero. You can, however, set it to point to the `FSSpec` for a file that is always stored at the same relative folder position from the target file. If you do specify a `fromFile`, the Alias Manager uses a different technique to resolve the alias, a technique which could, in certain situations, be more effective than the usual technique. See *Inside Macintosh*, Volume VI for details.

The second parameter, `target`, is a pointer to the `FSSpec` of the file whose alias you're creating. The third parameter, `alias`, is the pointer to a space for the alias record that **NewAlias** creates.

An alias record should generally be stored as an `'alis'` resource in the resource fork of the document that needs access to the file described by the alias. A preferences file for a communications program, for example, might contain `'alis'` resources describing the locations of the folders into which it transfers files from the online services it supports.

Since the File Manager and Resource Manager routines don't accept an alias record as a parameter, you have to convert it to an `FSSpec` first. Do this by calling the **ResolveAlias** routine:

```
pascal OSErr ResolveAlias( FSSpec *fromFile,
                           AliasHandle alias,
                           FSSpec *target,
                           Boolean *wasChanged );
```

As with **MakeAlias**, `fromFile` refers to the `FSSpec` for a file from which a relative resolution is to take place; set it to zero if you don't want relative resolution. The second parameter, `alias`, is a handle to the alias record to be resolved. (Use the handle returned by **GetResource** if you retrieved the alias from a resource.) On return, **ResolveAlias** returns the `FSSpec` of the target file at `target` and sets the `wasChanged` variable to true if the alias record was modified to more efficiently describe the current position of the target file. If the alias record is modified, be sure to update any copies of the alias you may have saved in a file on disk.

| Note ▶ |

When an application calls **ResolveAlias,** the user may be prompted to insert a particular disk or to log on to a particular server, depending on where the Alias Manager thinks it has to look for the target file.

You can also use the **MatchAlias** routine to resolve aliases, but only if you require greater control over the method of resolution. This low-level routine is described in *Inside Macintosh*, Volume VI.

▶ Preserving Aliases for Updated Files

Many applications, particularly those that load an entire document into memory at once, save an edited copy of a document back to disk in a temporary file; when the copy has been safely saved, the original is deleted and the copy is renamed to the name of the original document. This strategy prevents data loss if the system crashes during the save operation.

At first blush, the possible existence of aliases that refer to the document being edited makes this strategy less than appealing—even though the edited document is effectively saved back to disk under the same name as the original document, it is really a different file and aliases to the original document file would not refer to the edited document file.

The File Manager includes a new routine, **FSpExchangeFiles**, you can use to avoid this problem. **FSpExchangeFiles** swaps the contents of two files (on the same volume), effectively transferring the data in the edited file to the original, thus preserving existing aliases. It also swaps the modification dates for the two files, as you would expect.

Here is the function prototype for **FSpExchangeFiles**:

```
pascal OSErr FSpExchangeFiles( const FSSpec *source,
                               const FSSpec *dest );
```

The source parameter is a pointer to the FSSpec for the temporary file containing the edited data. The dest parameter is a pointer to the FSSpec for the original file.

The proper time to call **FSpExchangeFiles** is right after saving the edited copy of the document to a temporary file. After calling it, you would delete the copy of the document, leaving only the original document which now contains the edited data.

▶ Alias Files

You should be careful not to confuse an alias record, created by **NewAlias**, with an alias *file*, which you create from the Finder with the Make Alias command in the File menu. On the desktop, an alias file looks just like its target file, except that its name has an " alias" suffix and is italicized (you can rename an alias file just as you would a normal file, however).

Here are the vital statistics for an alias file that are of interest to programmers:

- `isAlias` bit of the `fdFlags` field of the file's `FInfo` record is set
- data fork of the file is empty
- resource fork contains an 'alis' resource (ID 0) describing the target file
- if the target file of the alias is an application, file type is 'adrp'

The `MakeAlias` routine in Listing 2-7 shows how to create a Finder-style alias file from inside an application. The routine calls `NewAlias` to create the alias record for the target file, then creates an alias file in the boot volume's Desktop Folder so that it appears on the Finder's desktop. You use **FindFolder** to determine the `vRefNum` and `dirID` of this folder, as described in the previous section. You also use the new Resource Manager routine, **FSpCreateResFile**, to create the alias file (with an initialized resource fork). Another new call, **FSpOpenResFile**, opens the resource fork so that the 'alis' resource can be added with **AddResource**.

Listing 2-7. MakeAlias, a routine for creating a Finder-style alias file

```
/* MakeAlias creates a standard Finder alias file for the target
        file given by theSpec and puts it in the Desktop Folder.
*/
OSErr MakeAlias( FSSpecPtr theFSSpec )
{
        Str255              aliasName = "\p";
        FSSpec              aliasSpec;
        OSErr               fileError;
        FInfo               theFInfo, targetFInfo;
        short               fileRef;
        AliasHandle         alias;

        fileError = NewAlias( 0L, theFSSpec, &alias );       /* create alias */
        if ( fileError ) return( fileError );

        /* Get type and creator of the target */
        FSpGetFInfo( theFSSpec, &targetFInfo );
        if ( targetFInfo.fdType == 'APPL' ) targetFInfo.fdType = 'adrp';

        if ( theFSSpec->name[0] > 25 ) theFSSpec->name[0] = 25;     /* chop stem
                                                                to 25 chars */

        /* Fill in the FSSpec for the alias file */
        ConcatString( aliasName, theFSSpec->name );
        ConcatString( aliasName, (StringPtr)"\p alias" );
        pStringCopy( aliasName, aliasSpec.name );
```

Listing 2-7. MakeAlias, a routine for creating a Finder-style alias file (continued)

```
        fileError = FindFolder( kOnSystemDisk, kDesktopFolderType,
                                kCreateFolder, &aliasSpec.vRefNum,
                                &aliasSpec.parID );

/* unlock and delete existing file: */

        fileError = FSpRstFLock( &aliasSpec );
        if ( !(( fileError == fnfErr ) || ( fileError == noErr )) )
                return( fileError );

        if ( fileError == noErr ) {

                fileError = FSpDelete( &aliasSpec );
                if ( fileError ) return( fileError );
        }

        FSpCreateResFile( &aliasSpec, targetFInfo.fdCreator,
                        targetFInfo.fdType, smSystemScript );
        fileError = ResError();
        if ( fileError ) return( fileError );

        fileError = FSpGetFInfo( &aliasSpec, &theFInfo );
        theFInfo.fdFlags = theFInfo.fdFlags | 0x8000;        /* set isAlias bit */
        FSpSetFInfo( &aliasSpec, &theFInfo );

        fileRef = FSpOpenResFile( &aliasSpec, fsCurPerm );
        if ( fileRef == -1 ) {

                fileError = ResError();
                return( fileError );
        }

        AddResource( (Handle)alias, rAliasType, 0, aliasName );
        fileError = ResError();

        CloseResFile( fileRef );
        return( fileError );
}
```

An application doesn't normally deal with alias files directly. When you Open or Print an alias for a document file from the Finder, for example, the Finder finds the target document by resolving the alias and passes it to the application instead. Similarly, if an application calls **StandardGetFile** or **CustomGetFile** to ask the user to select a file (see below), the FSSpec for an alias file is never returned—these routines automatically resolve the alias and return the FSSpec for the target application instead.

In those rare cases where you might have to deal with an alias file directly, you can easily find its target file using the **ResolveAliasFile** routine:

```
pascal OSErr ResolveAliasFile( FSSpec *theSpec,
                               Boolean resolveAliasChains,
                               Boolean *targetIsFolder,
                               Boolean *wasAliased );
```

In this routine, theSpec is the pointer to the FSSpec for the alias file you want to resolve. Set resolveAliasChains to true if you want **ResolveAliasFile** to resolve all aliases in the chain back to the original target file. (If resolveAliasChains is false and theSpec is the alias of another alias file, the FSSpec of that alias file is returned.)

On return, the FSSpec for the target file is in the theSpec variable, the targetIsFolder variable is true if the target file is a folder (or volume), and the wasAliased variable is true if theSpec did, indeed, refer to the FSSpec for an alias file. (If it didn't, the FSSpec that theSpec points to does not change and **ResolveAliasFile** really doesn't do anything.)

▶ The Standard File Package

The Standard File Package contains the routines for presenting the standard Open File and Save File dialog boxes shown in Figures 2-1 and 2-2. The Open File dialog lets the user browse through folders and volumes to locate a file; to select a file, the user clicks on its name and then clicks the Open button (or simply double-clicks on the name). The Save File dialog permits similar browsing and also provides an editable text field where the user can enter a name for the file to be saved. The user clicks the Save button to perform the operation.

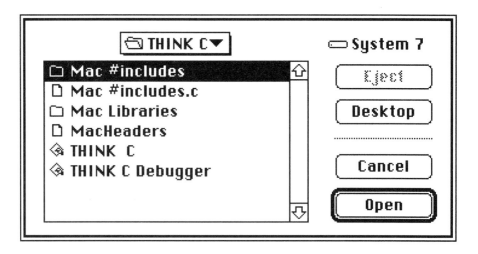

Figure 2-1. The standard Open File dialog box used by StandardGetFile

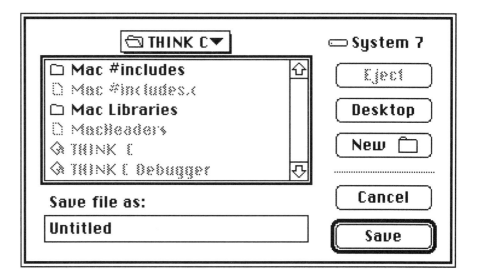

Figure 2-2. The standard Save File dialog box used by StandardPutFile

These two standard dialog boxes resemble the ones System 6.x applications use. Under System 7, however, you call two new routines to display them, **StandardGetFile** and **StandardPutFile**. The main reason for using these new routines is that they both return results in a `StandardFileReply` record and one of the fields of this record is an `FSSpec` record which the new File Manager routines need to open or create a file.

StandardGetFile

Here is the function prototype for **StandardGetFile**:

```
pascal void StandardGetFile( StringPtr prompt,
                             ProcPtr fileFilter,
                             short numTypes,
                             SFTypeList *typeList,
                             StandardFileReply *reply );
```

| Important ▶ |

Before describing **StandardGetFile**'s parameters, a note on how your application should react to the selection of a stationery-pad file (the `isStationery` bit in the `sfFlags` field of the `StandardFileReply` record for such a file is 1). By convention, your application must open an untitled copy of a stationery-pad file, not the original file, so that when the user tries to save the file back to disk, your application will ask for a new file name. This prevents accidental overwriting of the original stationery-pad file, which presumably contains a blank template that is not to be modified. The `CreateFileWindow` routine in the Skeleton application handles stationery-pad files in the proper way.

If your application handles stationery-pad files in the conventional way, set the `isStationeryAware` flag in its 'SIZE' resource (see Appendix B). If you don't, you will see the warning dialog shown in Figure 2-3.

Figure 2-3. The warning dialog that appears if an application's isStationeryAware flag is not set and the user tries to select a stationery-pad file from an Open File dialog

Now let's take a closer look at each of the parameters to **StandardGetFile**.

StandardFileReply—This record, shown in Listing 2-8, contains the results of the Open File operation. The two most important fields to note are sfGood, which is true if the user clicked the OK button, and sfFile, which is the FSSpec of the file the user selected. Other relevant fields are sfType, the file's type code; sfScript, the file's script system identification code; and sfFlags, the file's Finder flags. If sfGood is false, the user clicked the Cancel button and the application must abort the open operation.

Listing 2-8. The StandardFileReply record used by Standard File routines

```
typedef struct {
    Boolean     sfGood;        /* true = OK ; false = Cancel */
    Boolean     sfReplacing;   /* true = replacing existing file */
    OSType      sfType;        /* file type */
    FSSpec      sfFile;        /* FSSpec for the selection */
    ScriptCode  sfScript;      /* script system code */
    short       sfFlags;       /* Finder flags */
    Boolean     sfIsFolder;    /* selection is a folder */
    Boolean     sfIsVolume;    /* selection is a volume */
    long        sfReserved1;
    short       sfReserved2;
} StandardFileReply;
```

StandardGetFile checks the information given by the remaining three parameters to determine whether or not to display a particular file name in the scrollable list. This screening process is called *file filtering*.

typeList—This is a pointer to a list of file type codes (such as 'TEXT', 'APPL', and so on). Only files whose file types are in the list, and folder files, are passed to fileFilter for further filtering.

numTypes—This is the number of items in the list pointed to by typeList. If you specify a value of -1, however, the typeList parameter is ignored and *all* files are passed to fileFilter.

fileFilter—This is an optional file filter procedure that you provide. It receives CInfoPBRec information about each file whose type code is in the list pointed to by typeList (or all files if numTypes is -1) and returns a Boolean that tells **StandardGetFile** whether or not to display the file name in the scrollable list. If no special file filtering is needed, set fileFilter to 0L. The function prototype for a file filter follows:

```
pascal Boolean fileFilter( CInfoPBPtr PB );
```

The structure of the CInfoPBRec to which PB points is shown in Listing 2-4. The filter procedure can examine the values in this record to determine whether the file meets the desired criteria; if it does, the procedure returns false and **StandardGetFile** displays the file name. If it returns true, the file name is not displayed.

| Note ▶ | It is not possible to filter out folder files. They will appear in the list even if the file filter returns true. |

StandardPutFile

The function prototype for **StandardPutFile** follows:

```
pascal void StandardPutFile( StringPtr prompt,
                             StringPtr defaultName,
                             StandardFileReply *reply );
```

Here is the meaning of each parameter:

prompt—This is the prompting string that appears just above the editable text box where the user types in a file name.

defaultName—This is the file name that initially appears in the editable text box.

StandardFileReply—This record, shown in Listing 2-8, contains the results of the Save File operation. The two most important fields to note are sfGood, which is true if the user clicked the OK button, and sfFile, which is the FSSpec of the file the user entered. The other relevant field is sfReplacing which is true if a file already exists with the same FSSpec.

Take a look at the Skeleton program in Chapter 1 for examples of how to use **StandardGetFile** and **StandardPutFile**.

▶ Customized Open File and Save File Dialog Boxes

The Standard File Package also includes two new routines for presenting customized Open File and Save File dialog boxes to the user: **CustomGetFile** and **CustomPutFile**. These routines let you add more controls—such as radio buttons or check boxes—to the standard set used in Open File and Save File dialogs, making it possible to receive additional input from the user.

Don't you abuse the privilege of being able to use customized dialog boxes. Try to define custom boxes that look similar to the standard ones. Don't get fancy by repositioning the standard button items, for example—you will only confuse the user.

The function prototype for **CustomGetFile** follows:

```
pascal void CustomGetFile( FileFilterYDProcPtr fileFilter,
                           short numTypes,
                           SFTypeList typeList,
                           StandardFileReply *reply,
                           short dlgID,
                           Point where,
                           DlgHookYDProcPtr dlgHook,
                           ModalFilterYDProcPtr filterProc,
                           short *activeList,
                           ActivateYDProcPtr activateProc,
                           void *yourDataPtr );
```

Here is the meaning of each parameter:

StandardFileReply—This is the standard reply record described earlier in connection with the **StandardGetFile** routine.

dlgID—**CustomGetFile** displays the dialog box defined by the 'DLOG' resource whose ID is dlgID. The resource definitions for the standard

StandardGetFile dialog box and its nine 'DITL' items (both of which have a resource ID of -6042) are shown in Listing 2-9. The customized dialog box you define must include the same 'DITL' items, in the same order, although you can change the item names and bounding rectangles if you need to. Add the definitions of any new controls that you want to appear in the dialog box to the end of the list of required 'DITL' items.

Listing 2-9. The Rez source for the 'DLOG' and 'DITL' resources for a StandardGetFile dialog box

```
/* StandardGetFile dialog box */
resource 'DLOG' (-6042, "Get dialog", purgeable) {
    {0, 0, 166, 344}, dBoxProc, invisible, noGoAway, 0,
    -6042, "", noAutoCenter
};

/* StandardGetFile dialog item list */
resource 'DITL' (-6042, "Standard Get items") {
    {
    {135, 252, 155, 332}, Button { enabled, "Open" },
    {104, 252, 124, 332}, Button { enabled, "Cancel" },
    {0, 0, 0, 0}, HelpItem { disabled, HMScanhdlg { -6042 } },
    {8, 235, 24, 337}, UserItem { enabled }, /* volume icon and name */
    {32, 252, 52, 332}, Button { enabled, "Eject" },
    {60, 252, 80, 332}, Button { enabled, "Desktop" },
    {29, 12, 159, 230}, UserItem { enabled }, /* name list */
    {7, 12, 26, 230}, UserItem { enabled },       /* folder pop-up */
    {91, 251, 92, 333}, Picture { disabled, 11 }, /* dividing line */
    }
};
```

Here are the Rez definitions for the most common types of controls:

```
{top, left, btm, right}, Button { enabled, "Push Me" }
{top, left, btm, right}, CheckBox { enabled, "Check" }
{top, left, btm, right}, RadioButton { enabled, "Radio" }
{top, left, btm, right}, StaticText { disabled, "uneditable text" }
{top, left, btm, right}, EditText { enabled, "editable text" }
{top, left, btm, right}, Icon { disabled, myICONid }
{top, left, btm, right}, Picture { disabled, myPICTid }
{top, left, btm, right}, Control { enabled, myCNTLid }
```

Each of these control definitions begins with the bounding rectangle for the control and Rez's symbolic control type code. Following this are the two parameters each control type needs—the first indicates whether the control is enabled or disabled; the second is either the control name (for Button, CheckBox, RadioButton, StaticText, or EditText controls) or the ID of a resource that defines the control (for Icon, Picture, and Control controls).

Depending on how you're customizing the dialog box, you may need to change its bounding rectangle in the 'DLOG' resource so that it encompasses the new items you've added. Finally, you must assign a resource ID to the 'DLOG' and 'DITL' resources that falls in the allowable range for application use (128 to 32767).

> **where**—This point defines where **CustomGetFile** draws the dialog box on the screen—it is the coordinate of the top-left corner of the dialog box. If you specify a point of (-1,-1), **CustomGetFile** centers the dialog box on the screen.

> **yourDataPtr**—This is a pointer to a private data area that the application maintains. **CustomGetFile** passes this pointer to the fileFilter and dlogHook procedures described in this chapter.

> **typeList, numTypes,** and **fileFilter**—**CustomGetFile** filters files much like **StandardGetFile**, using the values of these three parameters for guidance. **CustomGetFile**'s file filter procedure, however, takes one additional parameter, yourDataPtr, a pointer to the application's private data structure. Here is the function prototype for the file filter procedure you provide:

```
pascal Boolean fileFilter( CInfoPBPtr PB,
                           void *yourDataPtr );
```

The private data structure that yourDataPtr points to can contain fields that tell fileFilter what set of filtering tests to perform. This makes it possible, for example, to use one fileFilter procedure for different **CustomGetFile** calls that require different filtering criteria. More importantly, you can use a dlgHook procedure (see the following section) to change the values stored in the private data area so that they reflect the state of a control that changes the file filtering criteria. This makes it possible for the user to change, on the fly, the types of files that are shown in the list. You will find an example of how to do this at the end of this section.

Another difference is that **CustomGetFile** gives fileFilter the ability to determine whether folder files should appear in the file list. (**StandardGetFile** does not provide this option and folder files are always shown.) In most cases you will want folders to appear, so return false if the file/folder bit (bit 4) of the ioFlAttrib field is set. This attribute field is part of the hFileInfo record inside CInfoPBRec. The appropriate line of code to use to make folder names appear is as follows:

```
if ( (*PB).hFileInfo.ioFlAttrib & 0x10 ) return( false );
```

where PB is the pointer to CInfoPBRec.

filterProc—This is a modal-dialog filter function for filtering and pre-processing events received from the Event Manager before they're passed on to **CustomGetFile**'s default filterProc. It is no different from standard modal-dialog filters described in the Dialog Manager chapter of *Inside Macintosh*, Volume I. Modal-dialog filters enable keyboard shortcuts for common operations by converting keystroke events into simulated mouse actions. The default filterProc used by **CustomGetFile** provides standard shortcuts (pressing Escape simulates clicking the Cancel button, for example) and should be sufficient for most purposes. Refer to *Inside Macintosh*, Volume I if you need to write a custom filter procedure—perhaps to add keyboard shortcuts for controls you add to a standard dialog box, for example. If you're not using a filterProc, set this parameter to 0L.

activateProc and **activeList**—You will need to pass an activateProc if your customized dialog box contains an extra control that can accept keystroke input and is not an editable text control—a list control, for example. **StandardGetFile** calls activateProc to highlight the control when the user tabs to it or clicks in it. (It also calls activateProc to unhighlight the control.) This provides the user with a visual cue as to what control will accept keyboard input. See *Inside Macintosh*, Volume VI for instructions on how to write activation procedures. The activeList parameter points to a table containing a count word followed by the IDs of all the controls you've added that can accept keystrokes (editable text fields excepted). If you're not using an activateProc, set the parameter to 0L.

dlgHook—This is the dialog-hook procedure that you provide, if necessary, to handle user interaction with any controls you've added to the standard dialog box template. Dialog-hook procedures are discussed in detail, after **CustomPutFile** and its parameters. If you're not using a dlgHook, set this parameter to 0L.

Here is the function prototype for **CustomPutFile**:

```
pascal void CustomPutFile( ConstStr255Param prompt,
                           ConstStr255Param defaultName,
                           StandardFileReply *reply,
                           short dlgID,
                           Point where,
                           DlgHookYDProcPtr dlgHook,
                           ModalFilterYDProcPtr filterProc,
                           short *activeList,
                           ActivateYDProcPtr activateProc,
                           void *yourDataPtr );
```

Let's now look at those parameters which have not already been described in connection with **CustomGetFile**, or which have slightly different meanings.

dlgID—**CustomPutFile** displays the dialog box defined by the 'DLOG' resource whose ID is dlgID. The resource definitions for the standard **StandardPutFile** dialog box and its 'DITL' with twelve items (both of which have a resource ID of -6043) are shown in Listing 2-10. You can customize this dialog box using the same general techniques described for **CustomGetFile**.

Listing 2-10. The Rez source for the 'DLOG' and 'DITL' resources for a StandardPutFile dialog box

```
/* StandardPutFile dialog box */
resource 'DLOG' (-6043, "Put dialog", purgeable) {
    {0, 0, 188, 344}, dBoxProc, invisible, noGoAway, 0,
    -6043, "", noAutoCenter
};

/* StandardPutFile dialog item list */
resource 'DITL' (-6043, "Standard Put items") {
    {
        {161, 252, 181, 332}, Button { enabled, "Save" },
        {130, 252, 150, 332}, Button { enabled, "Cancel" },
        {0, 0, 0, 0}, HelpItem { disabled, HMScanhdlg { -6043 } },
        {8, 235, 24, 337}, UserItem { enabled }, /* volume icon and name */
        {32, 252, 52, 332}, Button { enabled, "Eject" },
        {60, 252, 80, 332}, Button { enabled, "Desktop" },
        {29, 12, 127, 230}, UserItem { enabled }, /* name list */
        {7, 12, 26, 230}, UserItem { enabled }, /* folder pop-up */
        {119, 250, 120, 334}, Picture { disabled, 11 }, /* dividing line */
        {157, 15, 173, 227}, EditText { enabled, "" },  /* file name */
        {136, 15, 152, 227}, StaticText { disabled, "Save as: " },
        {88, 252, 108, 332}, UserItem { disabled }, /* New Folder button */
    }
};
```

prompt— This is the prompting string ('DITL' item #11). If you provide a prompt, it overrides the string specified in the resource.

defaultName—This is the name string that initially appears in the standard editable text control ('DITL' item #10). If you provide a name string, it overrides the string specified in the resource.

▶ Writing Dialog-Hook Procedures

A dialog-hook procedure processes item hits in a **CustomGetFile** or **CustomPutFile** dialog box. As noted, you need to supply a dialog-hook procedure when you add new controls to a standard Open File or Save File dialog box because the internal dialog-hook procedures handle activity only in the standard set of controls; they do not know how to handle additional controls that you define.

Here is the function prototype for a dialog-hook procedure:

```
pascal short myDialogHook( short theItem,
                           DialogPtr theDialog,
                           void *yourDataPtr );
```

The first parameter, theItem, is the number of the dialog item that has been hit. The second parameter, theDialog, is a pointer to the dialog record involved. Finally, yourDataPtr, is the pointer to the private data area that you passed to **CustomGetFile** or **CustomPutFile**. The dialog-hook procedure can share data with the application or the file-filter procedure via the private data area.

The item numbers passed to the dialog-hook procedure are either real 'DITL' item numbers or pseudo-item numbers that actually refer to requests for special actions. Listing 2-11 lists the numbers of the standard items as well as the pseudo-items.

Listing 2-11. Item numbers and pseudo-item numbers for StandardGetFile and StandardPutFile dialog-hook procedures

```
/* item numbers for standard dialog items */
enum {sfItemOpenButton = 1};        /* Save or Open button */
enum {sfItemCancelButton = 2};      /* Cancel button */
enum {sfItemBalloonHelp = 3};       /* Balloon help area */
enum {sfItemVolumeUser = 4};        /* Volume icon and name */
enum {sfItemEjectButton = 5};       /* Disk eject button */
enum {sfItemDesktopButton = 6};     /* Desktop button */
enum {sfItemFileListUser = 7};      /* Name in list clicked */
enum {sfItemPopUpMenuUser = 8};     /* Folder pop-up menu */
enum {sfItemDividerLinePict = 9};   /* (not generated) */
```

Listing 2-11. Item numbers and pseudo-item numbers for StandardGetFile and StandardPutFile dialog-hook procedures (continued)

```
enum {sfItemFileNameTextEdit = 10};  /* File name field clicked */
enum {sfItemPromptStaticText = 11};  /* (not generated) */
enum {sfItemNewFolderUser = 12};     /* New Folder button */

/* pseudo-item numbers for use by dlgHook routines */
enum {sfHookFirstCall = (-1)};       /* dialog has just opened */
enum {sfHookCharOffset = 0x1000};    /* offset for ASCII codes for lists */
enum {sfHookNullEvent = 100};        /* periodic null event */
enum {sfHookRebuildList = 101};      /* redisplay list of files */
enum {sfHookFolderPopUp = 102};      /* Folder pop-up menu */
enum {sfHookOpenFolder = 103};       /* Open button when folder selected */
enum {sfHookOpenAlias = 104};        /* selected item is an alias */
enum {sfHookGoToDesktop = 105};      /* user pressed Command-D */
enum {sfHookGoToAliasTarget = 106};  /* Option pressed when alias opened */
enum {sfHookGoToParent = 107};       /* user pressed Command-Up Arrow */
enum {sfHookGoToNextDrive = 108};    /* user pressed Command-Right Arrow */
enum {sfHookGoToPrevDrive = 109};    /* user pressed Command-Left Arrow */
enum {sfHookChangeSelection = 110};  /* reply record describes a new file */
enum {sfHookSetActiveOffset = 200};  /* offset for control to activate */
enum {sfHookLastCall = (-2)};        /* dialog is about to close */
```

Note ▶

sfHookRebuildList, sfHookChangeSelection, and sfHookSetActiveList are return values for a dialog-hook procedure. They are never passed to the dialog-hook procedure.

Important ▶

Note that item numbers 10 through 12 apply to **CustomPutFile** dialog boxes only. The item numbers for additional controls that you add begin at 10 for **CustomGetFile** dialog boxes, and 13 for **CustomPutFile** dialog boxes.

The dialog-hook procedure should check the value of theItem passed to it and process it as necessary. For example, it would check for the item number of an added control, such as a check box, and handle it by toggling the value of the control.

If the dialog-hook procedure does not handle theItem, it should return theItem as the result so that the internal dialog-hook procedure will handle it in the standard way. If you do handle `theItem`, return 0 or an item number the internal hook does not understand (such as the item number for a control you've added).

In practice, you'll probably need to use only a few of the pseudo-item numbers listed in Listing 2-11. Here are the more interesting events to which you might react:

- **sfHookFirstCall**—Your hook receives this event when the dialog box is first created. It can react to the event by initializing fields in the private data area and allocating any needed data structures.

- **sfHookLastCall**—Your hook receives this event when the dialog box is about to disappear. It should react by updating values in the private data area, if necessary, and disposing of any data structures created since the dialog box was first displayed.

- **sfHookNullEvent**—Your hook receives this event frequently to give it a chance to perform periodic actions such as updating a timer or continuing an animation sequence.

- **sfHookRebuildList**—Your hook will never receive this event, but it can return it to force the internal hook to redisplay the files in the current folder. Your hook will need to do this in situations where the user changes the value of a control that indicates the types of files to be displayed.

Warning ▶

You've got to be careful when dealing with the first three types of pseudo-events because they are generated not only for the main Open File or Save File dialog box but also for any subsidiary dialog boxes that appear. For example, when the user specifies a file name that already exists, **CustomPutFile** displays a dialog asking the user to verify that the original file is to be replaced. When this sub-dialog appears, your hook receives another `sfHookFirstCall` event; when it disappears, the hook receives `sfHookLastEvent`. Only react to an event associated with the dialog box in which you're interested. Do not, for example, perform your initialization code every time you receive a `sfHookFirstCall` event.

The `refCon` field of the window record in the dialog record indicates which dialog box is at the front—this value is `sfMainDialogRefCon` for the main dialog box, the one in which you'll usually be interested. Use the expression `((WindowPeek)theDialog)-> refCon` to access this field.

▶ An Example of Using CustomGetFile

Listing 2-12 shows the 'DLOG' and 'DITL' resources which define the customized Open File dialog box shown in Figure 2-4. This dialog box is the same as the one that **StandardPutFile** uses except that it includes a pop-up menu control for selecting the type of file that is to be shown in the scrolling list. The pop-up menu contains three items: *All files, Text,* and *MacWrite II.*

Listing 2-12. The Rez source for the 'DLOG' and 'DITL' resources (and related resources) for the CustomGetFile dialog box in Figure 2-4

```
#define        rCustomGet 1000
#define        rPopupMenu 2000

/* StandardGetFile dialog box */
resource 'DLOG' (rCustomGet, "CustomGet dialog", purgeable) {
     {0, 0, 181, 344}, dBoxProc, invisible, noGoAway, 0,
     rCustomGet, "", noAutoCenter
};

/* StandardGetFile dialog item list */
resource 'DITL' (rCustomGet, "Custom Get items") {
     {
     {135, 252, 155, 332}, Button { enabled, "Open" },
     {104, 252, 124, 332}, Button { enabled, "Cancel" },
     {0, 0, 0, 0}, HelpItem { disabled, HMScanhdlg { -6042 } },
     {8, 235, 24, 337}, UserItem { enabled },   /* volume icon and name */
     {32, 252, 52, 332}, Button { enabled, "Eject" },
     {60, 252, 80, 332}, Button { enabled, "Desktop" },
     {29, 12, 159, 230}, UserItem { enabled }, /* name list */
     {7, 12, 26, 230}, UserItem { enabled },        /* folder pop-up */
     {91, 251, 92, 333}, Picture { disabled, 11 },  /* dividing line */
/* our additional control definitions begin here: */
     {162, 12, 182, 212}, Control { enabled, 128 }; /* our pop-up control */
     }
};

resource 'CNTL' (128, "Popup control") {
     {0, 0, 20, 200}, /* boundsRect */
     popupTitleNoStyle+popupTitleLeftJust, /* style/justification */
     visible,
     50,            /* width of pop-up title area */
     rPopupMenu,    /* MENU resource ID */
     1008,          /* 1008 = pop-up procedure ID */
     0,             /* ResType (only for popupUseAddResMenu variation) */
     "Show"         /* title */
};

resource 'MENU' (rPopupMenu, "File type popup", preload) {
     rPopupMenu, textMenuProc,
     allEnabled,
     enabled, "File Type",
```

Listing 2-12. The Rez source for the 'DLOG' and 'DITL' resources (and related resources) for the CustomGetFile dialog box in Figure 2-4 (continued)

```
        {
                "All files",
                        noicon, nokey, nomark, plain;
                "Text",
                        noicon, nokey, nomark, plain;
                "MacWrite II",
                        noicon, nokey, nomark, plain;
        }
};
```

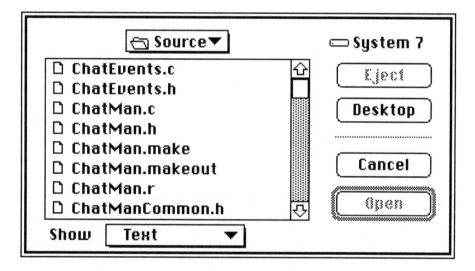

Figure 2-4. The customized CustomGetFile dialog box defined by the resources in Listing 2-12

The pop-up menu control was originally part of the Macintosh Communications Toolbox for System 6.x and has now become a standard system control. As shown in Listing 2-12, you define a pop-up menu control as a 'CNTL' resource. The 'CNTL' fields have the following initial values:

boundsRect—The boundary rectangle for the pop-up menu.

value—Specifies the styling and justification of the title of the pop-up menu. Here are the relevant mask values:

```
#define     popupTitleLeftJust     0x0000
#define     popupTitleCenterJust   0x0001
```

```
#define    popupTitleRightJust    0x00FF

#define    popupTitleBold         0x0100
#define    popupTitleItalic       0x0200
#define    popupTitleUnderline    0x0400
#define    popupTitleOutline      0x0800
#define    popupTitleShadow       0x1000
#define    popupTitleCondense     0x2000
#define    popupTitleExtend       0x4000
#define    popupTitleNoStyle      0x8000
```

Calculate the appropriate value to pass by adding one of the three justification masks to any combination of style masks (or to popupTitleNoStyle if no special styling is desired).

visible—Boolean indicating whether the control is visible (true) or invisible (false). You can also specify the constants visible and invisible defined in the Rez template for 'CNTL'.

max—Width of the pop-up menu title.

min—Resource ID of the 'MENU' resource containing the items to appear in the pop-up menu.

procID—Procedure ID of the pop-up menu control (1008) plus an optional variation code. Three variation codes are available:

- **popupFixedWidth** (1) The pop-up menu is not resized to fit long menu items. Instead, a long name is truncated and an ellipsis (…) is appended.

- **popupUseAddResMenu** (4) The items in the pop-up menu are formed by calling **AddResMenu** with the resource type stored in refCon. For example, to create a pop-up menu of font names, you would use this variation code and store 'FONT' in refCon.

- **popupUseWFont** (8) The font and font size of the window that owns the control, not the standard system font, is used to draw the pop-up menu.

refCon—If the control variation code is popupUseAddResMenu, this field contains a resource type, and the names of all resources of this type become pop-up menu items.

title—Name of the pop-up menu.

Note ▶

The names of many of these fields bear little relation to the types of data you store when defining the pop-up menu control. That's because the designers of the pop-up menu control had to bend a few rules to squeeze it into an old framework designed for simpler controls. After the pop-up menu control is loaded, the control fields take on their usual meanings, however.

In Listing 2-12, the 'CNTL' resource for the pop-up menu is tied to a standard 'MENU' resource containing the three file type choices of interest.

Listing 2-13 shows the GetOpenName routine for returning the name of the file selected by the user. Notice that it passes to **CustomGetFile** a pointer to a private data structure called GetHookRec which contains the typeCode field. This is where the dialog-hook procedure stores the current setting of the pop-up menu so that the file filter procedure can tell what filtering criteria to apply.

Listing 2-13. The file filter and dialog-hook procedures for the CustomGetFile dialog box in Figure 2-4

```
/* private data structure */
typedef struct {
     short     typeCode;
} GetHookRec;


void GetOpenName( StandardFileReply *toReply )
{
     Point      stdPosition = { -1, -1 };
     GetHookRec        myData;

     CustomGetFile( (FileFilterYDProcPtr)OpenCFilter, -1, 0L, toReply,
                    rCustomGet, stdPosition, (DlgHookYDProcPtr)MyGetHook,
                    (ModalFilterYDProcPtr)0L, 0L, (ActivateYDProcPtr)0L,
                    &myData );
}


/* Dialog-hook procedure for CustomGetFile */
pascal short MyGetHook( short theItem, DialogPtr theDialog,
                    GetHookRec *myDataPtr )
{
     short      itemType;
     Handle     itemHandle;
     Rect       itemRect;
     short      theValue;

     switch ( theItem ) {

        case sfHookFirstCall: /* initialization */
```

Listing 2-13. The file filter and dialog-hook procedures for the CustomGetFile dialog box in Figure 2-4 (continued)

```
                    if ( ((WindowPeek)theDialog)->refCon == sfMainDialogRefCon ) {
                        GetDItem( theDialog, 10, &itemType, &itemHandle, &itemRect );
                         SetCtlValue( (ControlHandle)itemHandle, 1 ); /* set pop-up val */
                        myDataPtr->typeCode = 1;
                    }
                    break;

            case 10:    /* Pop-up menu */
                GetDItem( theDialog, theItem, &itemType, &itemHandle, &itemRect );
                theValue = GetCtlValue( (ControlHandle)itemHandle );
                if ( theValue != myDataPtr->typeCode ) { /* if value has changed */

                    myDataPtr->typeCode = theValue;
                    theItem = sfHookRebuildList;        /* force rebuild of list */
                }
                break;
        }
        return( theItem );
}

/* File filter for CustomGetFile */
pascal Boolean OpenCFilter( CInfoPBPtr PB, GetHookRec *myDataPtr )
{
        OSType          theFileType;

        if ( (*PB).hFileInfo.ioFlAttrib & 0x10 ) return( false );  /* folders OK */

        theFileType = (*PB).hFileInfo.ioFlFndrInfo.fdType;

        switch ( myDataPtr->typeCode ) {
        PrintHex( myDataPtr->typeCode );
                case 1:             /* "All files" */
                    return( false );
                    break;

                case 2:             /* "Text only" */
                    if ( theFileType == 'TEXT' ) return( false );
                    break;

                case 3:              /* "MacWrite II" */
                    if ( (theFileType == 'MW2D') ) return( false );
                    break;
        }
        return( true );
}
```

Let's take a close look at the dialog-hook procedure and see how it ties in to the file filter procedure. The hook reacts to just two item numbers passed to it: sfHookFirstCall and the pop-up menu item number (10). It receives sfHookFirstCall when the dialog box first appears and responds by calling

SetCtlValue to initialize the value of the pop-up control to 1 (*All files*, the first menu item). It also initializes the value of typeCode in the private data area where the file filter will be looking for the value.

| Note ▶ | The hook reacts to sfHookFirstCall only if the refCon field of the dialog window is set to sfMainDialogRefCon—that is, only when the main dialog window first appears, not when any subsidiary dialog windows appear. |

When the hook receives a hit in the pop-up menu item, it first gets the current value of the pop-up control. If the value is different from the previous setting (stored at typeCode), the user wants to see a different set of files. The hook reacts by storing the new value at typeCode and returns sfHookRebuildList. Returning this pseudo-item number causes **CustomGetFile** to rebuild the file list. Since the file filter is aware of the new setting of the pop-up (it reads the value stored at typeCode), the new filtering criteria kick in, and only files of the selected type will appear.

| Keypoint ▶ | The file filter procedure also checks for folder files and allows them to appear. If the filter procedure doesn't do this, no folder files will appear, making it impossible for the user to move to another folder. |

▶ An Example of Using CustomPutFile

Listing 2-14 shows the 'DLOG' and 'DITL' resources that define the customized Save File dialog box shown in Figure 2-5. It differs from the **StandardPutFile** dialog box by including a check box called *Save as stationery*. By calling **CustomPutFile** with the resource ID of this dialog box and an appropriate dialog-hook procedure, an application can determine not only the name of the file to be saved, but also whether the stationery pad bit of the file is to be set.

Listing 2-14. The Rez source for the 'DLOG' and 'DITL' resources for the CustomPutFile dialog box in Figure 2-5

```
#define       rCustomPut 1001

/* StandardPutFile dialog box */
resource 'DLOG' (rCustomPut, "CustomPut dialog", purgeable) {
```

Listing 2-14. The Rez source for the 'DLOG' and 'DITL' resources for the CustomPutFile dialog box in Figure 2-5 (continued)

```
        {0, 0, 207, 344}, dBoxProc, invisible, noGoAway, 0,
        rCustomPut, "", noAutoCenter
};

/* StandardPutFile dialog item list */
resource 'DITL' (rCustomPut, "Custom Put items") {
    {
        {161, 252, 181, 332}, Button { enabled, "Save" },
        {130, 252, 150, 332}, Button { enabled, "Cancel" },
        {0, 0, 0, 0}, HelpItem { disabled, HMScanhdlg { -6043 } },
        {8, 235, 24, 337}, UserItem { enabled },    /* volume icon and name */
        {32, 252, 52, 332}, Button { enabled, "Eject" },
        {60, 252, 80, 332}, Button { enabled, "Desktop" },
        {29, 12, 127, 230}, UserItem { enabled },       /* name list */
        {7, 12, 26, 230}, UserItem { enabled },         /* folder pop-up */
        {119, 250, 120, 334}, Picture { disabled, 11 }, /* dividing line */
        {157, 15, 173, 227}, EditText { enabled, "" },  /* file name */
        {136, 15, 152, 227}, StaticText { disabled, "Save as: " },
        {88, 252, 108, 332}, UserItem { disabled },     /* New Folder button */
/* our additional control definitions begin here: */
        {186, 12, 204, 154}, CheckBox { enabled, "Save as stationery pad" };
    }
};
```

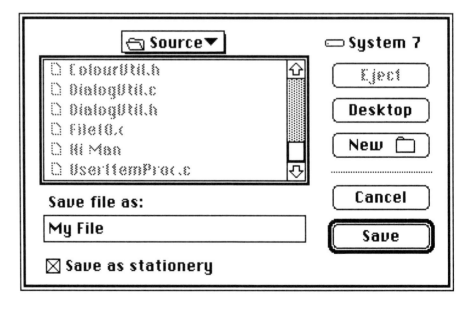

Figure 2-5. The customized CustomPutFile dialog box defined by the resources in Listing 2-14

The `GetSaveName` routine in Listing 2-15 shows how to present this custom dialog box and return the `StandardFileReply` record and the `isStationery` Boolean back to the caller. Notice that it passes the address of a private data structure, `PutHookRec`, to **CustomPutFile**. This structure contains the `stationeryFlag` field where the dialog-hook procedure stores the setting of the *Save as stationery* check box.

Listing 2-15 also shows the dialog-hook procedure needed to handle clicks of the added check box control. It reacts to only two item numbers—`sfHookFirstCall` and 13 (the number of the added check box item).

For `sfHookFirstCall`, the hook initializes the value of the check box control to false (off) using **SetCtlValue**. It also initializes `stationeryFlag` to the same value. In response to a click of the check box (item 13), the hook toggles the check box's value and stores the new value at `stationeryFlag`.

That's all there is to it. When the user dismisses the dialog box, the application simply checks the value at `myDataPtr->stationeryFlag` to determine the final state of the check box.

Listing 2-15. The dialog-hook procedure for the CustomPutFile dialog box in Figure 2-5

```
/* private data structure */
typedef struct {
    Boolean        stationeryFlag;
} PutHookRec;


void GetSaveName( StandardFileReply *toReply, Str255 defaultName, Boolean
*isStationery )
{
    Point     stdPosition = { -1, -1 };
    PutHookRec        myData;

    CustomPutFile( (StringPtr)"\pSave file as:", defaultName,
                    toReply, rCustomPut, stdPosition,
                    (DlgHookYDProcPtr)MyPutHook,
                    (ModalFilterYDProcPtr)0L,
                    0L, (ActivateYDProcPtr)0L, &myData );

    *isStationery = myData.stationeryFlag;
}


/* Dialog-hook procedure for CustomPutFile */
pascal short MyPutHook( short theItem, DialogPtr theDialog,
                    PutHookRec *myDataPtr )
{
    short     itemType;
    Handle    itemHandle;
    Rect      itemRect;
```

Listing 2-15. The dialog-hook procedure for the CustomPutFile dialog box in Figure 2-5 (continued)

```
short    theValue;

switch ( theItem ) {

   case sfHookFirstCall:
      if ( ((WindowPeek)theDialog)->refCon == sfMainDialogRefCon ) {
         myDataPtr->stationeryFlag = false;
         GetDItem( theDialog, 13, &itemType, &itemHandle, &itemRect );
         SetCtlValue( (ControlHandle)itemHandle, false );  /* check off */
      }
      break;

   case 13:        /* "Save as stationery" check box */
      GetDItem( theDialog, 13, &itemType, &itemHandle, &itemRect );
      theValue = GetCtlValue( (ControlHandle)itemHandle );
      SetCtlValue( (ControlHandle)itemHandle, !theValue );
      myDataPtr->stationeryFlag = !theValue;
   break;
}
return( theItem );
}
```

▶ Summary

In this chapter, we described the file system specification record (FSSpec) that System 7 uses to identify files and how several File Manager routines have been modified to use it. We also covered the special folders available in System 7, how to deal with aliases, and how to use the new Standard File Package to create custom Open File and Save File dialogs.

In the next chapter we will explore the issue of cooperative multitasking and show how to make your application a good citizen in a world where more than one application may be running at once.

3 ▶ Cooperative Multitasking

When the Macintosh was first unveiled in 1984, the operating system could run only one application at a time. To run another application, the user had to quit the current application to return to the Finder, then launch the other application. This was deemed to be acceptable on a computer limited to 128K of RAM.

A few years later, when more powerful Macintoshes with more memory were available, Apple boosted the power of the system by releasing a new version of Finder, called *MultiFinder*. MultiFinder manages multiple running applications and allows users to switch quickly between applications by clicking in a window or selecting the application from the Apple menu. It also allows applications to run in the background while a primary application runs in the foreground and interacts directly with the user if all running applications follow the rules in this chapter. Since the operating system does not totally control the multitasking, and requires support from the running applications, this feature is usually referred to as *cooperative multitasking*.

Important ▶

With earlier system software, MultiFinder is a user-selectable option—the user can choose to use the Finder even though there are few compelling reasons to do so. (One reason, unfortunately, is that applications still exist that are incompatible with MultiFinder.) Under System 7, however, there is no choice. The system always runs in a MultiFinder environment. To make matters confusing, Apple refers to this environment as Finder, not MultiFinder. Don't you be confused—almost everything you may have read about MultiFinder also applies to the new System 7 Finder.

In this chapter you will learn how to design an application that supports the cooperative multitasking features of System 7. Most of this information also applies to pre-System 7 applications; we're presenting it here to emphasize its importance under System 7 and because it has not been covered extensively in other Macintosh programming books.

By The Way ▶

Until *Inside Macintosh*, Volume VI, the only source of technical information about MultiFinder from Apple was *Programmer's Guide to MultiFinder*, available by mail order from the AppleProgrammer's and Developer's Association.

This chapter also covers the Process Manager—a new System 7 manager that you can use to obtain information about applications running in memory — and some memory management routines for dealing with free areas of memory that standard Memory Manager routines don't recognize.

▶ Running Multiple Applications

When the Finder launches an application, it first allocates a block of memory called a *partition*, inside of which the application loads and executes. The general structure of a Finder partition, shown in Figure 3-1, resembles the memory map for an application launched from the pre-System 7 Finder. The difference is that the partition does not necessarily use up all of the system's available RAM.

The important data areas inside a Finder partition are as follows:

- **Application heap**—This is where the application loads its resources and where standard Memory Manager routines allocate memory blocks. The heap grows upward, as necessary, towards the top of the stack.
- **Stack**—This is the 680x0 processor's stack space. The stack grows downward towards the top of the application heap as you pushmore data on the stack. The location of the top of the stack is given by the address in the 680x0 A7 register when the application is executing.
- **A5 World**—When an application is executing, the 680x0 A5 register contains the address of the base of a table of application parameters. Just below this table are the application's global variables, including the QuickDraw globals. Just above the table is the jump table containing entries for every inter-segment call the application makes. At the assembly-language level, applications access global variables and jump table entries by specifying offsets from the address in A5.

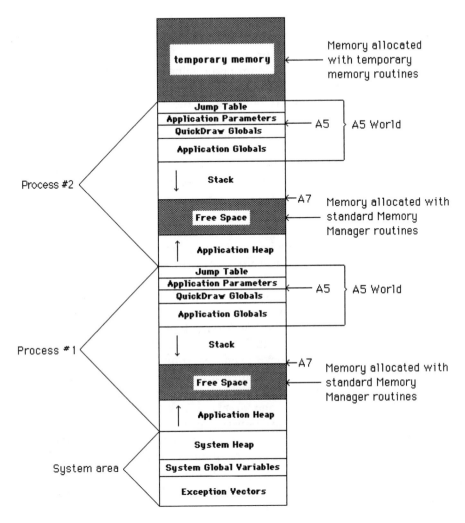

Figure 3-1. A Macintosh memory map

The Finder determines the size of the space to allocate for an application's partition by examining the application's 'SIZE' (ID -1) resource. The last two fields in this resource contain the preferred and minimum partition sizes, in bytes. (See the 'SIZE' resource for the Skeleton application in Listing 1-3 of Chapter 1 and also Appendix B.) The Finder tries to allocate a partition of the preferred size, but no larger, when it launches the application. If there's not enough memory available to do so, the Finder allocates the largest partition possible. The Finder will not launch the application if it is unable to allocate the minimum partition.

Choosing appropriate values for the preferred and minimum partition sizes is an art. For the preferred size, choose a number large enough to give your application elbowroom in most foreseeable situations. Don't just pick a large number, say 8 megabytes, because that would prevent the Finder from launching other applications on systems with limited RAM. To obtain a larger partition—for a monolithic spreadsheet, for example—the user can change the preferred size by editing the *Current size* field in the window the Finder displays when the user selects the Get Info command (in the File menu) after clicking on the application icon.

Choosing a minimum partition size involves more work. The best approach is to torture test your application in successively smaller partitions until you find a size below which your application just won't cut it. To set smaller partitions, just change the application's preferred partition size and relaunch the application.

The number of running applications System 7 can manage is limited only by available memory. The memory map in Figure 3-1 shows the general organization of memory in a situation where two applications, called *processes*, have been launched. The processes are independent of each other although they can send high-level events or Apple events to each other (see Chapter 4). When a process is executing, only its A5 World and its stack are active, and only the free memory inside its partition (or the system heap) can be allocated with NewHandle and NewPtr.

RAM that the system software is not using and that is not inside the partition of any process is called *temporary memory*. This is the source of memory for the partition the system allocates when the Finder launches an application; when an application quits, its memory partition returns to the pool of temporary memory. You will learn about the routines for dealing with temporary memory later in this chapter.

▶ Switching Between Applications

The *foreground application* is the one currently interacting with the user—its windows are in the frontmost plane of the screen, its menu bar appears at the top of the screen, and all user input is directed to it. All other applications in memory are *background applications*—their windows also appear on the screen, but they are unhighlighted and appear beneath the plane of the foreground application.

The user can bring a background application to the foreground in two ways:

- by picking the name of the desired application from the Application menu on the far side of the menu bar
- by clicking in an exposed window of the desired application

A background application automatically comes to the foreground if the current foreground application quits.

Switching in a new foreground application is called a *major switch*. When it occurs, the system sends a *suspend* event to the current foreground application and a *resume* event to the background application that is being brought to the foreground.

Your application must check for suspend and resume events and react accordingly. To do this, first include code to check for the osEvt event in the main event loop. (Suspend and resume events are actually subevents of osEvt.) Your event handler for osEvt can examine the high-order word of the message field of the event record to see if it is suspendResumeMessage. If it is, the resumeFlag bit of the message field will be 0 for a suspend event and 1 for a resume event. Here is the outline of a suspend/resume event handler, lifted from the Skeleton application in Chapter 1:

```
case osEvt:
     switch ( (event->message >> 24) & 0x0ff ) {
        case suspendResumeMessage:

            if ( ( event->message & resumeFlag ) == 0 ) { /* suspend */

            /* copy scrap to clipboard, deactivate controls */
            gInBackground = true;

            } else { /* resume */

            /* copy clipboard to scrap, activate controls */
            gInBackGround = false;

            }
        break;
     }
break;
```

Here is how an application should react to suspend and resume events:

- **Suspend events**—Deactivate the controls in the frontmost window and copy any private scrap (such as the TextEdit scrap) to the clipboard. Set to true a global variable (called gInBackground in Skeleton) indicating whether the application is currently running in the background.

- **Resume events**—Copy the clipboard to the private scrap you're using, if any, and activate the controls in your application's frontmost window. Set to false a global variable indicating whether the application is currently running in the background.

Note ▶

It's good practice to maintain a `gInBackground` global variable so that the application can quickly determine whether it's running in the foreground or background. You'll see in the next section how to make an application perform productively in the background.

By reacting to suspend and resume events in this way, an application switch will look just right to the user: The front window of the selected application will highlight and the suspended application's front window will be unhighlighted. The system automatically puts the menu bar of the selected application at the top of the screen and moves the windows of the suspended application to a lower plane.

Important ▶

Major switches can occur only if the foreground application is *not* displaying a modal dialog box. They only occur the first time the foreground application calls **WaitNextEvent** (or **EventAvail**) after retrieving the suspend event, not at some other arbitrary time.

▶ Operating in the Background

In the previous section you saw how to add code that allows the user to send the application to the background or bring it to the foreground. This section focuses on how to permit applications to continue processing quietly in the background. The operating system grants background applications processor time by performing a *minor switch*—the same as a major switch except that it does not bring the application to the foreground. A minor switch involves switching in the background's application execution environment, including its A5 World and stack. Unlike major switches, the user has no control over minor switches; they are handled transparently by the operating system.

▶ WaitNextEvent

Background processing doesn't happen automatically as it does under an operating system such as UNIX which supports traditional preemptive multitasking. Rather, it requires a bit of cooperation from the Finder and all other loaded applications, whether they're running in the foreground or background. These applications must explicitly relinquish processor time to the system so that the system can offer it to other applications that are waiting for a chance to continue executing. They do this by calling the **WaitNextEvent** routine in their event loops:

```
pascal Boolean WaitNextEvent( short mask,
                              EventRecord *event,
                              unsigned long sleep,
                              RgnHandle mouseRgn );
```

WaitNextEvent is the successor to **GetNextEvent**, the centerpiece of event loops for applications designed to run under the old Finder. **WaitNextEvent** returns true if an event is pending in the event queue. In this situation, the routine removes the event from the queue and places information about it in the event record given by event. As shown in Listing 3-1, the event record contains information about the event type and other related data (see *Inside Macintosh* for details). **WaitNextEvent** returns false if there is no pending event. In that case, the event record describes a null event—the what field is nullEvent.

Listing 3-1. The structure of the event record used by WaitNextEvent

```
typedef struct EventRecord {
       short what;          /* the message type */
       long message;        /* event-dependent data */
       long when;           /* time when event occurred (ticks) */
       Point where;         /* position of mouse when event occurred */
       short modifiers;     /* state of keyboard modifiers */
} EventRecord;
```

The mask parameter is a bit vector indicating which types of events **WaitNextEvent** should look for in the event queue (see Figure 3-2). **WaitNextEvent** ignores all types of events not permitted by mask, but does not remove them from the queue. In most cases you will specify a mask value of everyEvent, indicating that all events are of interest.

The parameter that is the key to cooperative multitasking is `sleep`—the maximum amount of time, in ticks (sixtieths of a second), your application will wait for **WaitNextEvent** to return a result if no non-null event is pending. **WaitNextEvent** returns true as soon as it receives a non-null event or false if a non-null event does not arrive before the `sleep` interval expires.

While **WaitNextEvent** waits for an event to arrive or the `sleep` interval to elapse, the operating system examines the states of other pending **WaitNextEvent** calls made by other running applications. If the system finds that the `sleep` interval for another application has elapsed, it performs a minor switch to that application and causes its **WaitNextEvent** call to return. If the other application is in the background, the operating system can resume execution of a portion of a background task, then call **WaitNextEvent** again to give another application a chance to gain control of the processor.

The value you pass in the `sleep` parameter depends on how frequently your application needs to regain control of the processor. If the application is in the foreground and needs to keep a TextEdit cursor blinking, for example, the appropriate value would be the number returned by **GetCaretTime** (usually 15 ticks). On the other hand, if the foreground application doesn't need to perform periodic tasks, it could specify the largest possible unsigned long value (-1). If the application is currently in the background performing a specific task, such as recalculating a spreadsheet or downloading a file, you should specify a `sleep` value appropriate to the circumstances. Pick a value that doesn't make the operation excessively long or prevent the proper execution of the operation.

The easiest way for your application to determine whether it's running in the background or foreground is to check the value of a Boolean variable that its event handler for suspend/resume events sets and clears, as described in the previous section.

To provide a framework that makes it possible to perform a task effectively in the background or foreground, structure your application so that all lengthy tasks are performed in a series of brief installments, with a call to **WaitNextEvent** after each installment. This serves two purposes: First, the user can put the application into the background (by performing a major switch) and bring it back to the foreground at will while the task continues executing; second, the application can receive the processing time to complete its task even when it is in the background. To prevent the foreground application from performing sluggishly, the length of each installment should be limited to no more than 15 ticks—the recommended minimum `sleep` value for an application running in the foreground.

The `DoLongTask` routine in Listing 3-2 illustrates how to implement these general techniques. The routine calls `DoPortion` to perform a part of a complete task and passes it an index (`taskIndex`) that `DoPortion` uses to deter-

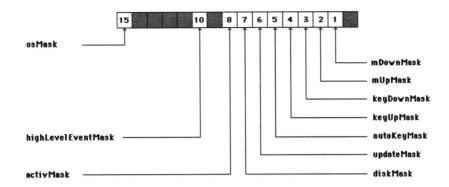

Notes:

• WaitNextEvent returns only event types enabled by the mask. Use the mask constant everyEvent to enable all events.

• You cannot mask out null events.

Legend:

mDownMask — mouse button pressed
mUpMask — mouse button released
keyDownMask — key pressed
keyUpMask — key released
autoKeyMask — key press auto-repeated
updateMask — window update event
diskMask — disk-inserted event
activMask — activate/deactivate event
highLevelEventMask — high-level event (including Apple event)
osMask — operating system event (suspend, resume, mouse-moved)

Figure 3-2. The event mask used by WaitNextEvent

mine where to begin processing its task. In the example, this index is a counter; in other applications it might be an address or any other data DoPortion needs to determine where to start processing. DoPortion returns after 15 ticks and DoLongTask immediately calls **WaitNextEvent** to give other applications processing time. This cycle repeats until DoPortion returns true to indicate that it has completed the entire task. (If DoPortion returns false, it also indicates in taskIndex where it stopped processing.)

Listing 3-2. DoLongTask: how to perform a long task in the background or foreground

```
/* DoLongTask performs a lengthy task in a way that permits the
   user to switch the application between foreground and
   background without interfering with the completion of the task.

   DoLongTask returns false if the task was cancelled because
   the user pressed Command-Period; otherwise it returns true.
*/
Boolean DoLongTask( void )
{
   EventRecord  event;
   char    key;
   short   taskIndex = 0;
   Boolean     taskComplete;

   do {

      taskComplete = DoPortion( &taskIndex );

      if ( WaitNextEvent( everyEvent, &event, 15L, 0L ) ) {

         switch ( event.what ) {

            case keyDown:    /* check for Command-period to cancel */
               key = event.message & charCodeMask;
               if ( ( key == '.' ) && (event.modifiers & cmdKey) )
                  return( false );
               break;

            case osEvt:
            case updateEvt:
               DoEvent( &event ); /* use main event loop handler */

               break;
         }
      }
   } while ( !taskComplete );
   return( true );
}

/* DoPortion processes a task from the position
   given by *taskIndex. If the task does not
   complete within 15 ticks (a minimum sleep
   value that other applications generally use),
   it stores, at *taskIndex, the position at which
   it left off, and returns false. It returns true
   if it completes the entire task.
*/
```

Listing 3-2. DoLongTask: how to perform a long task in the background or foreground (continued)

```
Boolean DoPortion( short *taskIndex )
{
    long    startTick = TickCount();
    WindowPtr wp;

    do {

        wp = FrontWindow();
        SetPort( wp );
        InvertRect( &wp->portRect ); /* invert window content */

        *taskIndex++;
        if ( *taskIndex == 1000 ) return( true );

    } while ( ( TickCount() - startTick ) < 15 );

    return( false );
}
```

Note ▶

While an application is performing a task as previously described, it normally needs to react to only two events that **WaitNextEvent** might return: osEvt (for suspend events when it's in the foreground or resume events when it's in the background) and updateEvt (for redrawing portions of windows that may become exposed while it's in the background). The DoLongTask routine handles these events by calling the event handler for the program's main event loop, DoEvent (in the Skeleton application). The next installment of the task can be executed when **WaitNextEvent** returns false to indicate that no event is pending or after handling osEvt or updateEvt. Notice that DoLongTask's event handler also examines keyDown events to see if the user pressed Command-period to cancel the task.

If your application is capable of performing useful tasks in the background, it must set the canBackground flag in its 'SIZE' resource to be granted processing time (see Appendix B). If the application doesn't do any background processing, it should clear this flag (specify the cannotBackground constant in the definition of the 'SIZE' resource). This will improve system performance because the system will not grant the background application processing time it doesn't need.

The other parameter you pass to **WaitNextEvent** is mouseRgn. This region describes the area where the mouse cursor is located. When the user moves the mouse outside this region, **WaitNextEvent** immediately returns an osEvt with mouseMovedMessage in the high-order byte of the message field of the event record. These events enable the application to change the shape of the cursor as the user moves the mouse to different areas of the screen. If your application doesn't need to change the cursor, it can specify a mouseRgn value of 0L.

The proper response to an osEvt event caused by movement of the mouse is as follows:

- Dispose of the current mouseRgn using **DisposeRgn.**
- Create a new region describing the area in which the mouse is currently located; do this using by calling **NewRgn** to create a new empty region, then calling routines like **SetRectRgn** and **RectRgn** to add areas to the region. (See *Inside Macintosh*, Volume I, pp. 181-187 for descriptions of routines that work with regions.)
- Pass the handle of the new region in the next call to **WaitNextEvent.**

When calling **WaitNextEvent** for the first time in an application, pass it a handle to an empty region returned by **NewRgn**. As soon as the mouse moves, the mouse-moved handler will receive control so it can set up the appropriate cursor.

▶ Notification Manager

An application running in the background must be prepared to concede that, in general, the user's attention will be focused on the foreground application. In fact, the user may forget about the background application entirely, especially if its windows are obscured by the foreground application. Therefore, if the background application needs to ensure that the user receives prompt notice of an important event, such as the completion of a specific task, it must do more than display a dialog box.

An application running in the background should use the services of the Notification Manager to get the user's attention. The Notification Manager provides four different cues that a background application can invoke:

- flashing a small icon (a 'SICN' resource that the application provides) on the right side of the menu bar atop the icon for the Application menu
- displaying a diamond mark to the left of the application's name in the Application menu

- playing a 'snd ' sound resource
- displaying an alert box in the foreground

Any one or any combination of these four notification cues may be used. To post a notification request, use **NMInstall**:

```
pascal OSErr NMInstall( NMRecPtr nmReqPtr );
```

The Notification Manager places the request in an internal queue which the operating system processes at its earliest opportunity. The nmReqPtr parameter is a pointer to a notification request record (NMRec), the structure of which is shown in Listing 3-3.

Listing 3-3. The structure of the NMRec used by the Notification Manager

```
typedef struct NMRec {
    QElemPtr    qLink;       /* internal use only */
    short       qType;       /* always set to nmType (8) */
    short       nmFlags;     /* internal use only */
    long        nmPrivate;   /* internal use only */
    short       nmReserved;  /* internal use only */
    short       nmMark;      /* 1 = put diamond mark next to name */
    Handle      nmIcon;      /* handle to 'SICN' resource */
    Handle      nmSound;     /* handle to 'snd ' resource */
    StringPtr   nmStr;       /* pointer to alert string */
    NMProcPtr   nmResp;      /* pointer to response procedure */
    long        nmRefCon;    /* constant for application use */
} NMRec, *NMRecPtr;
```

Before calling **NMInstall** to post the notification request, set up the fields of NMRec to indicate the types of notification cues you want, as follows:

- If you want a diamond mark to appear next to the application's name in the Application menu, store 1 at nmMark; otherwise store 0.
- If you want a small icon (defined by a 'SICN' resource) to flash on the right side of the menu bar, store a handle to it at nmIcon; otherwise store 0L. The handle must be nonpurgeable.
- If you want a sound (defined by a 'snd ' resource) to play, store a handle to it at nmSound; otherwise store 0L. Specify a value of –1L if you want to use the system beep sound. The handle must be nonpurgeable.
- If you want an alert dialog to appear in the foreground, store a pointer to

the string to appear in the box at nmStr. If you don't want an alert box to appear, store 0L at nmStr.

Three other fields must also be initialized:

- Store nmType at qType. This constant identifies NMRec as a notification request queue element.
- Store the address of a response procedure at nmResp or 0L if there is no response procedure. As soon as the notification process is complete, the Notification Manager calls the response procedure. Its duty is to remove the notification request (using the **NMRemove** routine described later); call **ReleaseResource** to free the nmIcon and nmSound handles, if necessary; then dispose of the NMRec itself (if space for it was allocated with **NewPtr** or **NewHandle**).

Here is the function prototype of a response procedure:

```
pascal void myResponse( NMRecPtr nmReqPtr );
```

If you store a value of –1L at nmResp, an internal response procedure is used that removes the notification request as soon as it completes.

Important ▶

Don't use the internal response procedure (or your own response procedure) if you're using the flashing icon cue or diamond cue—the cue may disappear before the user sees it. Do not use the internal response procedure if you need to dispose of data structures, such as nmIcon and nmSound handles, when the notification completes.

- Store any useful data your response procedure may need at nmRefCon. If you store the address in A5 at nmRefCon, for example, the procedure can gain access to the application's global variables, by using the value at nmRefCon to switch in the application's A5 World; which is not active when the response procedure gets control. Use the **SetCurrentA5** routine to return the current address in A5. The response procedure can use the **SetA5** routine to determine the current A5 address and restore the application's A5 address.

Important ▶

The response procedure must exit with the same address in A5 as on entry. Save and restore A5 if you need to change it.

Here are the function prototypes:

```
long SetCurrentA5( void );

long SetA5( long newA5 );
```

SetA5 stores the address given by newA5 in A5; the value it returns is the current A5 value.

Your choice of notification cue really depends on how critical it is for the user to react to the notification. The flashing icon, diamond, and sound cues are relatively unobtrusive and are appropriate in most situations. It is quite common to combine the icon and diamond cues, since one draws the user's eye to the Application menu and the other indicates which application needs attention. Sound cues are quite useful, but it's best to combine them with icon and diamond cues in case the user isn't near the computer when the sound plays.

An alert dialog should be used only if a crisis situation arises that requires immediate resolution. Apple's AppleLink communications software, for example, uses an alert dialog cue when it is about to hang up the telephone because of lack of online activity for an extended period.

Once you've posted a notification request with **NMInstall**, the request remains active until you remove it with **NMRemove**:

```
pascal OSErr NMRemove( NMRecPtr nmReqPtr );
```

NMRemove is called automatically if you store -1 in the nmResp field of NMRec when you call **NMInstall**. If you store the address of your own response procedure, you would typically call **NMRemove** in the procedure.

If you don't use a response procedure—perhaps because you're using a diamond or flashing icon cue that needs to remain in effect until the user brings the application to the foreground—matters become a bit more complicated. In this situation, you need to execute the code that would normally appear in the response procedure from inside the event handler for the resume event. The handler would do this only if a Boolean global variable, indicating whether a notification request is pending, was true. The application would set this variable to true just before calling **NMInstall** and set it to false after calling **NMRemove** in the event handler for suspend.

The `DoNotify` routine in Listing 3-4 shows how to make a notification request involving three cues: a system beep, a flashing icon, and a diamond mark. It assumes you have a `'SICN'` resource (ID 128) defining a small icon in the resource fork of the application—you can create one easily with ResEdit. To make the audible cue more interesting, pass a handle to your favorite `'snd'` resource in `nmSound`, instead of -1. You can easily create such a resource and add it to your application's resource fork with products like Farallon's SoundEdit software; on Apple systems that come with microphones, you can use the Sound control panel to add a `'snd '` resource to the System file. Use ResEdit to move it from there to your application file.

Listing 3-4. How to make a notification request

```
Boolean      gInBackground;
Boolean      gNotifying;
nmRec gNotifyRec;

/*  DoNotify shows how to install a notification request
    using NMInstall.
*/
void DoNotify( void )
{
    OSErr     nmError;

    if ( !gInBackground ) return;  /* don't do it if not in bkgnd */

    gNotifyRec.qType = nmType;
    gNotifyRec.nmMark = 1;  /* mark name with diamond */
    gNotifyRec.nmIcon = GetResource( 'SICN', 128 );  /* flash this icon */
    HNoPurge( gNotifyRec.nmIcon );  /* handle must be nonpurgeable */
    gNotifyRec.nmSound = (Handle)-1L;  /* or GetResource( 'snd ', resID ); */
    gNotifyRec.nmStr = 0L;  /* no alert box */
    gNotifyRec.nmResp = (NMProcPtr)0L;  /* or -1 for auto-remove */
    gNotifyRec.nmRefCon = 0L;

    nmError = NMInstall( &gNotifyRec );
    gNotifying = true;

    return;
}
```

Note ▶

The `NMRecPtr` that `DoNotify` passes to **NMInstall** refers to a *global* variable. It is not proper to refer to a local variable because the local will be long gone by the time the system processes the notification request. (Locals disappear, of course, when a routine ends.) Any string to which `nmStr` points should also be a global variable.

DoNotify does not use a response procedure because it wants the visual cues to remain visible until the user brings the application to the foreground. Instead, it sets to true a global Boolean variable, gNotifying, just before calling **NMInstall**. The event handler for the resume event should inspect this Boolean and, if it is true, remove the notification request with **NMRemove** and dispose of data structures. Here is the code you would use to do this:

```
if ( gNotifying ) {

    NMRemove( &gNotifyRec );
    if ( gNotifyRec.nmIcon ) ReleaseResource( gNotifyRec.nmIcon );
    /* uncomment the following line if you specified a 'snd ' alert: */
    /* if ( gNotifyRec.nmSound ) ReleaseResource( gNotifyRec.nmSound ); */
    gNotifying = false;
}
```

The last thing this code fragment does is set gNotifying to false to indicate that the notification request has been removed. You should also initialize gNotifying to false when the application first starts to run.

Important ▶

Use the services of the Notification Manager only when the application is running in the background. If the application is in the foreground, it is interacting directly with the user, so special notifications are unnecessary.

▶ Launching an Application

Many applications include a Transfer... item in the File menu for launching another application that the user picks from a standard Open File dialog box. This is often more convenient than switching to the Finder and trying to locate the application from the desktop.

You can use a new System 7 routine, **LaunchApplication**, to launch one application from inside another application:

```
pascal OSErr LaunchApplication( LaunchPBPtr LaunchParams );
```

LaunchApplication is a more powerful version of the **Launch** routine you would use in a System 6.x environment. Listing 3-5 shows the source code for a DoTransfer routine you could use to respond to the selection of a Transfer... item.

Listing 3-5. Using LaunchApplication to launch one application from another application

```
/*  DoTransfer transfers control to another application.
    It also sends the "open application" core AppleEvent
    to the application.
*/
void DoTransfer( void )
{
    StandardFileReply           reply;
    SFTypeList                  theTypeList = { 'APPL' };
    LaunchParamBlockRec         myLaunchStuff;
    AppParameters               myHLEvent;
    OSErr                       launchErr;

    StandardGetFile( 0L, 1, theTypeList, &reply );

    if ( reply.sfGood ) {

      myLaunchStuff.launchBlockID = extendedBlock;
      myLaunchStuff.launchEPBLength = extendedBlockLen;
      myLaunchStuff.launchFileFlags = 0;
      myLaunchStuff.launchControlFlags = launchContinue+launchNoFileFlags+
                                    launchUseMinimum;
      myLaunchStuff.launchAppSpec = &reply.sfFile;
      myLaunchStuff.launchAppParameters = &myHLEvent;

      myHLEvent.theMsgEvent.what = kHighLevelEvent;
      myHLEvent.theMsgEvent.message = kCoreEventClass;
      myHLEvent.theMsgEvent.where.v = (short)(kAEOpenApplication >> 16);
      myHLEvent.theMsgEvent.where.h = (short)(kAEOpenApplication & 0x0000FFFF);
      myHLEvent.theMsgEvent.when = TickCount();
      myHLEvent.eventRefCon = 0;
      myHLEvent.messageLength = 0;

      launchErr = LaunchApplication( &myLaunchStuff );
    }
}
```

The only parameter you pass to **LaunchApplication** is a pointer to a LaunchParamBlockRec record, the structure of which is shown in Listing 3-6.

Listing 3-6. The structure of the LaunchParamBlockRec used by the LaunchApplication routine

```
struct LaunchParamBlockRec {
    unsigned long      reserved1;           /* reserved */
    unsigned short     reserved2;           /* reserved */
    unsigned short     launchBlockID;       /* set to launchBlockID */
    unsigned long      launchEPBLength;     /* set to extendedBlockLen */
    unsigned short     launchFileFlags;
    LaunchFlags        launchControlFlags;
    FSSpecPtr          launchAppSpec;
    ProcessSerialNumber launchProcessSN;
    unsigned long      launchPreferredSize;
    unsigned long      launchMinimumSize;
    unsigned long      launchAvailableSize;
    AppParametersPtr   launchAppParameters;
};
```

Here is the meaning of each of the non-reserved fields of **LaunchParamBlockRec**:

launchBlockID—Set this to the constant extendedBlock.

launchPBLength—Set this to the constant extendedBlockLen.

launchFileFlags. LaunchApplication returns here the Finder flags for the launched application if the launchNoFileFlags flag in the launchControlFlags field is set.

launchControlFlags—The value you store in this field controls exactly how the application is launched. Determine the appropriate value by summing the flag values associated with the desired attributes. Here are the available flag values and how they affect a launch:

- **launchContinue** — Set this flag if you want the calling application to remain in memory after the other application launches. If it's not set, the calling application terminates.

- **launchNoFileFlags**—Set this flag if you want **LaunchApplication** to return the launched application's Finder flags in the launchFileFlags field.

- **LaunchUseMinimum** — Set this flag if you want **LaunchApplication** to launch the application in the largest available partition size that is less than the preferred size but larger than the minimum size. If you clear this flag, the file is launched only if a partition of the preferred size is available.

- **launchDontSwitch** — Set this flag if you don't want the launched application brought to the foreground after it is launched.
- **launchAllow24Bit** — If the operating system is in 32-bit mode, **LaunchApplication** normally displays a warning dialog if you try to launch an application whose is32BitCompatible flag is not set in its 'SIZE' resource. The user can either cancel the launch or proceed. The reason for the warning is that many pre-System 7 applications are 32-bit clean, but were written before Apple defined the use of the is32BitCompatible flag. Set the launchAllow24Bit flag to prevent the launching of applications that don't have the 32-bit clean flag set.
- **launchInhibitDaemon** — Set this flag if you want to prevent **LaunchApplication** from launching a background-only application. Such an application has the onlyBackground flag set in its 'SIZE' resource.

launchAppSpec—Put in this field the file system specification record (FSSpec) for the application file to be launched. If the user selected the file from a standard Open File dialog, as in the DoLaunch routine, set launchAppSpec to &replysfFile where reply is the StandardFileReply record.

launchProcessSN— LaunchApplication returns here the process serial number for the launched application. This number uniquely identifies a process running in memory.

launchPreferredSize—LaunchApplication returns here the preferred partition size (as specified in the application's 'SIZE' resource) for the launched application.

launchMinimumSize—LaunchApplication returns in this field the minimum partition size (as specified in the application's 'SIZE' resource) for the launched application.

launchAppParameters—Put a pointer to an AppParameters record in this field if you want to pass a high-level event to the launched application when it starts up; otherwise set this field to 0L. High-level events are covered in the next chapter. The DoTransfer routine in Listing 3-5 shows how to specify the "open application" event that the Finder sends when it launches an application.

▶ Temporary Memory

Temporary memory is a pool of unused memory that is not inside any Finder partition or the system heap. As a consequence, an application cannot use the traditional memory allocation routines, **NewHandle** and **NewPtr**, to allocate temporary memory. Those routines work only with free memory in the application heap or in the system heap.

It is possible, however, to allocate temporary memory using the **TempNewHandle** routine:

```pascal
pascal Handle TempNewHandle( Size logicalSize,
                             OSErr *resultCode );
```

Like **NewHandle**, **TempNewHandle** returns a handle to a block of memory of the size given by logicalSize. If the block could not be allocated, the returned handle is 0L and the resultCode variable contains the error code (memFullErr).

Under System 7 only, the handle returned by **TempNewHandle** can be dealt with as if it were returned by **NewHandle**. You can use standard Memory Manager routines to perform operations on the handle, including using **DisposHandle** to dispose of the handle, for example.

The only other special temporary memory routine you'll probably need to use is **TempMaxMem**:

```pascal
pascal Size TempMaxMem( Size *grow );
```

TempMaxMem returns the size of the largest available temporary memory block. The value it returns in the grow variable has no meaning; the grow parameter is there only to preserve the symmetry with the **MaxMem** routine.

You should design your application to be clever enough to recognize when useful amounts of temporary memory are available and then to use the space to make memory-intensive operations more efficient. However, your application must still be able to complete its tasks even if no temporary memory is available. Applications should never rely on the availability of temporary memory, because, unlike heap space whose size can be guaranteed, there is no way to guarantee the size of the temporary memory space. Indeed, if the user has several applications running in memory, a negligible amount of temporary memory may be available.

Important ▶

> The operating system allocates Finder partitions from temporary memory. Therefore, to allow the user to launch more applications from the Finder, you should not tie up huge blocks of temporary memory for long periods of time. Try to restrict your use of temporary memory to supporting brief tasks or modal tasks that cannot be switched to the background.

▶ Process Information

The Process Manager, new to System 7, provides information about the status of all processes in memory. Applications can use the Process Manager to gather interesting statistics about other processes; a debugger, for example, could use it to locate processes in memory. As you will see in Chapter 4, you'll probably use the Process Manager most frequently to determine whether an application in memory can accept Apple events from your application.

The system assigns a unique *process serial number* to each process running in memory. You provide this number when calling routines that require a target process. The structure of a `ProcessSerialNumber` record is shown in Listing 3-7.

Listing 3-7. The structure of the ProcessSerialNumber record

```
struct ProcessSerialNumber {
    unsigned long highLongOfPSN;
    unsigned long lowLongOfPSN;
};
```

The Process Manager provides two routines for determining the process serial numbers of the current process (the one whose A5 World is active; not necessarily the foreground process) and the foreground process. Here are the function prototypes:

```
pascal OSErr GetCurrentProcess( ProcessSerialNumber *PSN );

pascal OSErr GetFrontProcess( ProcessSerialNumber *PSN );
```

Both routines return the process serial number in the PSN variable.

To determine the process serial numbers of all active processes, make repeated calls to the **GetNextProcess** routine until it returns a procNotFound error:

```
pascal OSErr GetNextProcess( ProcessSerialNumber *PSN );
```

When you call **GetNextProcess**, pass it a serial number of a process in the PSN variable (or pass kNoProcess in the LowLongOfPSN field and 0L in the HighLongOfPSN field when calling **GetNextProcess** to get the first process). On return, **GetNextProcess** stores in the PSN variable the process serial number of the next process in its internal list of processes. If it does not find any more processes, it returns a procNotFound error.

Armed with a process serial number, you can learn all about the process by calling **GetProcessInformation**:

```
pascal OSErr GetProcessInformation( ProcessSerialNumberPtr *PSN,

                                      ProcessInfoRecPtr info );
```

This routine returns information in a ProcessInfoRec (see Listing 3-8) pointed to by info.

Listing 3-8. The structure of the ProcessInfoRec used by the GetProcessInformation routine

```
struct ProcessInfoRec {
        unsigned long              processInfoLength;
        StringPtr                  processName;
        ProcessSerialNumber        processNumber;
        unsigned long              processType;
        unsigned long              processSignature;
        unsigned long              processMode;
        Ptr                        processLocation;
        unsigned long              processSize;
        unsigned long              processFreeMem;
        ProcessSerialNumber        processLauncher;
        unsigned long              processLaunchDate;
        unsigned long              processActiveTime;
        FSSpecPtr                  processAppSpec;
};
```

Here is the meaning of each field of the `ProcessInfoRec` record:

processInfoLength— This field indicates the size of the record. Set this field to `sizeof( ProcessInfoRec )` before calling **GetProcessInformation**.

processName—Put a pointer to a 32-byte buffer in this field. **GetProcessInformation** returns in the buffer the name of the application. If you don't want the name returned, set this field to `0L`.

processNumber—Set this field to the process serial number of the application in which you are interested.

processType—**GetProcessInformation** returns here the file type for the application—`'APPL'` for a regular application, `'appe'` for a background-only application, or `'dfil'` for a desk accessory.

processSignature—**GetProcessInformation** returns here the creator type for the application.

processMode—**GetProcessInformation** returns here a bit vector that reflects the status of the mode bits in the application's `'SIZE'` resource. The mask values for the relevant bits are as follows:

```
enum {modeDeskAccessory              = 0x00020000};
enum {modeMultiLaunch                = 0x00010000};
enum {modeNeedSuspendResume          = 0x00004000};
enum {modeCanBackground              = 0x00001000};
enum {modeDoesActivateOnFGSwitch     = 0x00000800};
enum {modeOnlyBackground             = 0x00000400};
enum {modeGetFrontClicks             = 0x00000200};
enum {modeGetAppDiedMsg              = 0x00000100};
enum {mode32BitCompatible            = 0x00000080};
enum {modeHighLevelEventAware        = 0x00000040};
enum {modeLocalAndRemoteHLEvents     = 0x00000020};
enum {modeStationeryAware            = 0x00000010};
enum {modeUseTextEditServices        = 0x00000008};
```

Note that the first mask, `modeDeskAccessory`, does not correspond to a mode bit in the `'SIZE'` resource. If its bit is set, the application is a desk accessory, not a standard application.

processLocation—**GetProcessInformation** returns here the address of the base of the application's Finder partition.

processSize—**GetProcessInformation** returns here the number of bytes in the application's Finder partition.

processFreeMem—**GetProcessInformation** returns here the number of free bytes in the application's heap.

processLauncher—**GetProcessInformation** returns here the process serial number of the application that launched this process. If that application is no longer running, this number will be kNoProcess.

processLaunchDate—**GetProcessInformation** returns here the number of ticks since system start-up when the application was launched.

processActiveTime—**GetProcessInformation** returns here the total number of ticks during which the process has had control of the processor, either in the foreground or background.

processAppSpec—Put a pointer to a buffer for a FSSpec in this field; **GetProcessInformation** returns in the buffer the FSSpec of the application. If you don't want the FSSpec returned, set this field to 0L.

The ShowProcesses routine in Listing 3-9 shows how to use **GetNextProcess** to obtain the process serial numbers of all the applications in memory. For each serial number, the routine calls **GetProcessInformation** to determine the name, creator, and file type of the process, then displays the results in a line in the front window. Notice that ShowProcesses uses Skeleton's CRLF routine after drawing each line to advance the active drawing position to the left side of the next line.

Listing 3-9. Using Process Manager routines

```
/* Display the names, creators, and types of all
     processes running in memory.
*/
void ShowProcesses( void )
{
     ProcessSerialNumber     PSN;
     ProcessInfoRec          InfoRec;
     Str32                   theName;
     FSSpec                  theSpec;
     Str255                  typeString;

     InfoRec.processInfoLength = sizeof( ProcessInfoRec );
     InfoRec.processName = theName;
     InfoRec.processAppSpec = &theSpec;

     PSN.highLongOfPSN = 0;
     PSN.lowLongOfPSN = kNoProcess;
```

```
        while ( GetNextProcess( &PSN ) != procNotFound ) {
```

Listing 3-9. Using Process Manager routines (continued)

```
            GetProcessInformation( &PSN, &InfoRec );
            DrawString( InfoRec.processName );

            DrawString( (StringPtr)"\p (Signature: " );
            TypeToString( InfoRec.processSignature, typeString );
            DrawString( typeString );
            DrawString( (StringPtr)"\p  File type: " );
            TypeToString( InfoRec.processType, typeString );
            DrawString( typeString );

            DrawChar( ')' );

            CRLF();                      /* defined in Skeleton source */

    }
}

/* Convert an OSType to a character string.
*/
void TypeToString( OSType theType, Str255 typeString )
{
    long    typeNum;
    short   i;

    typeString[0] = 4;

    for ( i = 0; i <= 3 ; i++ ) {

            typeString[4-i] = (char)(theType & 0x000000FF);
            theType = theType >> 8;
    }
}
```

▶ Summary

In this chapter, we showed how to design an application that behaves properly in the System 7 multitasking environment. We also provided all the information you need to allow your application to operate in the background and to communicate with the user through the services of the Notification Manager.

Finally, we covered the Memory Manager's temporary memory routines and explored the routines the Process Manager provides so that you can get information about all the applications running on the system.

In the next chapter, we will examine one of the most important new System 7 managers—the Apple Event Manager. We will show you how two applications running on one system, or running on systems connected via a network, can send commands and data to each other.

4 ▶ Apple Events

System 7 introduces the high-level event to the Macintosh. A high-level event can be sent from one application to another. To make things more interesting, the receiving application can be running on the same Macintosh as the sender *or on any Macintosh connected to the same network*.

Using high-level events, applications can exchange data or send commands to one another. An accounting application might send a command to a spreadsheet telling it to prepare a complex chart for a given set of data, for example.

Of course, high-level events are useful only when the receiving application understands how to interpret and react to the commands or data sent along with them. In other words, the receiver must understand the protocol the sending application is using. To avoid a proliferation of proprietary protocols and to promote communication between the applications of different vendors, Apple has defined a standard high-level event protocol—the Apple Event Interprocess Messaging Protocol. High-level events sent by this protocol are called *Apple events*.

System 7 includes an Apple Event Manager you can use to handle the creation, sending, and receiving of Apple events. Your System 7 applications will always use this manager because, as you will see, there are several Apple events the Finder can send to an application when it starts up that the application *must* respond to.

115

This chapter will cover much of what you will need to know to deal with Apple events properly. Some of the topics are as follows:

- handling high-level events
- the structure of an Apple event
- installing handlers for incoming Apple events
- processing incoming Apple events
- creating and sending an Apple event
- supporting the required Apple events

▶ Preparing for High-Level Events

Application developers and users must attend to several basic chores to ensure that both an application and the Macintosh it is running on are configured to handle high-level events.

The developer of the application must, of course, include code to handle high-level events properly. This will be covered in much detail in the rest of this chapter. The developer must also set two flags in the application's 'SIZE' resource (see Appendix B):

- The isHighLevelEventAware flag tells the system that the application knows how to handle high-level events, including the required Apple events examined later in this chapter.
- The localAndRemoteHLEvents flag tells the system to send to the application high-level events it receives from other systems across the network. (You could set this flag to onlyLocalHLEvents if it doesn't make sense for your application to respond to remote events.)

The user must also carry out some responsibilities for an application to receive high-level events sent over the network. First, the user must enable the Macintosh system as a whole to receive remote high-level events. To do this, run the Sharing Setup control panel to see the window shown in Figure 4-1. If the program linking feature is currently off, click the *Start* button in the bottom pane of the window.

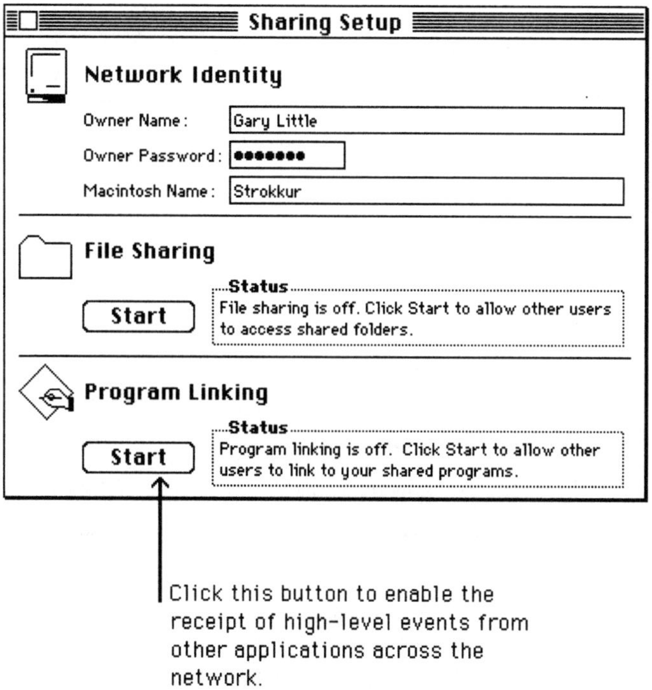

Figure 4-1. The Sharing Setup control panel lets you turn on Program Linking so that your system will process high-level events sent by other applications across the network

The next responsibility of the user is to configure the Macintosh to allow individual remote users to gain access. To do this, run the Users & Groups control panel and create new documents for each user you want to allow on your system (there should already be a document for <Guest>). When you double-click a Users & Groups document (its icon looks like a human head), you will see one of the types of windows shown in Figure 4-2. Check the Program Linking box to allow the remote user to send high-level events to your Macintosh.

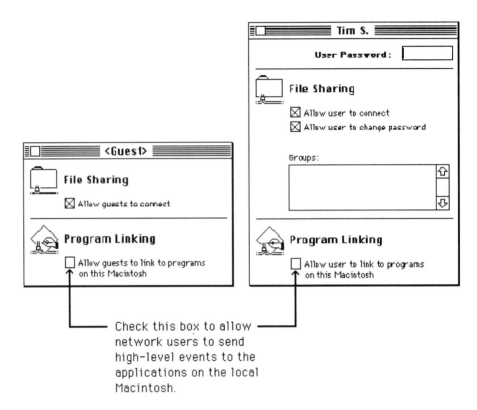

Check this box to allow
network users to send
high-level events to the
applications on the local
Macintosh.

Figure 4-2. You must explicitly grant remote users access to your Macintosh before they can send high-level events to your applications. Do this using the Users & Groups control panel to create users and specify their privileges. This figure shows the windows you see when you double-click on the Guest icon and the icon for a user named *Tim.S.*

The final responsibility of the user is to go to the Finder, select the application's icon, then choose the Sharing . . . item in the File menu to bring up the window shown in Figure 4-3. To enable the application to receive remote high-level events, check the *Allow remote program linking* box. You won't be able to check this box unless Program Linking has been turned on using the Sharing Setup control panel.

Note ▶

The check box in this window controls the state of the localAndRemoteHLEvents/onlyLocalHLEvents flag in the 'SIZE' resource. This allows the user to override the default setting provided by the developer of the application.

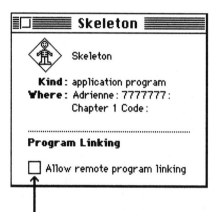

Check this box to allow high-level events received from an application across the network to be passed to the application.

Figure 4-3. The window brought up by the Sharing... item in the Finder's File menu when an application icon is selected. By checking the *Allow remote program linking* check box, the application will receive high-level events sent by applications running on systems across the network.

▶ The High-Level Event Mechanism

High-level events are sent from one application to another using the Event Manager's **PostHighLevelEvent** routine. This routine sends the contents of any arbitrary data buffer you specify to a target application (sometimes called a *server* application). The Event Manager uses the services of a low-level manager, the Program-to-Program Communications (PPC) Toolbox, to effect the transfer; the PPC Toolbox, in turn, transports data across the network using the Apple Data Stream Protocol (ADSP) implemented by the AppleTalk Manager.

The **PostHighLevelEvent** routine is not discussed in detail because you should avoid using it directly. Instead, use Apple Event Manager routines to construct a packet of data and send it to another application. This encourages you to use the standard Apple Event Interprocess Messaging Protocol rather than dreaming up your own unique protocol.

▶ Addressing a High-Level Event

A sender can specify the recipient of a high-level event using one of the following four data types:

- the application's signature
- the application's process serial number
- the target ID
- the session ID

If the target application is running on another computer on the network, you must specify either a target ID or a session ID—you can't specify a signature or a process serial number. The structure of a target ID record, which incorporates a session ID, is shown in Listing 4-1. Also shown are related data structures, PPCPortRec, LocationNameRec, and PortInfoRec.

Listing 4-1. The structures of the TargetID, PPCPortRec, LocationNameRec, and PortInfoRec records

```
struct TargetID {
    long sessionID;             /* session reference number */
    PPCPortRec name;            /* port name */
    LocationNameRec location;   /* port location */
    PPCPortRec recvrName;       /* reserved */
};

struct PPCPortRec {
    ScriptCode nameScript;              /* script of name */
    Str32 name;                         /* program name */
    PPCPortKinds portKindSelector;      /* variant: ppcByString or
                                                ppcByCreatorAndType */

    union {
        Str32 portTypeStr;              /* ppcByString - used by AE Manager */
        struct {
            OSType creator;             /* ppcByCreatorAndType */
            OSType type;
            } port;
        } u;
};
```

Listing 4-1. The structures of the TargetID, PPCPortRec,
LocationNameRec, and PortInfoRec records (continued)

```
struct LocationNameRec {
    PPCLocationKind locationKindSelector;   /* variant: ppcNoLocation
                                                        ppcNBPLocation or
                                                        ppcNBPTypeLocation   */
/* ppcNoLocation means the target application is local (not remote) */
union {
        EntityName nbpEntity;    /* ppcNBPLocation: NBP name entity */
        Str32 nbpType;           /* ppcNBPTypeLocation: NBP type string */
        } u;
};


struct PortInfoRec {   /* returned by PPCBrowser */
    unsigned char filler1;
    Boolean authRequired;
    PPCPortRec name;
};
```

Note ▶

If the recipient of an Apple event is the same as the sender (that is, the application is sending an event to itself), the fastest way to send the Apple event is to use a process serial number to identify the target.

In Chapter 3 you saw how to use the Process Manager's **GetNextProcess** and **GetProcessInformation** routines to determine the process serial numbers and signatures of all applications running on a system. You can use these routines to identify the target of a high-level event when you know the target is already running on the same computer. If the application isn't already running, you can first launch it by searching for it in the Finder's desktop database (see Chapter 9), then calling **LaunchApplication** (see Chapter 3).

The ApplicationIsRunning and LaunchMyApplication routines in Listing 4-2 assist you in locating a target application running on the same computer. You can call ApplicationIsRunning to determine if an application with a given signature is already running—if it is, a Boolean true is returned and you can use the signature or process serial number to identify the target. If the application is not already running, you can launch it by calling LaunchMyApplication. This routine uses the **PBDTGetAPPL** routine to search the desktop database of the boot volume for an application with a given signature. (You will learn more about the desktop database in Chapter 9; for more information on the **PBDTGetAPPL** routine, refer to *Inside Macintosh*, Volume VI.) When the application is found, LaunchMyApplication launches it using the **LaunchApplication** routine that you learned about in Chapter 3. Once the application is running, you can identify it by signature or by process serial number.

Listing 4-2. Routines for checking that an application is running and for automatically finding and launching an application that is not running

```
Boolean ApplicationIsRunning( OSType theSignature )
{
    ProcessSerialNumber    thePSN;
    ProcessInfoRec         theProcessInfo;
    OSErr                  theError;

    theProcessInfo.processInfoLength = sizeof( ProcessInfoRec );
    theProcessInfo.processName = 0L;
    theProcessInfo.processAppSpec = 0L;

    thePSN.highLongOfPSN = 0L;
    thePSN.lowLongOfPSN = kNoProcess;

    while ( GetNextProcess( &thePSN ) != procNotFound ) {

            GetProcessInformation( &thePSN, &theProcessInfo );
            if ( theProcessInfo.processSignature == theSignature )
                    return( true );
    }
    return( false );
}


OSErr LaunchMyApplication( OSType theSignature )
{
    DTPBRec                theDatabase;
    LaunchParamBlockRec    theLPB;
    FSSpec                 theFSSpec;
    OSErr                  myError;

    theDatabase.ioCompletion = 0L;
    theDatabase.ioNamePtr = 0L;
    theDatabase.ioVRefNum = -1;    /* search boot volume only */

    if ( ( myError = PBDTGetPath( &theDatabase ) ) != noErr )
                return( myError );
```

Listing 4-2. Routines for checking that an application is running and for automatically finding and launching an application that is not running (continued)

```
        theDatabase.ioIndex = 0;        /* most recent creation date */
        theDatabase.ioFileCreator = theSignature;
        theDatabase.ioNamePtr = (StringPtr)theFSSpec.name;

        if ( ( myError = PBDTGetAPPL( &theDatabase, false ) ) != noErr )
                    return( myError );

        theFSSpec.vRefNum = theDatabase.ioVRefNum;
        theFSSpec.parID = theDatabase.ioAPPLParID;

        theLPB.launchBlockID = extendedBlock;
        theLPB.launchEPBLength = extendedBlockLen;
        theLPB.launchFileFlags = 0;
        theLPB.launchControlFlags = launchContinue + launchNoFileFlags +
                                    launchUseMinimum + launchDontSwitch;
        theLPB.launchAppSpec = &theFSSpec;
        theLPB.launchAppParameters = 0L;

        return( LaunchApplication( &theLPB ) );
}
```

A more general technique for identifying a target—whether the target is local or running on another system—is to use the **PPCBrowser** routine. **PPCBrowser** puts up a dialog box similar to the one shown in Figure 4-4 allowing the user to select the desired target application. It returns a completed LocationNameRec and a PortInfoRec. You can construct a TargetID record by transferring the LocationNameRec to the location field of the TargetID and transferring the PortInfoRec.name field of the PortInfoRec to the name field of the TargetID.

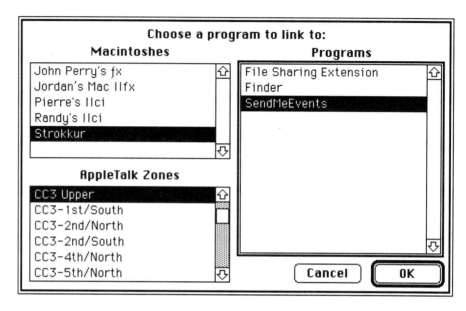

Figure 4-4. The dialog box PPCBrowser displays when you're connected to an internet. If you're not on an internet, the box titled *AppleTalk Zones* does not appear

The function prototype for **PPCBrowser** is as follows:

```
pascal OSErr PPCBrowser(ConstStr255Param prompt,
                        ConstStr255Param applListLabel,
                        Boolean defaultSpecified,
                        LocationNameRec *theLocation,
                        PortInfoRec *thePortInfo,
                        PPCFilterProcPtr portFilter,
                        ConstStr32Param theLocNBPType);
```

Here are the meanings of the parameters to **PPCBrowser**:

prompt—Defines the title of the dialog box. If you pass 0L, the title will be *Choose a program to link to:*.

applListLabel—Defines the heading that appears above the list of applications in the dialog box. If you pass 0L, the heading will be *Programs*.

defaultSpecified— If set to true, you're passing information about a default application in the records that theLocation and thePortInfo point to. If this application exists, its entry is highlighted when the dialog box first appears. (Presumably the default information you pass was returned by a previous call to **PPCBrowser**.) Set this parameter to false if you aren't providing information about a default application.

theLocation—On return, the LocationNameRec to which this parameter points contains information describing the selected application.

thePortInfo—On return, the PortInfoRec to which this parameter points contains information describing the selected application.

portFilter—Pass the address of a port filter procedure here, or OL if you aren't using a port filter procedure. As you will see, a port filter procedure restricts the types of applications **PPCBrowser** displays in its list of programs.

theLocNBPType—Pass a name-binding protocol (NBP) type string identifying the entities that **PPCBrowser** is to display in the Macintoshes list in the dialog box. If you specify OL (the usual case), **PPCBrowser** uses "PPCToolbox." This is the entity name the PPC Toolbox registers when the Macintosh starts up with Program Linking turned on or when you turn Program Linking on with the Sharing Setup control panel.

PPCBrowser returns an error code of userCanceledErr if the user clicks the Cancel button in the dialog box.

If you don't pass the address of a port filter procedure to **PPCBrowser**, the browser dialog shows all possible target programs for a high-level event. In some cases, however, you may wish to restrict the list of programs that are shown—you may want to display only programs with a particular signature or programs running on the same system, for example. To provide specialized filtering, write a port filter procedure that uses the following function prototype:

```
pascal Boolean myPPCFilter( LocationNamePtr locationName,
                            PortInfoPtr thePortInfo );
```

PPCBrowser calls this procedure each time it needs to decide whether to display the name of an application. If the procedure returns false, the name is not displayed; if it returns true, it is displayed.

The port filter procedure receives pointers to a program's LocationNameRec and PortInfoRec records. It inspects the data in these records to decide whether the program should be filtered. Listing 4-3 shows a filter you can use to force **PPCBrowser** to display only the names of programs that have a specific signature.

Listing 4-3. A typical port filter procedure for PPCBrowser

```
/* Port filter procedure for PPCBrowser */
/* Note: ApplCreator is a global defining an application signature */
pascal Boolean MyPPCFilter( LocationNamePtr locationName,
                              PortInfoPtr thePortInfo )
{
    StringPtr      s;
    OSType    theCreator;

/* include following line to filter out remote entities */
/* if ( !(locationName->locationKindSelector == ppcNoLocation) ) return( false );
*/

    if ( (thePortInfo->name).portKindSelector == ppcByCreatorAndType ) {

            theCreator = (thePortInfo->name).u.port.creator;

    } else { /* must be ppcByString */
/* Apple Event Manager uses ppcByString. The string is 8 characters
    long: a 4-byte creator followed by 'ep' and a 2-byte ID number */

            s = (thePortInfo->name).u.portTypeStr;

            if ( *s++ != 8 ) return( false ); /* unknown string */

            BlockMove (s &theCreator, 4);
    }

    if ( theCreator != ApplCreator ) return( false );
    return ( true );
}
```

▶ Receiving a High-Level Event

An application checks for high-level events in much the same way it checks for any other type of event—by calling **WaitNextEvent**. When **WaitNextEvent** retrieves a high-level event, the event record contains an event code of kHighLevelEvent in its what field. The message and where fields contain the event class and event ID for the event. These fields uniquely identify the high-level event and were provided by the sending application when it calls **PostHighLevelEvent** to send the event.

Note ▶

The proper response to a high-level event that is *not* an Apple event is to call **AcceptHighLevelEvent**. You will see later in this chapter that the proper response to a high-level Apple event is to call the **AEProcessAppleEvent** routine. You can check the event class and event ID in the event record to see if they match values for a high-level event (other than an Apple event) that you support.

If your application does not support high-level events that are not Apple events, you do not have to call **AcceptHighLevelEvent**. Since most applications will use Apple events exclusively, this chapter does not cover the **AcceptHighLevelEvent** routine in detail. If you want to learn more about it, refer to *Inside Macintosh*, Volume VI.

▶ Apple Event Interprocess Messaging Protocol

The preferred technique for sending high-level events between applications involves using the Apple Event Interprocess Messaging Protocol (AEIMP). High-level events sent using this protocol are called Apple events and are handled by routines in the Apple Event Manager.

The Apple Event Interprocess Messaging Protocol requires that the data you send via a high-level event be structured in a particular way. Much of this structure comes free as a result of using Apple Event Manager routines. Using a standard protocol like AEIMP makes it much easier for applications to work with one another, even if they were created by different programming teams.

Apple events are basically commands that direct the receiving application to perform particular tasks or return status information. Each event is uniquely defined by an event class and an event ID, both of which are usually represented by four-character mnemonic literal strings (instead of the equivalent 32-bit integers). Table 4-1 shows the four Apple events the Finder uses to communicate with a running application.

Table 4-1. The four required Apple events that the Finder sends to running applications

Event Class	Event ID	Parameter	Meaning
'aevt'	'oapp'	none	Open the application
'aevt'	'odoc'	list of aliases	Open the documents
'aevt'	'pdoc'	list of aliases	Print the documents
'aevt'	'quit'	none	Quit the application

The four general categories of Apple events are as follows:

- **Required**—These are the four events that the Finder can send to a running application (see Table 4-1). They will be sent to any application that has the `isHighLevelEventAware` flag in its `'SIZE'` resource set (see Appendix B).
- **Core**—These events define general operations that almost any Macintosh application should support. They are documented in the *Apple Event Registry*, published by Apple's Developer Technical Support group.
- **Functional-area**—These events define operations that are unique to a particular class of application (such as word processors, spreadsheets, and so on). They are also documented in the *Apple Event Registry*.
- **Custom**—These events are application-specific and may be published or unpublished, depending on the mood of the developer of the application. It is expected that many custom Apple events will eventually become de facto standards and migrate into the functional-area category.

If you wish to define an Apple event for a particular operation, check the *Apple Event Registry* to see if one has already been defined. If one has been defined, use it! Don't reinvent the wheel. If no published Apple event is available, you may go ahead and define your own. To do so, first assign a unique event class (your application's signature is a good choice), then assign an event ID that distinguishes it from other events with the same event class.

A complete Apple event definition also includes a description of any parameters that will be included with the event. The parameter for the Finder's `'aevt'` `'odoc'` (Open Document) event, for example, is a list of the aliases of file names to be opened. As you will see, each parameter is associated with a unique keyword.

▶ Apple Event Data Structures

You must become familiar with a few key Apple event data structures before you can confidently use Apple Event Manager routines. They are the following:

- `AEDesc`—descriptor record
- `AEKeyDesc`—keyword-specified descriptor record
- `AppleEvent`—Apple event record

The precise definitions for these records, and some related records, are shown in Listing 4-4.

Listing 4-4. The structures of the AEDesc, AEKeyDesc, AEDescList, AERecord, and AppleEvent records

```
struct AEDesc {
    DescType descriptorType;          /* data type specification */
    Handle dataHandle;                /* handle to the data */
};

struct AEKeyDesc {
    AEKeyword descKey;                /* keyword for the descriptor */
    AEDesc descContent;              /* the descriptor */
};

typedef AEDesc AEDescList;      /* an AEDesc with a descKey of 'list' */
typedef AEDescList AERecord;    /* a list of keyword-specified descriptors */
typedef AERecord AppleEvent;    /* an AERecord that defines an Apple event */
```

The descriptor record (AEDesc) is the basic building block. It is composed of a handle to a block of data and a descriptor type that indicates the contents of the data. Listing 4-5 contains a list of standard descriptor types. Notice that the list includes standard numeric types that you would find in any programming language, as well as complex structures such as file system specification records and lists.

Note ▶

AEDescList and AEAddressDesc records are special cases of an AEDesc record, and so may be used with all Apple Event Manager routines that act on AEDesc records. An AEDescList is an AEDesc whose descriptor type is typeAEList (a list of descriptor records). An AEAddressDesc is an AEDesc whose descriptor type is typeApplSignature, typeSessionID, typeTargetID, or typeProcessSerialNumber (in other words, the data describes the address of a target application).

Listing 4-5. Descriptor types for Apple event descriptor records

```
#define typeBoolean          'bool'   /* Boolean value */
#define typeChar             'TEXT'   /* block of characters */
#define typeSMInt            'shor'   /* 16-bit integer */
#define typeInteger          'long'   /* 32-bit integer */
#define typeSMFloat          'sing'   /* SANE single precision number */
#define typeFloat            'doub'   /* SANE double precision number */
#define typeLongInteger      'long'   /* 32-bit integer */
#define typeShortInteger     'shor'   /* 16-bit integer */
#define typeLongFloat        'doub'   /* SANE double precision number */
```

Listing 4-5. Descriptor types for Apple event descriptor records (continued)

```
#define typeShortFloat          'sing'   /* SANE single precision number */
#define typeExtended            'exte'   /* SANE extended number */
#define typeComp                'comp'   /* SANE computational number */
#define typeMagnitude           'magn'   /* unsigned 32-bit integer */
#define typeAEList              'list'   /* list of descriptor records */
#define typeAERecord            'reco'   /* list of keyword-specified
                                                descriptor records */
#define typeTrue                'true'   /* Boolean true value */
#define typeFalse               'fals'   /* Boolean false value */
#define typeAlias               'alis'   /* alias record */
#define typeEnumerated          'enum'   /* enumerated data */
#define typeType                'type'   /* descriptor type */
#define typeAppParameters       'appa'   /* launch parameters */
#define typeProperty            'prop'   /* Apple event property */
#define typeFSS                 'fss '   /* file system specification */
#define typeKeyword             'keyw'   /* Apple event keyword */
#define typeSectionH            'sect'   /* Edition Manager section handle */
#define typeWildCard            '****'   /* wildcard: matches any type */
#define typeNull                'null'   /* null or non-existent data */

#define typeApplSignature       'sign'   /* application signature */
#define typeSessionID           'ssid'   /* session ID */
#define typeTargetID            'targ'   /* target ID */
#define typeProcessSerialNumber 'psn '   /* process serial number */
```

The next step up from the descriptor record is the *keyword-specified descriptor record* or AEKeyDesc. An AEKeyDesc is similar to an AEDesc except that it also includes a keyword that serves as an identifying tag for the record. The Apple Event Manager reads the tag to determine to what *attribute* or *parameter* the AEDesc within the AEKeyDesc belongs. An attribute relates to a characteristic of an Apple event that is used primarily by the Apple Event Manager itself—the event class, event ID, and target address are all attributes, for example. A parameter relates to the data that the target application will retrieve and deal with explicitly. Parameters include numeric data and file names and are part of the definition for the Apple event that appears in the *Apple Event Registry*.

Listing 4-6 shows the keywords for standard Apple event parameters and attributes. Notice in particular the keyDirectObject keyword that identifies an Apple event's direct parameter. This is the primary (and many times only) parameter that most Apple events use.

Listing 4-6. Keywords for standard Apple event parameters and attributes

```
/* Keywords for Apple event parameters:

#define keyErrorNumber            'errn' /* error number */
#define keyErrorString            'errs' /* error string */
#define kAEAnswer                 'ansr' /* event ID for reply */
#define keyDirectObject           '----' /* direct parameter */

/* Keywords for Apple event attributes: */

#define keyTransactionIDAttr      'tran' /* transaction ID */
#define keyReturnIDAttr           'rtid' /* return ID */
#define keyEventClassAttr         'evcl' /* event class */
#define keyEventIDAttr            'evid' /* event ID */
#define keyAddressAttr            'addr' /* target address */
#define keyOptionalKeywordAttr    'optk' /* list of optional parms */
#define keyTimeoutAttr            'timo' /* timeout value */
#define keyInteractLevelAttr      'inte' /* user interaction level */
#define keyEventSourceAttr        'esrc' /* source address */
#define keyMissedKeywordAttr      'miss' /* first required parameter
                                            not yet retrieved */
```

The final important record is the `AppleEvent` record. This is the record you'll be building, sending, and receiving using Apple Event Manager routines. An `AppleEvent` record is an `AEDesc` with a descriptor type of `typeAppleEvent`. The data to which the `AEDesc` handle refers is a list of the keyword-specified descriptor records that completely describe the necessary attributes and parameters for the Apple event.

▶ Receiving Apple Events

Adding code to your application to handle incoming Apple events is quite straightforward. The first step is to prepare a list of the Apple events your application will support. This list should include the required Apple events sent by the Finder, other events in the *Apple Event Registry* that are appropriate to the application, and any custom events you've defined that are unique to the application.

Next, use the **AEInstallEventHandler** routine to install an event handler (that you provide) for each Apple event the application supports. This routine stores the address of the handler in an internal lookup table. When the Apple event corresponding to this handler arrives, and the application calls

AEProcessAppleEvent, the Apple Event Manager automatically calls this routine to handle the event. Here is the function prototype for **AEInstallEventHandler**:

```
pascal OSErr AEInstallEventHandler( AEEventClass theAEEventClass,
                                    AEEventID theAEEventID,
                                    EventHandlerProcPtr handler,
                                    long handlerRefcon,
                                    Boolean isSysHandler );
```

The parameters passed to **AEInstallEventHandler** are theAEEventClass (the event class), theAEEventID (the event ID), handler (the address of the Apple event handler you provide), handlerRefcon (an application-defined reference constant), and isSysHandler (a Boolean indicating whether the handler is to be added to the system dispatch table or the application's dispatch table).

How to write an event handler will be discussed in the next section.

As noted earlier, you use **WaitNextEvent** to retrieve high-level events (including Apple events) from the event queue, just like any other event type. When it retrieves a high-level event, the what field of the event record is kHighLevelEvent and the proper response to the event is to call the **AEProcessAppleEvent** routine. **AEProcessAppleEvent** checks for an event handler corresponding to the event class and event ID in the event record and dispatches control to it if it exists.

▶ Writing an Apple Event Handler

Here is the function prototype for an Apple event handler that you install with **AEInstallEventHandler**:

```
pascal OSErr myEventHandler( AppleEvent *theAppleEvent,
                             AppleEvent *reply,
                             long myRefcon );
```

The Apple Event Manager passes three parameters to the Apple event handler:

theAppleEvent—This is a pointer to the AppleEvent record describing the event.

reply—This is a pointer to the AppleEvent record that the Apple Event Manager sends back to the caller, if the caller requested a reply, when the handler exits. If an error occurs during processing, you can add a descriptive error string in this record (see "Error Handling" later in this chapter). You can also return any other useful data to the caller via the reply Apple event—the results of the operation, for example. The event class and event ID of a reply Apple event are kCoreEventClass and kAEAnswer, respectively.

myRefcon—This is the reference constant that the application passed to **AEInstallEventHandler** when it first installed the event handler. The application can use this constant for any convenient purpose.

If the Apple event handler did not encounter an error while processing the Apple event, it should return noErr; otherwise, it should return a meaningful error code documented in the description of the event in the *Apple Event Registry*. The Apple Event Manager automatically inserts the error code in the keyErrorNumber parameter of the reply Apple event so that the application that sent the Apple event can retrieve it to learn what went wrong.

▶ Extracting Parameters from an AppleEvent Record

Two routines are available for extracting parameters from the AppleEvent record passed to an Apple event handler: **AEGetParamDesc** and **AEGetParamPtr**. **AEGetParamDesc** returns a copy of the AEDesc record for the parameter whereas **AEGetParamPtr** returns the descriptor type and the data to which the AEDesc refers in buffers that you provide. Both routines return errAEDescNotFound if the requested parameter does not exist.

You will most often use **AEGetParamDesc** in situations where you're extracting an AEDesc that refers to a list of descriptor records (descriptor type: typeAEList). This is because the Apple Event Manager's list-processing routines (described later) require an AEDesc (coerced to an AEDescList) as an input. Otherwise, you will probably use **AEGetParamPtr** to retrieve the parameter's data directly.

Here is the function prototype for **AEGetParamDesc**:

```
pascal OSErr AEGetParamDesc( const AppleEvent *theAppleEvent,
                             AEKeyword theAEKeyword,
                             DescType desiredType,
                             AEDesc *result );
```

The meanings of each of the parameters are as follows:

theAppleEvent—A pointer to the AppleEvent record that was passed to the Apple event handler.

theAEKeyword—The keyword of the parameter you're interested in learning about. The names of the keywords for the parameters of Apple events are documented in the *Apple Event Registry*. Of course, if the event is a custom event that you have defined, you will already be familiar with the keywords its parameters use.

desiredType—Indicates the descriptor type to which the data referred to in the descriptor record is to be coerced. (You could specify, for example, typeFSS to coerce an alias type to a file system specification type, saving you the trouble of doing this explicitly.) Specify a value of typeWildCard if you don't want to coerce the type. Table 4-2 describes many of the built-in type coercions that the Apple Event Manager can perform. For information on how to write and install your own coercion handlers, see *Inside Macintosh*, Volume VI.

result—A pointer to a space where the AEDesc record is returned. Your application must reserve a space of sizeof(AEDesc) bytes before calling **AEGetParamDesc**. This descriptor must be disposed of with **AEDisposeDesc** when you're through with it.

Table 4-2. Type coercions supported by the Apple Event Manager (partial list)

Native Descriptor Type	Coerced Descriptor Type	Notes
typeChar	typeInteger typeLongInteger typeSMInt typeSMFloat typeShortInteger typeLongFloat typeShortFloat typeExtended typeComp typeMagnitude	Any string describing a number can be coerced to a numeric type.
typeInteger typeLongInteger typeSMInt typeSMFloat typeShortInteger typeLongFloat typeShortFloat typeExtended	typeChar	Any numeric type can be coerced to a text string representation.

Table 4-2. Type coercions supported by the Apple Event Manager (partial list) (continued)

Native Descriptor Type	Coerced Descriptor Type	Notes
typeComp		
typeMagnitude		
typeInteger	typeInteger	Any numeric type can
typeLongInteger	typeLongInteger	be coerced to any other
typeSMInt	typeSMInt	numeric type.
typeSMFloat	typeSMFloat	
typeShortInteger	typeShortInteger	
typeLongFloat	typeLongFloat	
typeShortFloat	typeShortFloat	
typeExtended	typeExtended	
typeComp	typeComp	
typeMagnitude	typeMagnitude	
typeAlias	typeFSS	An alias record can be coerced to a file system specification record.

Here is the function prototype for **AEGetParamPtr**:

```
pascal OSErr AEGetParamPtr( const AppleEvent *theAppleEvent,
                    AEKeyword theAEKeyword,
                    DescType desiredType,
                    DescType *typeCode,
                    Ptr dataPtr,
                    Size maximumSize,
                    Size *actualSize );
```

The first three parameters have the same meanings as the corresponding parameters of **AEGetParamDesc**. Here are the meanings of the remaining four parameters:

typeCode—The variable in which **AEGetParamPtr** returns the actual descriptor type of the specified parameter.

dataPtr—A pointer to a buffer in which the data referred to in the keyword-specified descriptor record for the parameter is returned. Your application must reserve space for this buffer before making the call to **AEGetParamPtr**.

`maximumSize`—The size of the buffer pointed to by `dataPtr`.

`actualSize`—The variable in which `AEGetParamPtr` returns the actual size of the data referred to in the keyword-specified descriptor record. If this value is greater than `maximumSize`, not all the data will have been retrieved, so you should call `AEGetParamPtr` again after allocating a buffer of `actualSize` bytes.

There is a pair of similar routines for extracting information about attributes from an `AppleEvent` record: `AEGetAttributePtr` and `AEGetAttributeDesc`. You won't use these routines very often since applications will rarely need to deal with attributes directly. The exception is the `keyMissedKeywordAttr` attribute discussed later in this chapter.

Note ▶

`AEGetParamDesc` and `AEGetAttributeDesc` both return an `AEDesc` record, which refers to a *copy* of the data referred to by the `dataHandle` field in the master descriptor the Apple Event Manager maintains. Your application must dispose of this record with the `AEDisposeDesc` routine when it has finished with it—this frees up the memory space occupied by the copy of the data. The function prototype for `AEDisposeDesc` is as follows:

```
pascal OSErr AEDisposeDesc( AEDesc *theAEDesc );
```

If you forget to dispose of descriptors you create, you will soon clog up the heap with used, but forgotten, memory blocks.

▶ Handling Lists of Descriptor Records

It is not uncommon for a parameter to an Apple event to consist of a list of descriptor records. The Finder's `kAEOpenDocuments` (`'odoc'`) and `kAEPrintDocuments` (`'pdoc'`) events, for example, each include a list of alias records describing a group of files to be opened or printed.

The Apple Event Manager includes three routines you can use to deal with lists of descriptors: `AECountItems`, `AEGetNthPtr`, and `AEGetNthDesc`.

Use **AECountItems** to return the number of items in a descriptor list. Here is its function prototype:

```
pascal OSErr AECountItems( const AEDescList *theAEDescList,
                              long *theCount );
```

The first parameter is a pointer to an AEDescList record. If the descriptor returned by **AEGetParamDesc** describes a list of descriptors, pass its address—coerced to an AEDescList—to **AECountItems**. The number of elements in the list is returned in the theCount variable.

To retrieve the data for a given descriptor record in a list, use **AEGetNthDesc** and **AEGetNthPtr**. Here are the function prototypes:

```
pascal OSErr AEGetNthDesc( const AEDescList *theAEDescList,
                      long index,
                      DescType desiredType,
                      AEKeyword *theAEKeyword,
                      AEDesc *result );

pascal OSErr AEGetNthPtr( const AEDescList *theAEDescList,
                      long index,
                      DescType desiredType,
                      AEKeyword *theAEKeyword,
                      DescType *typeCode,
                      Ptr dataPtr,
                      Size maximumSize,
                      Size *actualSize );
```

As is apparent, these routines are quite similar to **AEGetParamDesc** and **AEGetParamPtr**. Remember that the AEDescList type is equivalent to AEDesc. The only substantive difference is that they both take an index parameter indicating which element of the list is to be dealt with (the first element has an index of 1). Remember to use **AEDisposeDesc** to dispose of the descriptor returned by **AEGetParamDesc** once you've finished using it.

▶ Determining the Size of Parameters and Attributes

Sometimes you need to determine the size of an Apple event parameter that you've extracted or are about to extract. For example, if you're going to extract a parameter with **AEGetParamPtr**, it is helpful to know the size of the parameter in advance so that you can pass a buffer that is large enough to hold the result.

Three size-related routines are available to you: **AESizeOfParam**, **AESizeOfNthItem**, and **AESizeOfAttribute**. Here are their function prototypes:

```
pascal OSErr AESizeOfParam( const AppleEvent *theAppleEvent,
                            AEKeyword theAEKeyword,
                            DescType *typeCode,
                            Size *dataSize );

pascal OSErr AESizeOfAttribute( const AppleEvent *theAppleEvent,
                                AEKeyword theAEKeyword,
                                DescType *typeCode,
                                Size *dataSize );

pascal OSErr AESizeOfNthItem( const AEDescList *theAEDescList,
                              long index,
                              DescType *typeCode,
                              Size *dataSize );
```

Notice that you pass the same two input parameters to **AESizeOfParam** and **AESizeOfAttribute**: a pointer to the AppleEvent record (theAppleEvent) and the keyword for the Apple event parameter or attribute you're interested in (theAEKeyword). These routines return the descriptor type and the size of the descriptor data in the typeCode and dataSize variables.

AESizeOfNthItem returns the descriptor type and size of a list item. The two input parameters you pass to it are a pointer to the list descriptor (theAEDescList) and a list index (index).

▶ Checking for Completeness

It is good coding practice to verify that you have retrieved all required parameters for an Apple event *after you think you have done so*. Do this by using **AEGetAttributePtr** to retrieve information on the descriptor record for the attribute whose keyword is keyMissedKeywordAttr.

The data for the keyMissedKeywordAttr attribute is the descriptor type of a required parameter that has not yet been retrieved with **AEGetParamDesc** or **AEGetParamPtr**. The attribute is not present if all required parameters have already been retrieved; thus, if **AEGetAttributePtr** returns errAEDescNotFound you know that all is well. If it returns noErr, you forgot to retrieve an important parameter and you should exit the Apple event handler with an appropriate error code as the result.

Listing 4-7 shows a routine your Apple event handler can call to verify that it has retrieved all required parameters.

Listing 4-7. Call the RequiredCheck routine to determine if your Apple event handler has retrieved all required parameters. It has if RequiredCheck returns noErr.

```
OSErr RequiredCheck( AppleEvent *theAppleEvent )
{
     OSErr           myErr;
     DescType        typeCode;
     Size            actualSize;

     myErr = AEGetAttributePtr( theAppleEvent, keyMissedKeywordAttr,
                          typeWildCard, &typeCode, 0L, 0, &actualSize );

     if ( myErr == errAEDescNotFound ) return( noErr );
     if ( myErr == noErr ) return( errAEEventNotHandled );
     return( myErr );
}
```

▶ User Interaction Decisions

Once an application has extracted all the parameters from an Apple event, it may or may not have all the data it needs to perform the requested operation. Depending on the operation, more data may be needed from the user of the application that is processing the incoming Apple event—perhaps by displaying a data entry dialog box.

It is not proper to always interrupt the user to request this extra data. The correct approach is to call the **AEInteractWithUser** routine just before you would otherwise interact with the user. **AEInteractWithUser** checks two interaction preferences—one specified by the application using the **AESetInteractionAllowed** routine and one specified by the sender of the Apple event (see the description of **AESend** in the next section)—and returns one of three results:

- **noErr**—Interaction is permitted and the user has brought the application to the front (or the application was already at the front). **AEInteractWithUser** uses the services of the Notification Manager to prompt the user to bring the application to the front.

- **errAETimeout**—Interaction would have been permitted but the user didn't bring the application to the front within the specified period.

- **errAENoUserInteraction**—Interaction is not allowed.

If the result is not noErr, your application should try to complete the operation with a default set of data; if that's not appropriate, the Apple event handler should return an appropriate error code.

Here is the function prototype for **AEInteractWithUser**:

```
pascal OSErr AEInteractWithUser( long timeOutInTicks,
                                 NMRecPtr nmReqPtr,
                                 IdleProcPtr idleProc );
```

Here are the meanings of the parameters to **AEInteractWithUser**:

timeOutInTicks—The length of time, in ticks, that the application will wait for the user to bring the application to the foreground. If the application isn't brought to the foreground within this time period, **AEInteractWithUser** returns an errAETimeout error code. Two common values for this parameter are kAEDefaultTimeout (a default value of about one minute) and kNoTimeout (no time-out).

nmReqPtr—If **AEInteractionAllowed** determines that interaction is permitted, but the application is not in the foreground, it uses the Notification Manager to alert the user to bring the application to the foreground. This parameter is a pointer to a notification request record that **AEInteractWithUser** passes to **NMInstall** to issue the notification (see Chapter 3). If you specify a value of 0L, a default notification request record is used.

Note ▶	If the sending application sets the kAECanSwitchLayer flag in the sendMode parameter of the **AESend** routine (described in the next section), and the receiving application is running in the background, the receiving application comes to the foreground immediately. Notification Manager techniques are not used to prompt the user to bring the application to the foreground.

idleProc—A pointer to an idle procedure that deals with events—update, activate, and operating-system (suspend, resume, and mouse-moved)— that might occur while the **AEInteractWithUser** routine is waiting for the user to bring the application to the foreground. You will learn how to write an idle procedure in the next subsection.

The application's interaction preference that **AEInteractWithUser** inspects is set using the **AESetInteractionAllowed** routine:

```
pascal OSErr AESetInteractionAllowed( AEInteractAllowed level );
```

The three choices for the `level` parameter are:

- **kAEInteractWithSelf**—Allow interaction only if the source of the Apple event is the application itself.
- **kAEInteractWithLocal**—Allow interaction only if the source of the Apple event is an application running on the same Macintosh.
- **kAEInteractWithAll**—Always allow interaction.

As you will see in the next section, the sender of the Apple event indicates its interaction preference in the `sendMode` parameter of the **AESend** routine. If the preference is set to `kAENeverInteract`, no interaction will be allowed, regardless of the application's interaction preference setting.

▶ Writing an Idle Procedure

The function prototype for the idle procedure whose address you pass to **AEInteractWithUser** is as follows:

```
pascal Boolean myIdleProc( EventRecord *theEvent,
                           long *sleepTime,
                           RgnHandle *mouseRgn );
```

Here are the meanings of the three parameters:

theEvent—A pointer to the event record describing the event. The events that are passed to the idle procedure are `updateEvt`, `activateEvt`, `osEvt`, and `nullEvent`. In most cases, you will handle the first three types of events exactly as you do when you retrieve them in your main event loop. Handle a `nullEvent` by setting the value of `sleepTime` and `mouseRgn` and performing any periodic tasks required.

sleepTime—When the idle procedure receives its first `nullEvent`, it must return in this variable a tick count indicating how long it will wait for the next `nullEvent`. By specifying a value of no less than 15 ticks or so, the application can share processor time with all other running applications. The `sleepTime` parameter has the same meaning as it does for **WaitNextEvent** (see Chapter 3).

mouseRgn—When the idle procedure receives its first `nullEvent`, it must return a region handle in this variable. As described in Chapter 3 in the section on the parameters to the **WaitNextEvent** routine, a mouse-moved event (reported via a `osEvt`) is posted when the mouse moves outside this region. You can set this parameter to `0L` if you don't need to perform cursor management.

An idle procedure for **AEInteractWithUser** normally returns false to indicate that **AEInteractWithUser** should continue to wait for the user to bring the application to the front. It is difficult to think of a situation where true would be returned to force an immediate cancellation. As you will see in the next section, however, you will also use an idle procedure with the **AESend** routine (the routine you use to send an Apple event) when you specify that you want to wait for a reply from the receiver of the event. In this situation, you would want to allow the user to cancel the operation by typing Command-period, so you would check for that event in the idle procedure and return true if you found it.

Listing 4-8 shows a simple idle procedure that is suitable for use with **AEInteractWithUser**.

Listing 4-8. An idle procedure you can use with AEInteractWithUser

```
pascal Boolean myIdleProc( EventRecord *theEvent, long *sleepTime, RgnHandle
                                                        *mouseRgn )
{
    switch ( theEvent->what ) {

        case activateEvt:
        case updateEvt:
        case osEvt:
            DoEvent( theEvent );  /* use Skeleton's main event loop handler */
            break;

        case nullEvent:
            *mouseRgn = 0L;    /* no cursor management */
            *sleepTime = GetDblTime();
            /* insert here: any periodic tasks */
            break;

    }
    return( false );
}
```

▶ Error Handling

If an error occurs while processing an incoming Apple event, just exit the event handler with the error code as the result. (If no error occurred, exit with a noErr result.) The Apple Event Manager automatically sends a reply Apple event at the request of the sender of the original Apple event. The reply contains the error number as a parameter with a keyword of keyErrorString. A pointer to the AppleEvent record for this reply event is passed to the Apple event handler.

Optionally, you can also return an error *string* to the caller via the reply Apple event. To do this, add a parameter whose keyword is keyErrorString to the reply AppleEvent record. The data referred to by the parameter's AEDesc record has a descriptor type of typeChar and is a block of text with no length byte or trailing zero byte. In the next section you will see how to use **AEPutParamPtr** or **AEPutParamDesc** to add a keyword-specified descriptor record (which defines a parameter) to an AppleEvent record.

▶ Handling Required Apple Events

Table 4-1 summarized the required set of Apple events that every 7.0-specific application must support. You install handlers for any Apple event with the **AEInstallEventHandler** routine. These required events are sent by the Finder to an application that is running on the system, and each has an event class of kCoreEventClass ('aevt').

Here are more detailed descriptions of how you should react to these events:

kAEOpenApplication ('oapp')—The Finder sends this Apple event to the application when an application first starts up. The application should react by performing a "New" operation. For a text editor, for example, this would mean bringing up a new, untitled window. This event has no parameters.

kAEQuitApplication ('quit')—The Finder sends this Apple event to the application when it wants the application to quit (presumably because some sort of system error occurred). This event has no parameters.

kAEOpenDocuments ('odoc')—The Finder sends this event to an application when you open a document (or group of documents) from the Finder. This application has one parameter—a direct object (keyword: keyDirectObject) whose descriptor refers to a list of alias records (descriptor type: typeAEList). Your application should react by opening each document referred to in the list.

kAEPrintDocuments ('pdoc')—The Finder sends this event to an application when you print a document (or group of documents) from the Finder. This application has one parameter—a direct object (keyword: keyDirectObject) whose descriptor refers to a list of alias records (descriptor type: typeAEList). Your application should react by printing each document referred to in the list.

Look at the source code for the Skeleton application in Chapter 1 for examples of how to write the kAEOpenApplication and kAEQuitApplication handlers.

The handlers for kAEOpenDocuments and kAEPrintDocuments are similar. The only difference is that one will call your open routine for each document and the other will call your print routine.

Listing 4-9 shows a typical handler for kAEOpenDocuments. It begins by calling **AEGetParamDesc** to obtain the descriptor for the list of aliases (descriptor type: typeAEList) associated with the direct object parameter (keyword: keyDirectObject). It then calls RequiredCheck (Listing 4-7) to verify that this was the only required parameter. Finally, it processes each alias in the list by calling **AEGetNthPtr** to coerce the alias to a file system specification record (descriptor type: typeFSS) that can be passed to a routine that opens the file.

Listing 4-9. An event handler for the Finder's kAEOpenDocuments ('odoc') event

```
pascal OSErr HandleODOC( AppleEvent *theAppleEvent,
                                  AppleEvent *reply, long myRefCon )
{
    OSErr        myErr;
    AEDescList   docList;
    FSSpec       myFSS;
    long         itemsInList;
    AEKeyword    theKeyword;
    DescType     typeCode;
    Size         actualSize;
    long         i;
    Handle       winDataHndl;
    FInfo        theFInfo;
    Boolean      isStationery;

    myErr = AEGetParamDesc( theAppleEvent, keyDirectObject,
                                        typeAEList, &docList );
    if ( myErr ) return( myErr );

    myErr = RequiredCheck( theAppleEvent );
    if ( myErr ) return( myErr );

    myErr = AECountItems( &docList, &itemsInList );
    if ( myErr ) return( myErr );

    for (i = 1; i <= itemsInList; i++ ) {

      myErr = AEGetNthPtr( &docList, i, typeFSS, &theKeyword, &typeCode,
                                  (Ptr)&myFSS, sizeof( FSSpec ),
                                  &actualSize );
          if ( myErr ) return( myErr );

          FSpGetFInfo( &myFSS, &theFInfo ); /* check for stationery */
          isStationery = ( (theFInfo.fdFlags & 0x0800) != 0 );
          CreateFileWindow( &myFSS, isStationery ); /* Skeleton "Open" routine */
    }
    return( noErr );

}
```

▶ Sending Apple Events

Sending an Apple event is as easy as receiving one. There are five basic steps to follow:

- Determine the target address using one of the routines described at the beginning of this chapter (**PPCBrowser** or **GetNextProcess** and **GetProcessInformation**), then put the address into an address descriptor using **AECreateDesc**.
- Create the Apple event record by passing the address descriptor to **AECreateAppleEvent**.
- Add each parameter using **AEPutParamPtr** or **AEPutParamDesc**.
- Send the Apple event using **AESend**.
- Check for errors.

Let's review these steps one by one.

First, use **PPCBrowser** to allow the user to select the program that is to receive the Apple event. **PPCBrowser** returns a LocationNameRec and a PortInfoRec you can use to complete a TargetID record that we can use to create an address descriptor. Here's a sample code fragment:

```
TargetID            myTarget;
PortInfoRec         myPortInfo;
OSErr               myError;

myError = PPCBrowser( 0L, 0L, false, &(myTarget.location),
                      &myPortInfo, 0L, 0L );
if ( myError ) return;

BlockMove( &myPortInfo.name, &myTarget.name, sizeof( PPCPortRec ) );
```

Now that you've got a TargetID, you need to create a descriptor for it so that you can pass it to **AECreateAppleEvent**. Use the **AECreateDesc** routine to do this; here is the function prototype:

```
pascal OSErr AECreateDesc( DescType typeCode,
                           Ptr dataPtr,
                           Size dataSize,
                           AEDesc *result );
```

Since you're dealing with a TargetID, you will pass typeTargetID to **AECreateDesc** as the descriptor type. If you were using one of the other possible addressing techniques, you would use typeSessionID, typeApplSignature, or typeProcessSerialNumber. dataPtr is a pointer to the descriptor's data and dataSize is the size of the data. **AECreateDesc** returns the descriptor it creates in the space pointed to by result. This AEDesc must be disposed of with **AEDisposeDesc** when you're through using it.

Here is another code fragment (following from the earlier code fragment) showing how to make the call to **AECreateDesc** in your program:

```
AEAddressDesc        theAddressDesc;

myError = AECreateDesc( typeTargetID, &myTarget,
                        sizeof( TargetID ), &theAddressDesc );
```

Once you've created the address descriptor, you can create an empty Apple event record using the **AECreateAppleEvent** routine. The word *empty* actually refers to the parameters only. When **AECreateAppleEvent** creates a new record, it inserts all the attributes needed to describe an Apple event, notably the target address, the event class, and the event ID. Here is the function prototype for **AECreateAppleEvent**:

```
pascal OSErr AECreateAppleEvent( AEEventClass theAEEventClass,
                                 AEEventID theAEEventID,
                                 const AEAddressDesc *target,
                                 short returnID,
                                 long transactionID,
                                 AppleEvent *result );
```

Here are the meanings of the parameters passed to **AECreateAppleEvent**:

theAEEventClass—The event class for the Apple event you are sending.

theAEEventID—The event ID for the Apple event you are sending.

target—A pointer to the address descriptor describing the target application.

returnID—If you request a return receipt when sending an Apple event (with **AESend**), the return receipt Apple event will include a keyReturnIDAttr attribute containing the value of returnID you pass to **AECreateAppleEvent**. Thus, by specifying a unique returnID for each Apple event you create, you will always be able to determine what receipt corresponds to each Apple event. Alternatively, you can set returnID to kAutoGenerateReturnID to tell the Apple Event Manager to automatically generate a unique returnID for you. (Retrieve the value generated by calling the **AEGetAttributePtr** routine; the keyword for the attribute is keyReturnIDAttr.)

transactionID—When communicating with another application via the Apple event mechanism, you may want to exchange a series of events to complete a given operation. In this situation, you should use the same transactionID for each event in the series so that both participants can keep track of the transaction more easily. If the Apple event is not part of a transaction, specify the constant kAnyTransactionID.

result—Points to a space you've reserved for an AppleEvent record. **AECreateAppleEvent** returns the correctly-formatted AppleEvent record in this space. This AppleEvent record must be disposed of with **AEDisposeDesc** when you're through using it.

▶ Adding Parameters to an AppleEvent Record

The final step before actually sending the Apple event is to add any required parameters to the AppleEvent record. Most Apple events that require parameters require only one—the direct object (keyDirectObject). Consult the description of the Apple event in the *Apple Event Registry* for information on required parameters for any given Apple event.

The two routines for adding parameters are **AEPutParamPtr** and **AEPutParamDesc**. Use **AEPutParamPtr** in situations where you have the raw data for a parameter, but not the descriptor itself. Here is its function prototype:

```
pascal OSErr AEPutParamPtr( const AppleEvent *theAppleEvent,
                    AEKeyword theAEKeyword,
                    DescType typeCode,
                    Ptr dataPtr,
                    Size dataSize );
```

The first three parameters reflect the Apple event to which you are adding the parameter, the keyword for the parameter, and the descriptor type for the parameter's data. dataPtr points to the data itself and dataSize is the size of the data. For example, to add a direct object parameter to the AppleEvent record, you would make a call like this:

```
myError = AEPutParamPtr( &theAppleEvent, keyDirectObject,
                typeChar, myTextBlockPtr, sizeOfTextBlock );
```

This example adds a block of text (descriptor type: typeChar) that is sizeOfTextBlock bytes long.

If you already have your data formatted as a descriptor, use **AEPutParamDesc** instead. Here is its prototype:

```
pascal OSErr AEPutParamDesc( const AppleEvent *theAppleEvent,
                             AEKeyword theAEKeyword,
                             const AEDesc *theAEDesc );
```

The first two parameters have the same meaning as they do for **AEPutParamPtr**. The third parameter, theAEDesc, is a pointer to the descriptor record to be associated with the Apple event parameter.

▶ Descriptor Lists

A descriptor list is a descriptor record with a descriptor type of typeAEList. The data it refers to is a list of descriptor records, such as alias records (descriptor type: typeAlias) describing a group of files for a command to act on.

To create a descriptor list, use the **AECreateList** routine. Its function prototype is as follows:

```
pascal OSErr AECreateList( Ptr factoringPtr,
                           Size factoredSize,
                           Boolean isRecord,
                           AEDescList *resultList );
```

You will usually set the first two parameters to zero. However, if the data referred to by each element in the list will begin with the same sequence of data, pass a pointer to this common data in factoringPtr and the size of the data in factoredSize; this allows the Apple Event Manager to pack data more efficiently.

If you're creating a standard descriptor list, set the isRecord parameter to false. Set it to true to create an AppleEvent record (a list of keyword-specified descriptor records)—you won't do this very often since you usually create AppleEvent records using the **AECreateAppleEvent** routine.

The last parameter, resultList, points to a space where **AECreateList** returns a descriptor for the list it creates.

To add descriptors to the list, use the **AEPutDesc** routine. Its function prototype is as follows:

```
pascal OSErr AEPutDesc( const AEDescList *theAEDescList,
                        long index,
                        const AEDesc *theAEDesc );
```

The first parameter, theAEDescList, is the address of the descriptor list (returned by **AECreateList**) to which you are adding the descriptor given by theAEDesc. The index parameter indicates the position at which the descriptor is to be inserted in the list (the position count begins at 1); specify a value of 0 to add to the end of the list. If there is already a descriptor at the specified index position, it is replaced.

Since a descriptor list is simply an instance of a descriptor record, you can associate it with a parameter and add it to an AppleEvent record using the **AEPutParamDesc** routine. When doing so, don't forget to coerce the AEDescList parameter returned by **AECreateList** to the AEDesc type.

▶ Sending the Apple Event

The final step is to actually send the Apple event with the **AESend** routine. The function prototype for **AESend** is as follows:

```
pascal OSErr AESend( const AppleEvent *theAppleEvent,
                AppleEvent *reply,
                AESendMode sendMode,
                AESendPriority sendPriority,
                long timeOutInTicks,
                IdleProcPtr idleProc,
                EventFilterProcPtr filterProc );
```

Here are the meanings of each parameter passed to **AESend**:

theAppleEvent—A pointer to the AppleEvent record defining the Apple event you want to send. Dispose of this AppleEvent record with **AEDisposeDesc** when you're through using it (you should do this even if **AESend** returns an error.)

reply—A pointer to a space of size sizeof(AppleEvent) you've reserved for a reply AppleEvent record. If the sendMode parameter indicates you will wait for a reply to the Apple event you send, it will be returned here. Dispose of this AppleEvent record with **AEDisposeDesc** when you're through using it (you should do this even if **AESend** returns an error.) If **AESend** returns with a errAETimeout error—meaning a reply did not come back in time—the reply could still arrive later on. If you try to retrieve a parameter from the reply and the reply has still not arrived, you will get a errAEReplyNotArrived error.

sendMode—Contains flags you can use to set the reply mode, the interaction preference, and other miscellaneous behavior. To determine the value for sendMode, add together the values of the desired flags.

There are three reply modes to choose from, only one of which can be selected at a time. They are as follows:

- **kAENoReply**—The application does not want a reply (**AESend** returns as soon as it has sent the Apple event).

- **kAEQueueReply**—The application wants a reply, but it is to be put in the event queue when it arrives (**AESend** returns before the reply arrives).

- **kAEWaitReply**—The application wants a reply returned in the `reply` parameter (**AESend** does not return until the reply arrives).

If the reply mode is `kAEWaitReply`, the `timeOutInTicks`, `idleProc`, and `filterProc` parameters are relevant and should be given appropriate values.

There are three interaction preferences to choose from, only one of which can be selected at a time. They are as follows:

- **kAENeverInteract**—The receiving application should never interact with the user. This is the default if the Apple event is being sent to a remote application since there may be no user present at the remote system. As you saw in the previous section, **AEInteractWithUser** (called by the receiving application) will not bring the receiving application to the front if the sender specifies the `kAENeverInteract` interaction preference.

- **kAECanInteract**—The receiving application can interact with the user if it needs additional data to perform the requested operation. This is the default if the Apple event is being sent to a local application. The receiving application will be brought to the foreground (via **AEInteractWithUser**) only if the receiving application's interaction preference, set with **AESetInteractionAllowed**, permits it.

- **kAEAlwaysInteract**—The receiving application should always interact with the user, even if no additional data is needed from the user. The receiving application will be brought to the foreground (via **AEInteractWithUser**) only if the receiving application's interaction preference, set with **AESetInteractionAllowed**, permits it.

Each of the following three miscellaneous flags may also be selected:

- **kAECanSwitchLayer**—The receiving application, if it's running in the background, should immediately bring itself to the foreground when **AEInteractWithUser** is called. You would normally set this flag only in situations where the sender and receiver are running on the same Macintosh and you want complete control to pass to the receiving application.

- **kAEDontReconnect**—The Apple Event Manager should try to reconnect if the connection to the receiving application closes. If you don't set this flag, no reconnection is attempted.
- **kAEWantReceipt**—**AESend** should wait for the receiving application to send a return receipt before returning.

sendPriority—Can be set to either `kAENormalPriority` or `kAEHighPriority`. If the priority is `kAENormalPriority`, the usual case, the Apple event is placed at the end of the event queue of the receiving application. If the priority is `kAEHighPriority`, the Apple event is inserted in the queue ahead of all other Apple events. Use this priority only when it's important that the receiving application retrieve the Apple event as quickly as possible. This would be appropriate if the Apple event you're sending is for cancelling an Apple event transaction.

timeOutInTicks—The length of time, in ticks, that **AESend** should wait for a reply. If no reply is forthcoming within this time period, **AESend** returns an `errAETimeout` error code. Two common values for this parameter are `kAEDefaultTimeout` (a default time-out of about one minute) and `kNoTimeout` (no time-out).

idleProc—A pointer to an idle procedure that deals with events—update, activate, and operating-system (suspend, resume, and mouse-moved)—that might occur while the **AESend** routine is waiting for the reply to the Apple event or a return receipt. You saw how to write an idle procedure in the previous section on the **AEInteractWithUser** routine. A typical idle procedure for **AESend** looks like the one you would use for **AEInteractWithUser** except that it should also include code to check whether a Command-period keyboard event is in the event queue—particularly if no time-out period is specified. If Command-period is pressed, the idleProc can return true and **AESend** will terminate with an `errAEWaitCanceled` error. Here is a code fragment you can put at the beginning of an idle procedure to implement this behavior:

```
EventRecord    testEvent;
Boolean             gotKbd;
char           key;

gotKbd = GetOSEvent( keyDownMask, &testEvent );  /* get next kbd event */

if ( gotKbd ) {

    key = testEvent.message & charCodeMask;
    if ( ( key == '.' ) && ( testEvent.modifiers & cmdKey ) )
            return( true );

}
```

Important ▶

An application's idle procedure can take control to check for a Command-period cancelation request only if other applications running on the Macintosh periodically relinquish control of the processor using the techniques described in Chapter 3 by periodically calling **WaitNextEvent**. If the application that receives the Apple event is running on the same Macintosh and doesn't periodically relinquish control while it's processing the Apple event, the user of the calling application won't be able to cancel the operation. The moral is to ensure that the Apple event handlers you write follow the cooperative multitasking guidelines you learned about in Chapter 3.

filterProc—A pointer to a filter procedure you can provide to handle Apple event activity that occurs while you're waiting for a reply. By providing a filter procedure, you can design your application to respond to Apple events while it is waiting for a response. For information on how to write a filter procedure, see *Inside Macintosh*, Volume VI.

▶ Checking for Errors

AESend returns an error code of noErr if the Apple Event Manager was able to send the Apple event successfully. Common error conditions that can occur are errAEEventNotHandled (the receiver did not not have an Apple event handler installed to handle the event), errAETimeout (no reply was received within the time-out period), and errAEWaitCanceled (the idle procedure returned true, presumably because the user canceled the wait for a reply or a receipt by typing Command-period).

Note ▶

The error code that **AESend** returns does *not* reflect the error code returned by the Apple event handler that the target application invoked to process the incoming Apple event. That error code is returned as a typeLongInteger in the keyErrorNumber parameter of the reply AppleEvent record. As you saw in the previous section, the target application's Apple event handler can also optionally return an error string as a typeChar in the keyErrorString parameter of the reply.

Use **AEGetParamPtr** to retrieve the keyErrorNumber parameter from the reply Apple event to determine if the event was handled without error. If **AEGetParamPtr** returns an errAEDescNotFound error, no error number descriptor was in the reply, so, by convention, there was no error. If the descriptor does exist, its data (a long) reflects the error code.

Here is a code fragment you can use to provide complete error checking once you've successfully sent an Apple event to a target application:

```
AppleEvent          theReply;
DescType            actualType;
long                actualSize;
long                eventError;

myError = AEGetParamPtr( &theReply, keyErrorNumber,
                         typeLongInteger, &actualType,
                         &eventError, sizeof( eventError ),
                         &actualSize );

if ( myError != errAEDescNotFound ) {

    if ( eventError != noErr ) { SysBeep(1); return; }

}

/* all OK if you reach here */
```

▶ Example: Sending an Apple Event to ToolServer

The DoDeRez routine in Listing 4-10 is a complete example of how to send an Apple event to another application. In this case, the other application is Apple's ToolServer program, a Macintosh Programmer's Workshop tool-execution environment. The Apple event you're sending tells ToolServer to execute the MPW DeRez tool so that you can obtain a Rez source description of a particular resource. The description, returned in **AESend**'s reply AppleEvent record, is placed on the clipboard by the DoDeRez routine. Refer to Appendix A for an introduction to the Rez and DeRez tools.

The characteristics of the Apple event used in this example are as follows:

- **event class**—kToolServerEventClass ('misc')
- **event ID**—kTSReplyOutput ('dosc')
- **parameter**—keyDirectObject
- **descriptor type**—typeChar (a block of text)

This event, described in the ToolServer documentation, tells ToolServer to execute the tool command stored in the text block referred to by the descriptor. The output of the command, a block of text, is returned in **AESend**'s reply Apple event as the data for the direct object parameter.

The DeRez command string you attach to the direct parameter is of the form:

```
DeRez 'filename' -only ''∂''resType'∂''(resID)' 'typesFile' > dev:console
```

The values for filename (the pathname of the file containing the resource), resType (the resource type), resID (the resource ID), and typesFile (the name of the file containing the Rez resource template) are passed as parameters to the DoDeRez routine.

The DoDeRez routine uses the techniques described to obtain the target address, create a descriptor for it, create the AppleEvent record, and put the direct parameter into the AppleEvent record. The routine then calls **AESend** with sendMode set to kAEWaitReply and timeOutInTicks set to kNoTimeout. This means it will wait indefinitely for ToolServer to complete the operation and send a reply. (It uses an idle procedure that cancels the operation if the user types Command-period; if it didn't, the application would freeze if the receiver didn't send a reply.)

The result of the operation (a block of text) is returned as the data for the direct parameter of the reply record. The DoDeRez routine obtains a handle to the data by calling **AEGetParamDesc** to get the AEDesc for the direct parameter, then retrieving the dataHandle field of the AEDesc record; the routine uses **AESizeOfParam** to determine the size of the data. With the handle and size in hand, it copies the data to the clipboard using the **PutScrap** routine.

Notice how careful DoDeRez is to dispose of descriptor records before returning. Don't forget to be just as careful in your own routines that use the Apple Event Manager to create descriptor records, including AppleEvent records.

Listing 4-10 Sending an Apple event to the ToolServer application

```
#define      ToolServerCreator    'MPSX' /* ToolServer signature */
#define      kToolServerEventClass 'misc' /* event class */
#define      kTSReplyOutput        'dosc' /* event ID - put result in reply */

/* Call the DoDeRez routine to return (on the clipboard) the Rez source
      code for the resource given by theResType, theResID, and filePath.
      The typesName parameter is the name of the Rez template file.
      Both filepath and typesName are C strings.
*/
void DoDeRez( char filePath[], char typesName[], ResType theResType,
                        long theResID )
{
      Str255                typeString, IDString;
```

Listing 4-10 Sending an Apple event to the ToolServer application (continued)

```
char                    myTSCommand[512];

Str255                  myPrompt = "\pChoose a ToolServer to link to:";
Str255                  myListTitle = "\pToolServer hosts:";
TargetID                myTarget;
PortInfoRec             myPortInfo;
OSErr                   myError, sendError;

AEAddressDesc           theAddressDesc;
AppleEvent              theAppleEvent, theReply;
AEDesc                  theResultDescriptor;
DescType                theDescriptorType, actualType;
long                    theResultSize, actualSize;
long                    eventError;

Str255                  numberString, MPWErrorString;

TypeToCString( theResType, typeString ); /* convert res type to string */
NumToCString( theResID, IDString );      /* convert res ID to string */

myTSCommand[0] = 0;
strcat( myTSCommand, "DeRez '" );
strcat( myTSCommand, (char *)filePath );
strcat( myTSCommand, "' -only ''∂''" );
strcat( myTSCommand, (char *)typeString );
strcat( myTSCommand, "'∂''(" );
strcat( myTSCommand, (char *)IDString );
strcat( myTSCommand, ")' '" );
strcat( myTSCommand, (char *)typesName );
strcat( myTSCommand, "' > dev:console" );

myError = PPCBrowser( myPrompt, myListTitle, false, &(myTarget.location),
                      &myPortInfo,
                      (PPCFilterProcPtr)ToolServerFilter, 0L);

if ( myError ) return;

BlockMove( &myPortInfo.name, &myTarget.name, sizeof( PPCPortRec ) );

myError = AECreateDesc( typeTargetID, &myTarget, sizeof( TargetID ),
                        &theAddressDesc );

myError = AECreateAppleEvent( kToolServerEventClass, kTSReplyOutput,
                              &theAddressDesc, kAutoGenerateReturnID,
                              kAnyTransactionID, &theAppleEvent );

myError = AEDisposeDesc( &theAddressDesc ); /* we don't need it anymore */

myError = AEPutParamPtr( &theAppleEvent, keyDirectObject, typeChar,
                         myTSCommand, strlen( myTSCommand ) );

sendError = AESend( &theAppleEvent, &theReply, kAEWaitReply,
```

Listing 4-10 Sending an Apple event to the ToolServer application
(continued)

```
                                kAENormalPriority, kNoTimeOut, myIdleProc, 0L );

myError = AEDisposeDesc( &theAppleEvent ); /* we don't need it anymore */

if ( sendError ) {

        myError = AEDisposeDesc( &theReply );
        SysBeep( 1 );
        return;

}

myError = AEGetParamPtr( &theReply, keyErrorNumber, typeLongInteger,
                            &actualType, &eventError,
                            sizeof( eventError ),
                            &actualSize );

if ( myError != errAEDescNotFound ) {

        if ( myError ) {

                        myError = AEDisposeDesc( &theReply );
                        SysBeep( 1 );
                        return;

        } else {

                if ( eventError != noErr ) {

                        myError = AEDisposeDesc( &theReply );
                        SysBeep( 1 );
                        return;

                }
        }

}

myError = AEGetParamDesc( &theReply, keyDirectObject, typeChar,
                            &theResultDescriptor );

if ( myError ) { /* no direct object exists! */

        myError = AEDisposeDesc( &theReply );
        SysBeep( 1 );
        return;

}

myError = AESizeOfParam( &theReply, keyDirectObject,
                            &theDescriptorType, &theResultSize );
```

Listing 4-10 Sending an Apple event to the ToolServer application (continued)

```
        myError = ZeroScrap();
        myError = PutScrap( theResultSize, 'TEXT',
                                *theResultDescriptor.dataHandle );

        myError = AEDisposeDesc( &theResultDescriptor );
        myError = AEDisposeDesc( &theReply );

        return;
}


/* Filter procedure for PPCBrowser */
pascal Boolean ToolServerFilter( LocationNamePtr locationName,
                                    PortInfoPtr thePortInfo )
{
        StringPtr       s;
        OSType          theCreator;

        if ( (thePortInfo->name).portKindSelector == ppcByCreatorAndType ) {

                theCreator = (thePortInfo->name).u.port.creator;

        } else { /* must be ppcByString */
/* AppleEvent Manager uses ppcByString. The string is 8 characters
    long: a 4-byte creator followed by 'ep' and a 2-byte ID number */

                s = (thePortInfo->name).u.portTypeStr;

                if ( *s++ != 8 ) return( false );

                theCreator = *(OSType *)s;
        }

        if ( theCreator != ToolServerCreator ) return( false );
        return ( true );
}


pascal Boolean myIdleProc( EventRecord *theEvent, long *sleepTime,
                                RgnHandle *mouseRgn )
{
        EventRecord     testEvent;
        Boolean         gotKbd;
        char            key;

        gotKbd = GetOSEvent( keyDownMask, &testEvent ); /* get next kbd event */

        if ( gotKbd ) {             /* check for Command-period */

                key = testEvent.message & charCodeMask;
                if ( ( key == '.' ) && ( testEvent.modifiers & cmdKey ) )
```

Listing 4-10 Sending an Apple event to the ToolServer application (continued)

```
                                    return( true );
        }

        switch ( theEvent->what ) {

                case activateEvt:
                case updateEvt:
                case osEvt:
                        DoEvent( theEvent );  /* call main event loop handler */
                        break;

                case nullEvent:
                        *mouseRgn = 0L;         /* no cursor management */
                        *sleepTime = GetDblTime();
                        /* insert here: any periodic tasks */
                        break;

        }

        return( false );
}


/* Convert an OSType to a C-string.
*/
void TypeToCString( ResType theType, Str255 typeString )
{
        short   i;

        for ( i = 0; i <= 3 ; i++, theType = theType >> 8 )
                typeString[3-i] = (char)(theType & 0x000000ff);

        typeString[4] = 0;
}


/* Convert a number to a C-string.
*/
void NumToCString( long theNumber, Str255 theString )
{
        short   i, length;

        NumToString( theNumber, theString );

        for (i = 1, length = theString[0]; i <= length ; i++ )
                theString[i-1] = theString[i];

        theString[i-1] = 0;
}
```

▶ Summary

In this chapter you saw how to use the Apple Event Manager to send and receive Apple events that pass from one application to another, either locally or across a network. Apple events can be used to remotely control the operation of another application or request its status information. You can use events described in the *Apple Event Registry* or define your own if you need any new ones. You also examined the required Apple events in detail and learned how to support them in your applications.

One important client of the Apple Event Manager is the Edition Manager. It uses a set of Apple events to facilitate the live copying and pasting of data between diverse applications. You will read about the Edition Manager in the next chapter.

5 ▶ Edition Manager

The Edition Manager is a new System 7 manager that uses a set of high-level Apple events to control the transfer of data from one application to another through an intermediate file called an *edition*. Transferring data between applications is obviously not a new concept. The novelty of an Edition Manager transfer, however, is that it takes place *asynchronously* either locally or across a network—the sender and receiver do not have to be running at the same time for the transfer to occur, nor do they have to be running on the same computer. Furthermore, one application can transmit data for use by multiple applications and does not need to know which applications will use the data.

In this chapter, you will learn how your applications can benefit from the Edition Manager as you study the following topics:

- the meaning of the terms *section, publisher, subscriber*, and *edition*
- the new menu items that applications need to implement to support the Edition Manager
- managing publishers and subscribers
- supporting publisher and subscriber options
- Apple events used by the Edition Manager

Before you can use the features of the Edition Manager, your application must call the **InitEditionPack** routine once when it first starts up (after it confirms than System 7 is running). **InitEditionPack** takes no parameters and returns an error code of type OSErr. If the error code returned is `memFullErr`, there was not enough memory available to support Edition Manager operations and the application should either quit immediately or continue with Edition Manager features disabled.

▶ Edition Manager Overview

Every Macintosh user knows how easy it is to copy data from one application to another via the clipboard. This technique provides an effective, though sometimes tedious, means of pulling together information from multiple documents, even if each document was created by a different application. There are two problems with this approach, however:

- If the information in one of the documents changes, the user must manually copy and paste it into every document that relies on that information.
- The user must have access to all the applications used to create the component documents as well as the documents themselves.

Under System 7, applications can use the Edition Manager to avoid the problems inherent in the clipboard technique. In particular, applications that use the Edition Manager can be configured so that any data in their documents that originated with another application is updated automatically whenever the other application modifies the data. Furthermore, users no longer need access to the application that created the data or even the document containing the original data (unless the user is also the "keeper" of the original data) because there is no need to transfer the data to the clipboard.

The Edition Manager provides a "super clipboard" that any application across the network can access. The "super clipboard" can contain multiple clippings and can automatically transfer modified data to all documents that refer to it.

Each clipping on this "super clipboard" is a file known as an *edition*. To create an edition, a user selects information within a document and *publishes* it. Users "paste" this information into their documents by *subscribing* to the edition that contains the information. Since editions are disk files, it is easy for an application on one Macintosh to publish data to which any application running on another Macintosh on the same network can subscribe.

The Edition Manager allows for either automatic or manual updating of both the published and the subscribed data. The application should allow the user to control this behavior to suit the needs of each document.

The selection area within the publishing document that is saved to an edition is known as a *publisher*. Any changes made to the publisher should be saved to the edition file; this does not happen automatically—it is the responsibility of your application to do the publishing. From the user's perspective, everything happens transparently; from the developer's perspective, however, there's plenty of behind-the-scenes work to be done.

Documents can subscribe to multiple editions. For example, a word processing file containing a chapter of a book may subscribe to several different editions (one for each listing, table, or figure in the chapter, for example). The listings, tables, and figures would be created by another application (being used by the staff artist) that publishes them; changes would automatically be reflected in the word processing file each time it's opened. This is much simpler than having to remember whether the listings, tables, and figures are current before the chapter goes to press and then having to paste them in manually if they're not. Each area of a document that is associated with an edition is known as a *subscriber*.

A subscribing application should treat the contents of each subscriber as a single object. Users should be able to make stylistic changes to the entire subscriber (changing its color, rotating it, and so on), but should *not* be able to change a subscriber's contents. The only time a subscriber's contents should change is when the publisher updates the edition file.

When the creator of an edition changes the contents of the edition, the Edition Manager sends a special Read Section Apple event to all open documents that have subscribed to that edition. If a document containing a subscriber is not open at the time the publisher updates the edition, the Read Section Apple event telling the application to update the subscriber is deferred and is not sent until the document is open.

▶ Edition Manager Menu Items

Applications that tap into the Edition Manager's publish and subscribe capabilities must provide several standard menu items and two standard dialogs to ensure consistency across applications. Since publish and subscribe operations are analogous to copy and paste, the menu items that provide user control over the Edition Manager should be included in the Edit menu.

Users need menu items to initiate the following tasks:

- publishing information to an edition
- subscribing to an edition
- controlling options for publishing and subscribing
- forcing editions to be disconnected (so they stop receiving or sending changes)
- toggling the highlighting of publishers and subscribers within a document

The first three items should be in all applications that support publishing and subscribing; the last two items are optional, but are highly recommended because they provide complete control and feedback to users.

A typical application's Edit menu, showing the optional items for controlling publish and subscribe, is shown in Figure 5-1. Another view of the same menu, with items whose names have been toggled or checked, is shown in Figure 5-2.

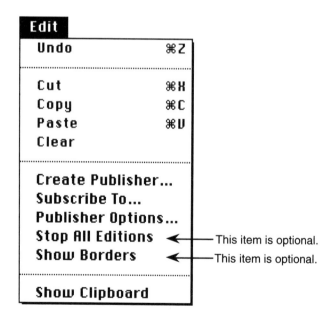

Figure 5-1. A complete Edit menu for a typical System 7 application

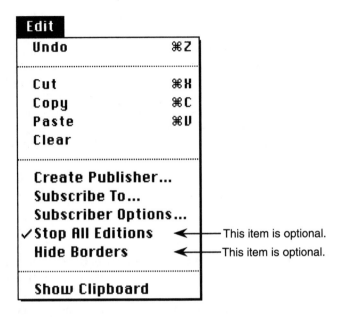

Figure 5-2. Another view of the Edit menu for a typical System 7 application showing the Subscriber Options... and Hide Borders items (these items toggle with Publisher Options... and Show Borders, respectively)

The Create Publisher... item is for creating a new edition file. It should be enabled any time the user has selected something in the frontmost document window. Later in this chapter you will see how to ask the user for the name of the edition for the publisher and how to create that file.

The Subscribe To... item is for adding a subscriber to an open document. It should be enabled any time the front window in the application can accept new data. Later in this chapter you will see how to ask the user for the name of the edition file to be subscribed to and how to incorporate the data within an edition into a document.

The third item toggles between Publisher Options... and Subscriber Options... depending on whether the user has selected a publisher or a subscriber within a document. If neither is selected, this item should read Publisher Options... and be disabled. The standard dialogs your applications should display in response to the selection of this menu item are discussed later in this chapter.

The Stop All Editions item disconnects all publishers and subscribers in a document from their editions. For publishers, this means changes to their contents should not be written to their edition files when a Write Section Apple event is received. For subscribers, this means changes made to edition files by their publishers will not be reflected in subscribers when a Read Section Apple event is received. (These events are described at the end of the chapter.) Individual publishers and subscribers can also be disconnected by setting their update mode to manual (as explained later in this chapter), but the Stop All Editions item provides a convenient way to turn on or off all publishers and subscribers within a document. When editions are stopped, the Stop All Editions item should have a check mark placed next to it (as shown in Figure 5-2).

▶ Drawing Borders

The final standard menu item toggles between Show Borders and Hide Borders and controls whether borders should be drawn around publishers and subscribers within the document. When borders are shown, they should be drawn differently for publishers and subscribers. The standard publisher border is three pixels wide drawn with a 50 percent gray line. The standard subscriber border is the same width, but uses a 75 percent gray line. To prevent the border from overwriting the data within the publisher or subscriber, both types of borders should be outset 1 pixel from the rectangle that frames the publisher or subscriber.

A border should also be drawn around a publisher when the user clicks within it. When a user clicks within a subscriber, the entire contents of the subscriber should be selected and the subscriber treated as a single unit of information.

Listing 5-1 shows the source code for a routine that draws the proper border around a rectangular publisher or subscriber. Pass this routine a pointer to the rectangle that surrounds the publisher or subscriber, a Boolean indicating whether the border is for a publisher or a subscriber, and a Boolean indicating whether the rectangle is specified in global or local coordinates. Use **SetPort** to set the active port to the window containing the publisher or subscriber before calling this routine.

Listing 5-1. General purpose border drawing routine

```
/* The following routine draws either a publisher border or a subscriber */
/* border around the rect that's passed to it. First Boolean indicates */
/* whether a publisher (true) or subscriber (false) border should be */
/* drawn. Second Boolean indicates whether theRect is in local coords */
/* (true) or global coords (false). The window being drawn into should */
/* be set as the current grafPort before this routine is called. */
```

Listing 5-1. General purpose border drawing routine (continued)

```
void DrawOneBorder( Rect theRect, Boolean shouldDrawPub,
                            Boolean isInLocalCoords )
{
    PenState oldPenState;      /* buffer for current pen state */
    Point  myTL, myBR;         /* no topLeft/botRight in interfaces */

    GetPenState( &oldPenState );       /* buffer current pen's state */

    if ( shouldDrawPub ) {     /* is this for a publisher or subscriber? */
        PenPat( gray );        /* publisher gets 50% gray border */
    } else {
        PenPat( dkGray );      /* subscriber gets 75% gray border */
    }

    if ( !isInLocalCoords ) {   /* rect should be in local coordinates */
        SetPt( &myTL, theRect.left, theRect.top );
        SetPt( &myBR, theRect.right, theRect.bottom );
        LocalToGlobal( &myTL );
        LocalToGlobal( &myBR );
        SetRect( &theRect, myTL.h, myTL.v, myBR.h, myBR.v );
    }

    /* Borders are drawn 3 pixels wide, outset one pixel from image, use */
    /* pen size of 3,3 and widen rect by 4 pixels (3 for pen's width + 1 */
    /* for outset from section) */
    InsetRect( &theRect, -4, -4 ); /* outset by using negative amounts */
    PenSize( 3,3 );                 /* pen is 3 x 3 wide */
    FrameRect( &theRect );          /* draw it! */

    SetPenState( &oldPenState );       /* restore original pen state */
}
```

▶ Sections

Publishers and subscribers are known collectively as *sections* and the key
data structure for dealing with them is the *section record*. The anatomy of
a section record is shown in Listing 5-2.

Listing 5-2. The structure of a SectionRecord record

```
struct SectionRecord {
    SignedByte version;       /* always 0x01 in System 7.0 */
    SectionType kind;         /* stSubscriber or stPublisher */
    UpdateMode mode;          /* auto or manual */
    TimeStamp mdDate;         /* last change in document */
    long sectionID;           /* app. specific, unique per document */
    long refCon;              /* application specific */
    AliasHandle alias;        /* handle to alias record for edition */
```

Listing 5-2. The structure of a SectionRecord record (continued)

```
    long subPart;                           /* used internally */
    struct SectionRecord **nextSection;     /* used internally */
    Handle controlBlock;                    /* used internally */
    EditionRefNum refNum;                   /* used internally */
};
```

The meanings of the fields in `SectionRecord` are as follows:

version—The version of the `SectionRecord` data structure. For System 7.0, this field is always 1.

kind—Indicates whether the section is a publisher or a subscriber. Use the following constants defined in the Editions.h interface file:

```
    #define stSubscriber 0x01 /* section type = subscriber */
    #define stPublisher  0x0A /* section type = publisher */
```

mode—Determines whether editions and subscribers are automatically or manually updated. Use the following constants defined in the Editions.h interface file:

```
    #define sumAutomatic 0  /* subscriber update mode - Automatically */
    #define sumManual    1  /* subscriber update mode - Manually */
    #define pumOnSave    0  /* publisher update mode - update when doc saved */
    #define pumManual    1  /* publisher update mode - Manually */
```

mdDate—The date this section was last modified. For subscribers, the Edition Manager compares the value in this field with the modification date stored in the corresponding edition. If the edition's `mdDate` field contains a more recent date than that of a subscriber, the Edition Manager brings the subscriber up to date by sending a Read Section Apple event to the application. This Apple event is discussed at the end of this chapter. For publishers, the application should update this field whenever a publisher's data changes so that the date stored in the edition file will be updated when you save the publisher data to the edition. Use the **GetDateTime** routine to return the current date in the format required for `mdDate`.

sectionID—Contains a unique number identifying the section within the document. The first section should have an ID of 1 and no section should be given the value 0 or -1.

refCon—Not used by the Edition Manager. This field has been set aside for applications to use as they see fit.

alias—The handle to the alias record identifying the edition associated with this section.

subPart—This field is private and should not be used by applications.

nextSection—This field is private and should not be used by applications.

controlBlock—This field is private and should not be used by applications. The Edition Manager assigns each edition a unique control block for its own tracking purposes.

refNum—This field is private and should not be used by applications.

▶ Creating New Sections

Both the SectionRecord and the alias to its corresponding edition file (stored in the alias field) are created by a single call to **NewSection**. The function prototype for **NewSection** follows:

```
pascal OSErr NewSection( const EditionContainerSpec *container,
                         const FSSpec *sectionDocument,
                         SectionType kind,
                         long sectionID,
                         UpdateMode initialMode,
                         SectionHandle *sectionH );
```

The meanings of the parameters used by **NewSection** are as follows:

container—The EditionContainerSpec describing the edition file associated with this section. **NewSection** uses container to create an alias record for the document and puts a handle to it in the section record's alias field. For more information on the EditionContainerSpec data type, see the "Publishing" section later in this chapter.

sectionDocument—The FSSpec for the document that contains the publisher or subscriber for which this section record is being created. If the document has never been saved, pass 0L for this parameter—you can specify the FSSpec later, after you have saved the document, by calling the **AssociateSection** routine described below.

kind—Indicates whether the section is a publisher or a subscriber. Use the following constants defined in the Editions.h interface file:

```
#define stSubscriber 0x01      /* section type = subscriber */
#define stPublisher 0x0A       /* section type = publisher */
```

sectionID—Contains a unique number identifying the section within the document. The first section should have an ID of 1 and no section should be given the value 0 or -1.

initialMode—Determines whether editions are initially updated automatically or manually (the user can change this setting later if desired by using an options dialog described below). Use the following constants defined in the Editions.h interface file:

```
#define sumAutomatic 0 /* subscriber update mode - Automatically */
#define sumManual    1 /* subscriber update mode - Manually */
#define pumOnSave    0 /* publisher update mode - update when doc saved */
#define pumManual    1 /* publisher update mode - Manually */
```

sectionH—The handle to the newly created SectionRecord is returned in this variable. This variable is set to 0L if the call to **NewSection** fails.

The two most common error codes that **NewSection** returns are actually only warnings: multiplePublisherWrn and notThePublisherWrn. A multiplePublisherWrn error occurs if another publisher is already registered to the edition; in most situations it's not appropriate to have more than one publisher for an edition, so you may want to warn the user and proceed only if the operation is confirmed. The notThePublisherWrn error occurs if another publisher was the last section to write to the edition; this serves to alert you that another publisher has recently updated the edition and that perhaps you shouldn't.

▶ Section Management

Each application is responsible for tracking the sections that are part of a document. The source code samples in this chapter implement a tracking system by maintaining a linked list of handles to a custom data structure called a sectionInfo record (one record for each section in the document) that includes miscellaneous information about a section, a handle to the section record, and a handle to the next sectionInfo record in the list. A handle to the beginning of the linked list is stored in the private data area accessed via the handle stored in the `refCon` field of the window record. The structure of the `sectionInfo` record, which is suitable for tracking sections in a TextEdit document, is shown in Listing 5-3.

Listing 5-3. The structure of the custom sectionInfo record

```
struct sectionInfo {
    long          siSectionID;   /* ID of this section */
    Boolean       siIsPublisher; /* true = publisher, false = subscriber */
    short         siTextStart;   /* text starting position */
    short         siTextEnd;     /* text ending position */
    SectionHandle siSectionHndl; /* handle to section's SectionRecord */
    struct sectionInfo ** siNextSectionInfo; /* hndl to next sectionInfo */
};
typedef struct sectionInfo sectionInfo, *siPtr,**siHandle;
```

The fields in the `sectionInfo` data structure are as follows:

siSectionID—The ID for the section. This ID is also part of the section record, but repeating it here saves you a handle dereference each time you need this information.

siIsPublisher—A Boolean indicating whether the section is a publisher (true) or a subscriber (false). You could extract the same information from the `kind` field of the Section Record, but repeating it here saves you a handle dereference each time you need this information.

siTextStart—The offset to the start of the TextEdit data that is in the section. The application must update this field if the offset changes when the user edits the TextEdit document.

siTextEnd—The offset to the end of the TextEdit data that is in the section. The application must update this field if the offset changes when the user edits the TextEdit document.

siSectionHndl—A handle to the section record.

siNextSectionInfo—Set to `0L` if this is the last section in the list. If there are more sections after this one in the linked list, this field should be set to the handle to the `sectionInfo` structure for the next section.

▶ Loading and Saving Sections

When you create a section using **NewSection**, you will create both a section record and an alias record for the edition. Both of these records should be stored as resources in the document's resource fork when the file is saved—give them the same resource ID so you can pair them up more easily when the file is loaded. Use the resource type `'sect'` (rSectionType) for section records and `'alis'` (rAliasType) for alias records. The `SaveSectionToFork` routine in Listing 5-4 shows how to save a given section to the resource fork of a document.

Listing 5-4. A routine for saving a section record and its corresponding alias record to the resource fork of a document

```
/* Save the section record (and associated alias resource) given
    by theSectionH to the resource fork of the document file given
    by docName. This code assumes the resource fork is empty to
    begin with; if it isn't you would first have to remove any
    existing 'sect' (and 'alis') resource with the same ID as the
    one you are adding.

    ApplCreator and DocumentType are constants for the application
    signature and the document file type, respectively.
*/
OSErr SaveSectionToFork( FSSpec *docName, SectionHandle theSectionH )
{
    OSErr              fileError, myErr;
    short              fileRef;
    SectionHandle      tempSectionHndl;
    AliasHandle        tempAliasHndl;

    /* create the resource fork (in case it doesn't already exist) */
    FSpCreateResFile( docName, ApplCreator, DocumentType,
    smSystemScript );

    /* open resource fork */
    fileRef = FSpOpenResFile( docName, fsCurPerm );
    if ( fileRef == -1 ) {
            fileError = ResError();
            return( fileError );
    }

    /* copy section record so we can attach it to Resource Mgr */
    tempSectionHndl = theSectionH;
    myErr = HandToHand( (Handle *)&tempSectionHndl );

    /* copy alias record so we can attach it to Resource Mgr */
    tempAliasHndl = (**tempSectionHndl).alias;
    myErr = HandToHand( (Handle *)&tempAliasHndl );

    /* write 'sect' resource */
    AddResource( (Handle)tempSectionHndl, rSectionType,
```

Listing 5-4. A routine for saving a section record and its
corresponding alias record to the resource fork of a document
(continued)

```
                                   (**tempSectionHndl).sectionID, 0L );

    /* write 'alis' resource */
    AddResource( (Handle)tempAliasHndl, rAliasType,
                         (**tempSectionHndl).sectionID, 0L );

    CloseResFile( fileRef );
    return( noErr );
}
```

When you load a document, you should also load all its 'sect'
(rSectionType) resources and corresponding 'alis' (rAliasType)
resources from the resource fork, detach the resource handles so the
Resource Manager no longer owns them, then store the alias handles in
the corresponding section records. You can use the LoadSectionsFromFork
routine shown in Listing 5-5 to do this. LoadSectionsFromFork also
creates a linked list of private sectionInfo records (described above) for
each section and stores a handle to the start of the linked list in the
private data area accessed via a handle stored in the window's refCon
field. It also registers each section using the technique described in the
next subsection.

Listing 5-5. A routine for loading section records and
corresponding alias records from the resource fork of a
document. This routine also builds a linked list of sectionInfo
records and registers the sections

```
/* Load all sections (and corresponding aliases) from the
   resource fork of the document, create the linked
   list of sectionInfo records, and add it to the
   private data area referenced via the refCon of the
   window record. */
void LoadSectionsFromFork( FSSpec *docName, WindowPtr wp )
{
    short            initialRefNum, refNum;
    short            sectionCount, i;
    winPrivateHndl   thePrivate;
    SectionHandle    theSectionH;
    AliasHandle      theAliasH;
    OSErr            myErr;
    Boolean          wasUpdated;
    short            textStart, textEnd;
```

Listing 5-5. A routine for loading section records and corresponding alias records from the resource fork of a document. This routine also builds a linked list of sectionInfo records and registers the sections (continued)

```
/* Get handle to private data area. One of the fields in
   this area, winsiHndl, is a handle to start of the
   linked list of sectionInfo records (Listing 5-3). */
thePrivate = (winPrivateHndl)GetWRefCon( wp );

refNum = FSpOpenResFile( docName, fsCurPerm );

initialRefNum = CurResFile();
UseResFile( refNum );

/* get number of 'sect' resources */
sectionCount = Count1Resources( rSectionType );

for ( i=1 ; i <= sectionCount ; i++ ) {

    /* get nth 'sect' resource */
    theSectionH = (SectionHandle)Get1IndResource( rSectionType, i );
    DetachResource( theSectionH ); /* claim ownership of handle */

    /* 'alis' resource ID is the same as the 'sect' resource ID,
       which is the same as the sectionID in the section record
       (because that's the way we planned it when we saved
       the section) */
    theAliasH = (AliasHandle)Get1Resource( rAliasType,
                            (**theSectionH).sectionID );
    DetachResource( theAliasH ); /* claim ownership of handle */

    /* place alias handle into section record */
    (**theSectionH).alias = theAliasH;

    /* Register the section; we can ignore possible errors.
       If wasUpdated comes back true, mark the section record as
       "dirty" and save it to disk when the document is closed.
       (We don't do it here, but you should.) */
    myErr = RegisterSection( docName, theSectionH, &wasUpdated );

    /* Get the offsets to the start and end of the text block
       associated with this section. GetSectionTextRange
       traverses a data structure you maintain that maps sections
       to text ranges. */
    GetSectionTextRange( wp, theSectionH, &textStart, &textEnd );

    AddSectionToList( thePrivate, theSectionH, textStart, textEnd );
}
```

Listing 5-5. A routine for loading section records and corresponding alias records from the resource fork of a document. This routine also builds a linked list of sectionInfo records and registers the sections (continued)

```
        CloseResFile( refNum );
        UseResFile( initialRefNum );
}

/* Add a sectionInfo record to the end of the linked list.
    (See Listing 5-3 for the structure of sectionInfo.)
    A handle to the first element in the list is stored in
    the winsiHndl field of the window's private data area.
    You access this area via a handle stored in the window's
    refCon field. */
void AddSectionToList( winPrivateHndl thePrivate, SectionHandle theSectionH,
                        short textStart, short textEnd )
{
    siHandle   newsiHndl, tempsiHndl;

    /* set up the new sectionInfo record */
    newsiHndl = (siHandle)NewHandle( sizeof ( sectionInfo ) );
    (**newsiHndl).siSectionID = (**theSectionH).sectionID;
    (**newsiHndl).siIsPublisher = ( (**theSectionH).kind == stPublisher );
    (**newsiHndl).siSectionHndl = theSectionH;
    (**newsiHndl).siTextStart = textStart;
    (**newsiHndl).siTextEnd = textEnd;
    (**newsiHndl).siNextSectionInfo = nil;

    /* Find the end of the linked list and save the new element */

    tempsiHndl = (**thePrivate).winsiHndl; /* get 1st element */

    if ( tempsiHndl ) {    /* nil unless sections exists */
        /* walk list to find last sectionInfo record */
        while ( (**tempsiHndl).siNextSectionInfo ) {
            tempsiHndl = (**tempsiHndl).siNextSectionInfo;
        }
        (**tempsiHndl).siNextSectionInfo = newsiHndl;
    } else {
        (**thePrivate).winsiHndl = newsiHndl;
    }
}
```

When you save a document's 'sect' and 'alis' resources, you must also save a custom resource that contains the data needed to map each section with the portion of the document with which it is associated. For the simple case of a TextEdit document, for example, you would save an array, each element of which contains a section ID, the offset to the start of the section data, and the offset to the end of the section data. This data permits you to construct fully the private `sectionInfo` record you maintain for each section.

▶ Registering and Unregistering Sections

When you create a new section by calling **NewSection**, it is automatically registered so that the Edition Manager knows about it. The Edition Manager sends Apple events to publishers and subscribers telling publishers to write or subscribers to read an edition only if the publishers and subscribers are registered. (See the "Apple Events Used by the Edition Manager" section of this chapter for more information on these events.) The Edition Manager performs its duties more efficiently and quickly when it only has to track registered sections.

When opening a document that already contains publishers or subscribers, do not call **NewSection**. Instead, retrieve the section records and alias records from the document's resource fork as described above and register each section by calling **RegisterSection**. The function prototype for **RegisterSection** is:

```
pascal OSErr RegisterSection( const FSSpec *sectionDocument,
                SectionHandle sectionH,
                Boolean *aliasWasUpdated );
```

The parameters used by **RegisterSection** are the following:

sectionDocument—The FSSpec of the document containing the section that is being registered.

sectionH—A handle to the section record for the section being registered.

aliasWasUpdated—After the call to **RegisterSection**, this variable indicates whether the alias referred to in the section record was updated to more efficiently describe the location of the document. If this variable is true, your application should update the 'alis' resource for the section by writing the new alias record to the resource fork of the document. In practice, you don't usually write the updated information back to disk right away—you simply mark the section record as "dirty" and save it just before the user closes the document.

Two common errors that **RegisterSection** can return for a subscriber section are `userCanceledErr` and `containerNotFoundWrn`. The `userCanceledErr` error occurs if the user clicked the Cancel button when asked to log on to the server on which the edition container is located. The `containerNotFoundWrn` error is a warning that occurs if the edition container cannot be located (perhaps because it was deleted).

For a publisher, if **RegisterSection** returns a `containerNotFoundWrn`, it creates an empty edition file and sends a Write Section Apple event to your application—when the application receives the Write Section event, it saves the publisher to the edition. See the "Apple Events Used by the Edition Manager" section for more information.

When a document containing a section is closed, your application should unregister each section it contains by calling **UnRegisterSection**. (You should also call **UnRegisterSection** if you cancel a section; see the "Publisher and Subscriber Options" section in this chapter.) This tells the Event Manager not to send any more Apple events relating to it and simplifies its housekeeping chores. The function prototype for **UnRegisterSection** is the following:

```
pascal OSErr UnRegisterSection( SectionHandle sectionH );
```

The `sectionH` parameter is a handle to the section record for the section being unregistered.

▶ Associating Sections

Whenever you change the name of the document with which a section record is associated, you should call **AssociateSection** to ensure the Edition Manager knows about the change. This allows the Edition Manager to manage the section properly and effectively; for a publisher, for example, it means the Finder will be able to automatically open the document that created an edition when you open the edition file from the Finder.

If the `sectionDocument` parameter was set to `0L` when **NewSection** was called to create a publisher because the document hadn't been saved to disk yet, you need to call **AssociateSection** once the document has been saved.

You may also want to call **AssociateSection** after you save a copy of a document in response to a Save As… command or when you copy a section from one document to another. Do this for publishers only if you want the copy to be brought up—not the original—when the user requests that the publisher be opened. (You may want to prevent the user from creating multiple publishers to the same edition, however. This can lead to confusion.)

The function prototype for **AssociateSection** is as follows:

```
pascal OSErr AssociateSection( SectionHandle sectionH,
                               const FSSpec *newSectionDocument );
```

The parameters used by **AssociateSection** are the following:

sectionH—A handle to the section record for the publisher.

newSectionDocument—The FSSpec of the document containing the section whose handle is passed in sectionH.

After calling **AssociateSection**, your application should save the updated section record, and the alias record to which it refers, to the document's resource fork using the techniques described earlier in this chapter.

▶ Publishing

An edition is similar to the clipboard in that you can save publisher data to it in a variety of formats, allowing the subscriber to deal with the richest format it can handle. The most common edition formats have the following identifiers: 'TEXT' (a block of text), 'PICT' (a QuickDraw picture), and 'snd ' (a sound).

New editions are created when the user selects the Create Publisher... menu item from the Edit menu and specifies a name for the edition file. (This item should only be highlighted when something in the document has been selected.) Once the edition file has been created and opened, the publisher can be created and saved to the edition.

An existing publisher whose data has been modified should update its edition file either automatically when the document is saved to disk or only when the user clicks the *Send Edition Now* button in the publisher options dialog box (see the "Publisher and Subscriber Options" section in this chapter). Update editions automatically when the document is saved only when the value stored in the mode field of the section record is pumOnSave.

Before you learn how to publish a section record to an edition, you need to understand two other data structures: the EditionContainerSpec and the NewPublisherReply.

An `EditionContainerSpec` is an expanded version of a file specification record and identifies the edition file associated with a given section. The structure of an `EditionContainerSpec` is shown in Listing 5-6.

Listing 5-6. The structure of an EditionContainerSpec record

```
struct EditionContainerSpec {
    FSSpec theFile;
    ScriptCode theFileScript;
    long thePart;
    Str31 thePartName;
    ScriptCode thePartScript;
};
```

The fields in an `EditionContainerSpec` are the following:

theFile—The file specification for the edition file, or *edition container*. As explained in Chapter 2, an `FSSpec` is made up of three components: a volume reference number (`vRefNum`) identifying the disk volume, a directory ID (`parID`) identifying the parent folder, and the name of the file itself (`name[64]`).

theFileScript—The script code of the file name given by `theFile`.

thePart—Not currently used, but should be set to `kPartsNotUsed` to ensure compatibility with future releases of the Edition Manager.

thePartName—Not used in System 7.0.

thePartScript—Not used in System 7.0.

The second important data structure is the `NewPublisherReply` record and is used in connection with the **NewPublisherDialog** routine. This routine displays the standard publisher dialog box shown in Figure 5-3 which allows the user to specify the name of the edition in which the publisher is to be saved. The function protoype for **NewPublisherDialog** is as follows:

```
pascal OSErr NewPublisherDialog( NewPublisherReply *reply );
```

The sole parameter to **NewPublisherDialog** is a pointer to a `NewPublisherReply` record. The structure of `NewPublisherReply` is shown in Listing 5-7.

Listing 5-7. The structure of a NewPublisherReply record

```
struct NewPublisherReply {
      Boolean canceled;
      Boolean replacing;
      Boolean usePart;
      Handle preview;
      FormatType previewFormat;
      EditionContainerSpec container;
};
```

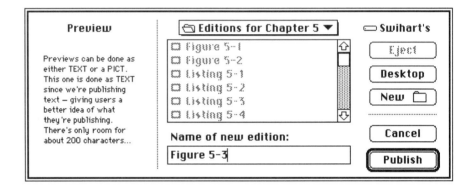

Figure 5-3. The standard publisher dialog box

The fields in a NewPublisherReply record are as follows:

canceled—Set to true by the Edition Manager if the user clicks the Cancel button (see Figure 5-3).

replacing—Set to true by the Edition Manager if the user selects an edition file that already exists and has verified that its contents should be replaced. It is set to false if a new edition file needs to be created. You can create new edition containers by calling **CreateEditionContainerFile.**

usePart—Always set this field to false.

preview—Holds the handle to the preview data. As you will see, the preview data should be of type 'TEXT', 'PICT', 'snd ', or 'prvw'.

`previewFormat`—Describes the format of the data whose handle is in the `preview` field. This field should be set to `'TEXT'`, `'PICT'`, `'snd '`, or `'prvw'`.

`container`—This is where you specify the file system specification describing the default file name and location for the edition. When **NewPublisherDialog** ends, this field identifies the file actually specified by the user.

▶ Publisher Previews

Notice the Preview area on the left side of the publisher dialog box in Figure 5-3. Your application is responsible for providing the content of this 120-pixel-square area for any edition it creates. It is also responsible for saving the preview data to the edition container using the **WriteEdition** routine. The purpose of the preview is to remind users of the contents of the publisher.

The preferred edition format for a preview is a QuickDraw picture that you've tuned to look attractive in the 120x120 preview area. It should be added to the edition file in the `kPreviewFormat` (`'prvw'`) format. Users will see the preview when subscribing to your edition from other applications or when they double-click on an edition container file in the Finder. The preview data is generally not used in any other way by the subscribing application.

If you don't save a preview in the `kPreviewFormat` format, the Edition Manager generates a preview picture from data in the `'TEXT'`, `'PICT'`, or `'snd '` format that may have been saved to the edition.

The preview derived from the `'TEXT'` format is made up of the first few characters in the text block. About 200 characters of unstyled text can be squeezed into such a preview. The preview derived from the `'PICT'` format is a QuickDraw picture scaled to fit the 120-pixel-square preview area. The preview for the `'snd '` format is a loudspeaker icon.

▶ Creating Editions

Create new edition containers by calling **CreateEditionContainerFile**. The function prototype for **CreateEditionContainerFile** is as follows:

```
pascal OSErr CreateEditionContainerFile( const FSSpec *editionFile,
                                         OSType fdCreator,
                                         ScriptCode editionFileNameScript );
```

The parameters used by **CreateEditionContainerFile** are the following:

> **editionFile**—The FSSpec for the edition container to be created. Use the value returned in the container.theFile field of the NewPublisherReply record returned by **NewPublisherDialog**.

> **fdCreator**—The creator type of the application creating this edition. This parameter should be set to your application's creator type (see Chapter 9 for more information on creator types).

> **editionFileNameScript**—The script code of the file name used for the edition container being created. Use the value returned in the container.theFileScript field of the NewPublisherReply record returned by **NewPublisherDialog**.

▶ Opening Editions

Before a section can be published, an edition container must be opened by calling **OpenNewEdition**. The function prototype for **OpenNewEdition** is as follows:

```
pascal OSErr OpenNewEdition( SectionHandle publisherSectionH,
                OSType fdCreator,
                const FSSpec *publisherSectionDocument,
                EditionRefNum *refNum );
```

The parameters used by **OpenNewEdition** are the following:

> **publisherSectionH**—The section handle to the publisher that will be written to the edition container being opened.

> **fdCreator**—The creator type of the application creating this edition. This parameter should be set to your application's creator type (see Chapter 9 for more information on creator types).

> **publisherSectionDocument**—A pointer to the FSSpec of the document containing the publisher that will write the data to the edition container being opened. This FSSpec is used to create an alias record for the document and is stored in the edition file. Pass 0L for this parameter if the document containing the publisher has not yet been saved.

Note ▶	If you create an edition with a FSSpec pointer of 0L (meaning the document containing the section is untitled and has never been saved), you must eventually call **OpenNewEdition** again and pass the document's FSSpec to update the edition's record of which document owns the edition. This is important since users should be able to double-click on the edition file from the Finder and automatically open the application that created it. If the document's FSSpec was never recorded in the edition, the Finder will be unable to do this.

refNum—The reference number for the edition container is returned in this variable. If you aren't permitted to write to this container (because the file is locked or someone else is accessing it), 0L is returned.

The two common errors that **OpenNewEdition** can return are flLckdErr and permErr. The flLckdErr code is returned if another application (perhaps running on another Macintosh across the network) is currently reading the edition.

The permErr code is returned if the edition is already associated with a registered publisher that is not on the local system. Multiple publishers are permitted only when they reside on the same computer.

Your application should allow the user to select the edition file to publish to by calling **NewPublisherDialog** and then, if the replacing field of the NewPublisherReply record is false (meaning the user specified a new edition rather than an existing one), create the new edition container by calling **CreateEditionContainerFile**. Finally, the application should open the edition container for writing by calling **OpenNewEdition**.

▶ Publishing Sections

Once the edition container has been opened, use **WriteEdition** to write the data being published. The function prototype for **WriteEdition** is as follows:

```
pascal OSErr WriteEdition( EditionRefNum whichEdition,
                           FormatType whichFormat,
                           const void *buffPtr,
                           Size buffLen );
```

The parameters used by **WriteEdition** are the following:

whichEdition—The refNum of the open edition container. This is the refNum returned by **OpenNewEdition**.

whichFormat—Indicates the format of the data being written. To properly support the exchange of common data types with other applications, you should try to save data to the edition file in both the 'TEXT' and 'PICT' formats (using separate calls to **WriteEdition**). To save styled text to an edition, save the text itself in the 'TEXT' format and the styling information in the 'styl' format. In addition, don't forget to save the publisher preview in the 'prvw' format.

buffPtr—A pointer to the buffer containing the data to be written

buffLen—The number of bytes of data to be written to the edition container. This data is in the buffer pointed to by buffPtr.

WriteEdition returns standard file system and Memory Manager errors that occur if there are problems encountered when saving the publisher to disk.

▶ Closing Editions

After writing the data, close the edition container by calling **CloseEdition**.The function prototype for **CloseEdition** is as follows:

```
pascal OSErr CloseEdition( EditionRefNum whichEdition,
                                  Boolean successful );
```

The parameters used by **CloseEdition** are the following:

whichEdition—Set to the refNum of the open edition container.

successful—If your application was successful in writing the data to the edition container (using **WriteEdition**), set this parameter to true. If the write failed, set this parameter to false. When set to true, **CloseEdition** causes the Edition Manager to set the edition container's modification date to the mdDate field in the publisher's section record. It also causes the Edition Manager to send a Read Section Apple event to all registered subscribers of this edition informing them that new data is ready to be read. (For more information on Apple events sent by the Edition Manager, see the "Apple Events Used by the Edition Manager" section later in this chapter.)

You now have all the information you need to publish data to edition containers. Listing 5-8 shows the source code for creating a new edition container, including a simple example of how to publish to it.

Listing 5-8. Source code for creating an edition and writing a publisher to it

```
/* The following routine is responsible for publishing the front
      window's current TextEdit selection in an edition file. Only
      the 'TEXT' format is supported, but other formats should be
      easy to add.

   This code assumes a handle to a private data structure has
   been stored in the window's refCon field. This private data
   structure has the following definition:

   typedef struct {
        FSSpec    winFSSpec;      - file specification for the document
        siHandle winsiHndl;       - handle to first sectionInfo record
                                  - (defined in Listing 5-3)
        long winSectionID;        - the section ID
        TEHandle winTEHndl;       - handle to the TextEdit record
   } winPrivate, **winPrivateHndl;
*/
void DoCreatePublisher( void )
{
    winPrivateHndl        myPrivHndl;        /* handle to window's private data */
    TEHandle              tempTEHndl;        /* temporary handle to TE field */
    Boolean               aliasChanged;
    SectionHandle         mySectionHndl;
    long                  mySectionID;       /* ID of the section being created */
    OSErr                 myErr;
    NewPublisherReply     myReply;           /* needed for NewPublisherDialog */
    EditionContainerSpec  mySpec;
    Handle                myData;            /* handle to info to write out */
    Handle                myPreviewHndl;     /* handle to preview */
    siHandle              newsiHndl, tempsiHndl;
    Str63                 defaultName = "\pGary's Edition";

    /* Note: this code assumes the front window has a TextEdit record and a
          selection range. Disable the Create Publisher… menu item if it
          doesn't so that you don't have to do any error checking here. */

    myPrivHndl = (winPrivateHndl)GetWRefCon( FrontWindow() );
    HLock( (Handle)myPrivHndl );

    /* set the section's ID to the last section ID for this document + 1 */
    mySectionID = (**myPrivHndl).winSectionID + 1;

    tempTEHndl = (**myPrivHndl).winTEHndl; /* simplifies life */
    HLock( (Handle)tempTEHndl );

    /* Get a handle to the preview data - we're using 'TEXT' */
    DoGetTextPreview( tempTEHndl, &myPreviewHndl );
```

Listing 5-8. Source code for creating an edition and writing a publisher to it (continued)

```
/* initialize mySpec */
/* use GetLastEditionContainerUsed info for everything but the name */
myErr = GetLastEditionContainerUsed( &mySpec );
BlockMove( defaultName, mySpec.theFile.name, sizeof( defaultName ) );

/* initialize the fields of myReply */
myReply.container = mySpec;
myReply.previewFormat = 'TEXT';        /* using text for preview */
myReply.preview = myPreviewHndl;       /* handle to the preview */
myReply.usePart = false;               /* always set to false */

/* prompt the user to specify an edition file */
/* (we won't bother checking for an error; you should) */
myErr = NewPublisherDialog(&myReply);

/* free the memory allocated by DoGetTextPreview() */
if ( myPreviewHndl ) { DisposHandle( (Handle)myPreviewHndl ); }

if ( !myReply.canceled ) {      /* if 'Cancel' wasn't hit, carry on...*/
    if ( !myReply.replacing ) {
        /* if replacing was false, create a new edition container */
        myErr = CreateEditionContainerFile( &myReply.container.theFile,
                          ApplCreator,
                          myReply.container.theFileScript);
        if ( myErr ) {
            PrintString( "\pError during CreateEditionContainerFile" );
            HUnlock( (Handle)myPrivHndl );
            HUnlock( (Handle)tempTEHndl );
            return;
        }
    }

    /* Create new publisher */
    myErr = NewSection( &myReply.container, &(**myPrivHndl).winFSSpec,
                    stPublisher, mySectionID, pumOnSave,
                    &mySectionHndl );

    if ( !myErr ) {
        /* new section was created, set up sectionInfo record */
        newsiHndl = (siHandle)NewHandle( sizeof( sectionInfo ) );
        (**newsiHndl).siSectionID = mySectionID;
        (**newsiHndl).siIsPublisher = true; /* true = publisher */
        (**newsiHndl).siSectionHndl = mySectionHndl;
        (**newsiHndl).siNextSectionInfo = nil;

        /* get its contents */
        DoGetPubContents( tempTEHndl, &myData );

        /* Write it out! */
        myErr = DoWriteContents( mySectionHndl,
                          &(**myPrivHndl).winFSSpec, myData );
```

Listing 5-8. Source code for creating an edition and writing a publisher to it (continued)

```
            DisposHandle( myData );    /* free the memory used by myData */

            /* record new value of last section used in document */
            (**myPrivHndl).winSectionID = mySectionID;

            /* store handle to new sectionInfo record at end of linked list */
            tempsiHndl = (**myPrivHndl).winsiHndl;
            if ( tempsiHndl ) {   /* nil unless sections exists */
                /* walk list to find last sectionInfo record */
                while ( (**tempsiHndl).siNextSectionInfo ) {
                    tempsiHndl = (**tempsiHndl).siNextSectionInfo;
                }
                (**tempsiHndl).siNextSectionInfo = newsiHndl;
            } else {
                (**myPrivHndl).winsiHndl = newsiHndl;
            }

        } else {
            /* we didn't get a new section, so punt */
            PrintString( "\pError in NewSection" );
        }
    }
    HUnlock( (Handle)myPrivHndl );
    HUnlock( (Handle)tempTEHndl );
}


/* The following routine is responsible for opening the edition,
    writing the publisher data, and closing the edition.
*/
OSErr DoWriteContents( SectionHandle theSectionHndl,
                    FSSpecPtr docsSpecPtr, Handle theData )
{
    OSErr           myErr, ignoreErr;
    EditionRefNum    theEdRefNum;      /* refNum for edition container */

    SetCursor( *GetCursor( watchCursor ) );     /* wristwatch cursor */

    HLock( (Handle)theSectionHndl );
    /* stuff current time into mdDate, so subscribers get update notice */
    GetDateTime( &(**theSectionHndl).mdDate );
    HUnlock( (Handle)theSectionHndl );

    /* Open the edition for writing */
    myErr = OpenNewEdition( theSectionHndl, ApplCreator,
                        docsSpecPtr, &theEdRefNum );
    if ( !myErr ) {   /* if the open was successful, write to it! */

        HLock( theData );

        /* write the publisher data */
        myErr = WriteEdition( theEdRefNum, 'TEXT', *theData,
```

Listing 5-8. Source code for creating an edition and writing a publisher to it (continued)

```
                            GetHandleSize( theData ) );

        HUnlock( theData );

        if ( myErr ) {
            ignoreErr = CloseEdition( theEdRefNum, false );  /* write failed */
        } else {
            ignoreErr = CloseEdition( theEdRefNum, true );  /* write is OK */
        }
    }
    InitCursor();    /* normal cursor */
    return ( myErr );
}

/* This routine returns a handle to the preview data in the
    thePreviewHandle variable. The data is a block of text
    extracted from the TextEdit record.
*/
void DoGetTextPreview( TEHandle theTERecord, Handle *thePreviewHandle )
{
    char *dataPtr;
    long dataSize;

    dataPtr = *( (**theTERecord).hText );
    dataPtr += (**theTERecord).selStart;
    dataSize = (**theTERecord).selEnd - (**theTERecord).selStart;
    if ( dataSize > 200 ) dataSize = 200;
    PtrToHand( dataPtr, thePreviewHandle, dataSize );
}

/* This routine returns a handle to the data to be published in the
    thePubData variable. The data is a block of text extracted from
    the TextEdit record.
*/
void DoGetPubContents( TEHandle theTERecord, Handle *thePubData )
{
    char *dataPtr;
    long dataSize;

    dataPtr = *( (**theTERecord).hText );
    dataPtr += (**theTERecord).selStart;
    dataSize = (**theTERecord).selEnd - (**theTERecord).selStart;
    PtrToHand( dataPtr, thePubData, dataSize );
}
```

▶ Subscribing

As you learned above, an application should provide a Subscribe To... menu item so that users can subscribe to an existing edition file. You enable this item any time a paste operation makes sense.

The application should react to the selection of the Subscribe To... item by presenting the standard subscriber dialog box shown in Figure 5-4.

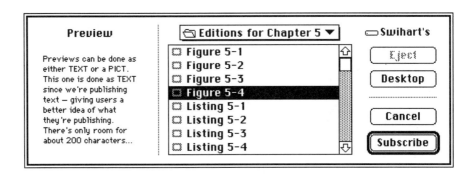

Figure 5-4. The standard subscriber dialog box

Notice the Preview area on the left side of the subscriber dialog box. As you saw earlier, the application that created the edition is responsible for providing the content of the preview area. Your application could also use this preview as a fast way to represent the data within a subscriber instead of displaying the entire subscriber. (The preview is usually stored in the edition in the 'prvw' format and you can read it by calling **ReadEdition**, described below.)

Bring up the subscriber dialog box by calling the **NewSubscriberDialog** routine which requires a pointer to a NewSubscriberReply record as its sole parameter. The structure of NewSubscriberReply is shown in Listing 5-9.

Listing 5-9. The structure of a NewSubscriberReply record

```
struct NewSubscriberReply {
        Boolean canceled;
        unsigned char formatsMask;
        EditionContainerSpec container;
};
```

The fields in a `NewSubscriberReply` are as follows:

canceled—Set to true by the Edition Manager if the user clicks the Cancel button (see Figure 5-4).

formatsMask—Set this before calling **NewSubscriberDialog** to reflect the formats you want to subscribe to. The Edition Manager uses this mask to filter out editions that do not contain the desired formats (similar to file filtering in a standard open file dialog). Each format is represented by a constant (defined in the Editions.h interface file); more than one format can be specified by adding the appropriate constants together. The standard formats that applications should support are the following:

```
#define kTEXTformatMask 'TEXT'
#define kPICTformatMask 'PICT'
#define ksndFormatMask  'snd '
```

Note ▶

Refer to *Inside Macintosh*, Volume VI for information on how to deal with editions that contain non-standard formats.

container—Before calling **NewSubscriberDialog**, store here the EditionContainerSpec of the last edition file created by a call to **NewSection** from any application on the user's computer (call **GetLastEditionContainerUsed** to obtain this information). This edition file becomes the default and its name will be highlighted when the dialog appears. The edition file actually selected by the user will be returned in this FSSpec field of container, overwriting the default settings supplied by your application if the user picks an edition other than the default.

Using the edition container returned by **GetLastEditionContainerUsed** simplifies the user's interaction with other applications on the same computer since it lets them publish a new edition from one application and have that edition as the default to subscribe to from another application. This is similar to copying something to the clipboard in one application and having that data available for immediate pasting in another application.

The function prototype for **GetLastEditionContainerUsed** is the following:

```
pascal OSErr GetLastEditionContainerUsed( EditionContainerSpec *container );
```

The sole parameter passed to **GetLastEditionContainerUsed** is a pointer to the space for an EditionContainerSpec record that this routine returns. The fields within this record reflect the edition container that was last referenced by a call to **NewSection** from any application running on the computer. If no calls to **NewSection** have been made on the user's computer, the fields in the EditionContainerSpec returned by **GetLastEditionContainerUsed** will be set to safe values so that the returned value is always a usable default when calling **NewSubscriberDialog**.

After calling **GetLastEditionContainerUsed**, and using the information it returns to prepare your NewSubscriberReply record, call **NewSubscriberDialog** to allow users of your application to select the edition to which they want to subscribe. The sole parameter to **NewSubscriberDialog** is a pointer to a NewSubscriberReply record. The function prototype for **NewSubscriberDialog** is the following:

```
pascal OSErr NewSubscriberDialog( NewSubscriberReply *reply );
```

After determining which edition a user wants to subscribe to, your application should *not* open the edition and start reading its contents. Instead, create a new section for the subscriber and return to your main event loop. The Edition Manager will register your newly created section, detect that this section needs to be updated, and send an Apple event to your application telling it to read the section. This Read Event, and how to react to it, is described in the "Apple Events Used by the Edition Manager" section later in this chapter.

Listing 5-10 shows the source code for a routine that allows the user to select an edition to subscribe to and to create a subscriber section.

Listing 5-10. Source code for selecting and creating a new subscriber

```
/* The following routine is responsible for creating a subscriber
    at the insertion point in the front window. This routine does
    NOT read the subscriber's content - we wait for the Read Event
    to come from the Edition Manager and handle it with our Apple
    event handler.

    This code assumes a handle to a private data structure has
```

Listing 5-10. Source code for selecting and creating a new subscriber (continued)

```
                been stored in the window's refCon field. This private data
                structure has the following definition:

                typedef struct {
                    FSSpec   winFSSpec;        - file specification for the document
                    siHandle winsiHndl;        - handle to first sectionInfo record
                                               - (defined in Listing 5-3)
                    long     winSectionID;     - the section ID
                    TEHandle winTEHndl;        - handle to the TextEdit record
                } winPrivate, **winPrivateHndl;
*/
void DoCreateSubscriber(void)
{
    winPrivateHndl          myPrivHndl;    /* handle to window's private data */
    Boolean                 aliasChanged;
    SectionHandle           mySectionHndl;
    long                    mySectionID;
    OSErr                   myErr;
    NewSubscriberReply      myReply; /* for NewSubscriberDialog */
    siHandle                tempsiHndl, newsiHndl;

    /* Note: this code assumes the front window has a TextEdit record. */

    myPrivHndl = (winPrivateHndl)GetWRefCon( FrontWindow() );
    HLock( (Handle)myPrivHndl );

    /* initialize container's spec */
    myErr = GetLastEditionContainerUsed( &myReply.container );

    /* set mask to allow only editions with TEXT in them */
    myReply.formatsMask = kTEXTformatMask;

    /* ready to prompt user to select an edition file */
    /* (we won't bother checking for an error; you should) */
    myErr = NewSubscriberDialog( &myReply );

        if ( !myReply.canceled ) {         /* if 'Cancel' wasn't hit, carry on...*/
            /* set this section's ID */
            mySectionID = (**myPrivHndl).winSectionID + 1;

            /* Create new subscriber */
            myErr = NewSection( &myReply.container, &(**myPrivHndl).winFSSpec,
                                stSubscriber, mySectionID,
                                sumAutomatic,
                                &mySectionHndl );

            if ( !myErr ) {
            /* new section has been created, record new section's info */
                newsiHndl = (siHandle)NewHandle( sizeof( sectionInfo ) );
                (**newsiHndl).siSectionID = mySectionID;
                (**newsiHndl).siIsPublisher = false; /* false=subscriber */
                (**newsiHndl).siSectionHndl = mySectionHndl;
```

Listing 5-10. Source code for selecting and creating a new subscriber (continued)

```
                    (**newsiHndl).siNextSectionInfo = nil;

                    /* record new value of last section used in this document */
                    (**myPrivHndl).winSectionID = mySectionID;

             /* store handle to new sectionInfo record at end of linked list */
                    tempsiHndl = (**myPrivHndl).winsiHndl;
                    if ( tempsiHndl ) {      /* nil unless sections exist */
                        /* walk list to find last sectionInfo record */
                        while ((**tempsiHndl).siNextSectionInfo) {
                            tempsiHndl = (**tempsiHndl).siNextSectionInfo;
                        }
                        (**tempsiHndl).siNextSectionInfo = newsiHndl;
                    } else {
                        (**myPrivHndl).winsiHndl = newsiHndl;
                    }
                }
            }
        HUnlock( (Handle)myPrivHndl );
    }
```

▶ **Publisher and Subscriber Options**

▶ Publisher Options

When the user selects a publisher within a document, the application should enable the Publisher Options... menu item in the Edit menu. If the user selects this item, or double-clicks on the publisher, the standard publisher options dialog (see Figure 5-5) should be displayed. This dialog allows the user to specify whether the selected publisher will be updated *On Save* (automatically every time the document is saved) or *Manually* (only at the specific request of the user).

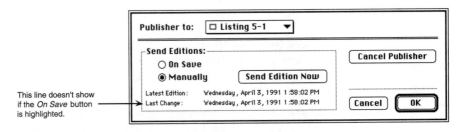

Figure 5-5. The standard publisher options dialog

A publisher with its update mode set to *On Save* should have its contents written to its edition every time the document containing the publisher is saved, but only if the contents of the publisher have changed since the last time the document was saved. This minimizes the time it takes to save a document with many publishers since only those publishers that have been changed and are set to *On Save* need to be written to their edition files. Your application is responsible for determining when a publisher needs to be saved to its edition file; this is not handled automatically by the Edition Manager.

An immediate transfer of a publisher's contents to its edition can be forced by clicking the *Send Edition Now* button in the publisher options dialog, regardless of whether that publisher is normally sent *Manually* or *On Save*. This provides a method of quickly updating individual editions without having to save the entire document, and it is the only way to update an edition whose publisher update mode is *Manually*.

You can display the publisher options dialog by calling **SectionOptionsDialog**. The sole parameter to this routine is a pointer to a `SectionOptionsReply` record. Some of the fields in a `SectionOptionsReply` record are set by the application before calling **SectionOptionsDialog** and others are set by the Edition Manager in response to user selections in the dialog. The structure of a `SectionOptionsReply` record is shown in Listing 5-11.

Listing 5-11. The structure of a SectionOptionsReply record

```
struct SectionOptionsReply {
    Boolean canceled;       /* set by Edition Manager */
    Boolean changed;        /* set by Edition Manager */
    SectionHandle sectionH; /* set by the application */
    ResType action;         /* set by Edition Manager */
};
```

The fields in a `SectionOptionsReply` record for a publisher are as follows:

canceled—Set to true by the Edition Manager if the user clicks the Cancel button. If this field is set to false, the user dismissed the publisher options dialog by clicking one of the other three buttons. Examine the `action` field to determine which button was clicked.

changed—Set to true by the Edition Manager if the publisher's section record changed—selecting a different update mode causes this to happen. If this field is true, the section record for this publisher, stored as a 'sect' resource in the document containing the publisher, needs to be updated to reflect the change.

sectionH—The handle to the section record for the currently selected publisher. The kind field within the section record tells the Edition Manager whether this is the section record for a publisher or subscriber (it will be set to stPublisher for a publisher).

action—There are three possible actions that the user can request from the publisher options dialog if the operation was not canceled. This field indicates which one of these actions was requested. Each action is represented by a four-character string. The possible actions and their meanings are:

- 'cncl'—User clicked the *Cancel Publisher* button.
- 'writ'—User clicked the *Send Edition Now* button.
- '   '—User clicked the *OK* button (four blank spaces are used for the action code).

If the action code returned is 'cncl', the application should unregister the publisher from its edition, dispose of the memory used by the alias handle stored in the alias field of the section record, then dispose of the memory used for the section record itself. Use the following three lines of code to do all this:

```
myErr = UnRegisterSection( theSectionH );
DisposHandle( (**theSectionH).alias ); /* only if alias is not nil */
DisposHandle( theSectionH );
```

The application should also remove references to the publisher in any private data structures it uses to track the sections in a document.

Important ▶	Usually, you should not delete the edition file—editions can, in rare circumstances, have multiple publishers (only one of which should be active at a time). Also, your application may support a Revert command and this is easier to implement if the edition file is still around. If you do ever need to delete an edition, do so just before the application quits and use the **DeleteEditionContainerFile** routine; it takes a pointer to an FSSpec for the edition as its only parameter and returns an error code of type OSErr. **DeleteEditionContainerFile** works only if the publisher to the edition is unregistered.

If the action code returned is 'writ', the application should immediately write the current contents of the publisher to its edition container. It can do this by calling a routine such as the **DoWriteContents** routine included in Listing 5-8. If **DoWriteContents** returns an error, you should warn the user by displaying an appropriate dialog box.

If the action code returned is '   ' (four blank spaces—0x20202020), the user dismissed the publisher options dialog by clicking the *OK* button.

▶ Subscriber Options

When a user selects a subscriber within a document, the application should change the name of the Publisher Options... item in the Edit menu to Subscriber Options... and should enable the item. If the user selects this item or double-clicks the subscriber, the standard subscriber options dialog (see Figure 5-6) should be displayed. This dialog allows the user to specify whether the selected subscriber will be updated *Automatically* (whenever its edition changes) or *Manually* (only at the specific request of the user).

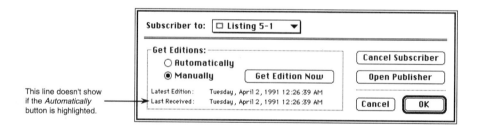

Figure 5-6. The standard subscriber options dialog

A subscriber with its update mode set to *Manually* has its contents updated only when the user clicks the *Get Edition Now* button in the subscriber options dialog.

You can display the subscriber options dialog by calling **SectionOptionsDialog**. The sole parameter to this routine is a SectionOptionsReply record. As described in the previous subsection, the sectionH field in the SectionOptionsReply record needs to be set by the application before calling **SectionOptionsDialog**; the other fields are set by the Edition Manager in response to user's selections in the dialog.

The fields in a `SectionOptionsReply` record for a subscriber are as follows:

canceled—Set to true by the Edition Manager if the user clicks the Cancel button. If this field is set to false, the user dismissed the subscriber options dialog by clicking one of the other four buttons. Examine the `action` field to determine which button was clicked.

changed—Set to true by the Edition Manager if the subscriber's section record changed—selecting a different update mode causes this to happen. If this field is true, the section record for this subscriber, stored as a `'sect'` resource in the document containing the subscriber, needs to be updated to reflect the change.

sectionH—The handle to the section record for the currently selected subscriber. The `kind` field within the section record tells the Edition Manager whether this is the section record for a publisher or subscriber (it will be set to `stSubscriber` for a subscriber).

action—Four possible actions that the user can request from the publisher options dialog if the operation was not canceled. This field indicates which one of these actions was requested. Each action is represented by a four character string. The possible actions and their meanings are as follows:

- `'cncl'`—User clicked on the *Cancel Subscriber* button.
- `'read'`—User clicked on the *Get Edition Now* button.
- `'    '`—User clicked on the *OK* button (four blank spaces are used for the `action` code).
- `'goto'`—User clicked on the *Open Publisher* button.

If the action code returned is `'cncl'`, the application should unregister the subscriber from its edition, dispose of the memory used by the alias handle stored in the `alias` field of the section record, then dispose of the memory used for the section record itself. Do not delete the information in the document that was imported from the edition—simply stop treating the information as a subscriber. Use the following three lines of code to do all this:

```
myErr = UnRegisterSection( theSectionH );
DisposHandle( (**theSectionH).alias ); /* only if alias is not nil */
DisposHandle( theSectionH );
```

The application should also remove references to the subscriber in any private data structures it uses to track the sections in a document.

If the action code returned is `'read'`, the application should immediately retrieve the current contents of the subscriber's edition container. This allows the user to force a specific subscriber to be updated as discussed earlier in this section. It can do this by calling a routine such as the **DoReadContents** routine included in Listing 5-14.

If the action code returned is `'    '` (four blank spaces—0x20202020), the user dismissed the subscriber options dialog by clicking the *OK* button.

If the action code returned is `'goto'`, the application should send an Apple event to the Finder telling it to open the document that contains the publisher for this edition. To do this, the application should first locate the edition container in question by calling **GetEditionInfo**. The function prototype for **GetEditionInfo** is as follows:

```
pascal OSErr GetEditionInfo( const SectionHandle sectionH,
                             EditionInfoRecord *editionInfo );
```

The parameters passed to **GetEditionInfo** are as follows:

sectionH—A handle to the section record for the currently selected subscriber.

editionInfo—Points to a space for an `EditionInfoRecord`. **GetEditionInfo** returns the subscriber's edition information record here.

The structure of an `EditionInfoRecord` is shown in Listing 5-12.

Listing 5-12. The structure of an EditionInfoRecord record

```
struct EditionInfoRecord {
    TimeStamp crDate;  /* date EditionContainer was created */
    TimeStamp mdDate;  /* date of last change */
    OSType fdCreator;  /* file creator */
    OSType fdType;     /* file type */
    EditionContainerSpec container;  /* the Edition */
};
```

The meanings of the fields in an `EditionInfoRecord` are as follows:

crDate—The date and time the edition was created.

mdDate—The date and time at which the edition was last updated.

fdCreator—The creator type of this edition.

fdType—The file type of this edition.

container—The `EditionContainerSpec` (explained earlier in this chapter) for this edition.

If **GetEditionInfo** cannot locate the edition file, it returns a `fnfErr` error code. This may happen if the file has been deleted or moved.

The Apple event for opening the document containing the publisher can be sent to the Finder by calling **GoToPublisherSection**, with its sole parameter pointing to the `container` field in the `EditionInfoRecord` obtained by the call to **GetEditionInfo**. The function prototype for **GoToPublisherSection** is as follows:

```
pascal OSErr GoToPublisherSection( const EditionContainerSpec
                                        *container );
```

This routine also sends a Scroll Section Apple event to the publisher after the publisher has been registered by the application containing it. This event is described in the next section.

▶ Apple Events Used by the Edition Manager

The Edition Manager defines four Apple events that each application that uses the Edition Manager must support. Some of these events are sent to the application that created an edition and others are sent to applications whose documents contain subscribers to that edition.

Applications must prepare to deal with these Apple events in the usual way—by installing high-level event handlers for them with **AEInstallEventHandler** and reacting to `kHighLevelEvent` events by calling **AEProcessAppleEvent**. Refer to Chapter 4 if this sounds mysterious.

The four Edition Manager Apple events each use the event class of `sectionEventMsgClass` (`'sect'`). The event IDs are as follows:

`'cncl'`	Cancel Section
`'read'`	Read Section
`'scrl'`	Scroll Section
`'writ'`	Write Section

Each of these Apple events passes a single parameter in the direct parameter (the keyword for which is `keyDirectObject`). The parameter is a handle to a section record and its data type is `typeSectionH`. The meaning of each of these Apple events is briefly described in Table 5-1.

Table 5-1. Apple events used by the Edition Manager and their destinations

Event Name	Event ID	Apple Event's Destination	Meaning
Cancel Section	'cncl'	Not sent at present	(provide handler for future compatibility)
Read Section	'read'	Subscriber's application	Read new information from edition
Scroll Section	'scrl'	Publisher's application	Scroll document so publiser is visible
Write Section	'writ'	Publisher' application	Write published material to edition file

When you call **AEInstallEventHandler** to install the handlers for the Edition Manager-related Apple events, the first parameter you specify should be `sectionEventMsgClass` (the event class). The second parameter (the event ID) should be set to one of the following constants:

```
sectionCancelMsgID      for the Cancel Section ('cncl') handler
sectionReadMsgID        for the Read Section ('read') handler
sectionScrollMsgID      for the Scroll Section ('scrl') handler
sectionWriteMsgID       for the Write Section ('writ') handler
```

Each Edition Manager-related Apple event deals with only one section at a time. Call **AEGetKeyPtr** to retrieve a handle to the `SectionRecord` to which the event relates.

Since it is possible that the section was unregistered after the Apple event was placed in the event queue, verify that the affected section is still registered before acting on a section referred to in the event. A section's registration status can be determined by passing its section handle as the sole parameter to **IsRegisteredSection**. If the error code returned by **IsRegisteredSection** is `notRegisteredSectionErr` (defined in the interface file Errors.h), the section is not registered and you should ignore the Apple event.

▶ Cancel Section

The System 7.0 version of the Edition Manager does not use Cancel events, but you should still provide a handler for them to ensure compatibility with future releases of system software. Handle this event just as you would handle a user clicking on the *Cancel Publisher* or *Cancel Subscriber* button in the publisher or subscriber options dialog box described earlier in this chapter. In particular, it should unregister the section, dispose of the alias record inside the section record, then dispose of the section record itself.

▶ Read Section

When a publisher updates its edition, the Edition Manager sends a Read Section event to all applications that have sections registered as subscribers to the edition and whose update mode is set to automatic. (Read Section events are never sent to a subscriber that has its update mode set to manual.) Your application should handle the Read Section event by updating a subscriber, but only if the Stop All Editions item in the Edit menu is *not* marked. To determine the item's mark character, use the following statement:

```
GetItemMark( GetMHandle( mEdit ), iStopEditions, &theMark );
```

where `mEdit` is menu ID for the Edit menu and `iStopEditions` is the Stop All Editions item number. If the character returned in the `theMark` variable (a `char`) is not `noMark`, simply exit the event handler and return `noErr`. Otherwise, respond to the Read Section event by opening the edition file for the subscriber, reading the new contents, and closing the edition file.

Opening an edition file to subscribe to its contents is slightly different from opening it to publish new contents. Instead of calling **OpenNewEdition**, call **OpenEdition**. The function prototype for **OpenEdition** is as follows:

```
pascal OSErr OpenEdition( SectionHandle subscriberSectionH,
                          EditionRefNum *refNum );
```

The parameters used by **OpenEdition** are the following:

subscriberSectionH—The handle to the section record for the sub-scriber whose data is about to be read from the edition. You obtain this handle from the direct parameter of the Read Section Apple event.

refNum—The reference number for the opened edition is returned in this variable.

Once the edition has been successfully opened, you can read its contents by calling **ReadEdition**. The function prototype for **ReadEdition** is as follows:

```
pascal OSErr ReadEdition( EditionRefNum whichEdition,
                          FormatType whichFormat,
                          void *buffPtr,
                          Size *buffLen );
```

The parameters used by **ReadEdition** are the following:

whichEdition—The refNum for the edition container returned by **OpenEdition**.

whichFormat—The format of the data to be read. To support the exchange of common data types with other applications, your application should be able to deal with both the 'TEXT' and the 'PICT' formats. The formats of the data read from an edition are the same as those read from the clipboard. Editions can contain data in more than one format, but each format must be read by a separate call to **ReadEdition**.

buffPtr—Set to a pointer to the buffer where the data being read is to be placed. The buffer must be large enough to hold the number of bytes specified by the buffLen parameter.

buffLen—Indicates the number of bytes to be read from the edition container—these bytes will be read into the buffer pointed to by buffPtr. After the read operation finishes, this variable is set by the Edition Manager to the actual number of bytes read. If the value returned is the same value that was passed to **ReadEdition**, more data is waiting to be read from the requested format and you should continue to call **ReadEdition** until all of the data has been read. All data has been read when the returned value of buffLen is smaller than the requested value.

Once you've read all of the desired formats from an edition, close it by calling **CloseEdition**. **CloseEdition** was described earlier in this chapter but the description will be repeated here because the meaning of the last parameter changes slightly when closing an edition file that has been read. The function prototype for **CloseEdition** is as follows:

```
pascal OSErr CloseEdition( EditionRefNum whichEdition,
                           Boolean successful );
```

The parameters used by **CloseEdition** are the following:

whichEdition—Set to the refNum of the open edition container.

successful—If your application was able to read the data from the edition container, set this parameter to true; otherwise, set it to false. When set to true, **CloseEdition** causes the Edition Manager to adjust the mdDate field in the subscriber's section record so that it is the same as the edition container's modification date. You should save the updated section record to the document's resource fork so that you don't get an unnecessary Read Section event the next time the section is registered.

▶ Scroll Section

The subscriber options dialog (discussed in the "Publisher and Subscriber Options" section of this chapter) provides an *Open Publisher* button that allows users to launch the application that published that edition and load the document containing the publisher. Once the publishing application has been launched, the Edition Manager sends it a Scroll Section Apple event; the application should react to it by scrolling the document so that the publisher appears in the visible portion of the document's window.

▶ Write Section

Your application should handle the Write Section event by writing a publisher to an edition, but only if the Stop All Editions item in the Edit menu is *not* marked. Use the technique described above in connection with the Read Section event to determine whether this item is marked.

If editions are not stopped and a Write Section event comes in, the receiving application should open the edition for the section with **OpenNewEdition**, write the contents of the section to it with **WriteEdition**, then close the edition with **CloseEdition**.

A Write Section event is automatically generated when you create a new publisher by calling **NewSection** or when you register an existing publisher with **RegisterSection** and the edition container does not already exist or cannot be found. In these situations, the edition container is automatically created before you receive the Write Section event.

Earlier in this chapter, you learned how to create a new publisher by explicitly creating the edition file first by calling **CreateEditionContainerFile**. When you do this, then call **NewSection** to create the new publisher, no Write Section event is generated because the edition file already exists. Thus, you have to write to the edition file immediately by calling **WriteEdition**. An alternative technique for creating a new publisher and writing it to its edition is simply to call **NewSection**—the Edition Manager will create the edition file for you and the Write Section event handler will write the publisher data to it.

Listing 5-13 shows the source code for installing handlers for all four Edition Manager-related Apple events. Listing 5-14 shows the source code for the four handlers used in the Skeleton application.

Listing 5-13. The source code for installing the Apple event handlers for Apple events used by the Edition Manager

```
/* The following routine installs the four handlers for */
/* the Apple events defined by the Edition Manager. */
void DoEditionsAEInstallation( void )
{
    /* Install the handler for Cancel Events */
    AEInstallEventHandler( sectionEventMsgClass, sectionCancelMsgID,
                           (EventHandlerProcPtr)DoCancelEdition,
                           0L, false );

    /* Install the handler for Read Events */
    AEInstallEventHandler( sectionEventMsgClass, sectionReadMsgID,
                           (EventHandlerProcPtr)DoReadEdition,
                           0L, false );

    /* Install the handler for Scroll Events */
    AEInstallEventHandler( sectionEventMsgClass, sectionScrollMsgID,
                           (EventHandlerProcPtr)DoScrollEdition,
                           0L, false );

    /* Install the handler for Write Events */
    AEInstallEventHandler( sectionEventMsgClass, sectionWriteMsgID,
                           (EventHandlerProcPtr)DoWriteEdition,
                           0L, false );

}
```

Listing 5-14. The source code for Skeleton's handlers for the Apple events used by the Edition Manager

```
/*  The following routines assume a handle to a private data
    structure has been stored in the window's refCon field.
    This private data structure has the following definition:

    typedef struct {
        FSSpec   winFSSpec;        - file specification for the document
        siHandle winsiHndl;        - handle to first sectionInfo record
                                   - (defined in Listing 5-3)
        long     winSectionID;     - the section ID
        TEHandle winTEHndl;        - handle to the TextEdit record
    } winPrivate, **winPrivateHndl;
*/


/* The following routine is called when a 'Cancel Section' event occurs */
pascal OSErr DoCancelEdition( AppleEvent *theAppleEvent, AppleEvent *reply,
                              long myRefCon )
{
    WindowPtr        wp;                 /* pointer to section's window */
    SectionHandle    mySectionHndl;
    OSErr            myErr, ignoreErr;
    DescType         typeCode;
    Size             actualSize;
    FSSpec           tempSpec;           /* FSSpec for section's edition file */
    Boolean          aliasChanged;

    SetCursor( *GetCursor( watchCursor ) ); /* wristwatch cursor */

    /* extract the section handle from the direct parameter */
    myErr = AEGetKeyPtr( theAppleEvent, keyDirectObject, typeSectionH,
                         &typeCode, (Ptr)&mySectionHndl,
                         sizeof( mySectionHndl ), &actualSize );

    if ( !myErr ) {
        /* make sure section is unregistered */
        ignoreErr = UnRegisterSection( mySectionHndl );

        /* Tip on canceling a publisher: don't delete the edition
            with DeleteEditionContainerFile right now. To support
            revert or undo, flag the section record as canceled and
            delete the edition when the file is being closed. The
            section is a publisher if (**mySectionHndl).kind is
            equal to stPublisher. */

        /* Find the window associated with this section.
            (DoFindSectionWindow scans the sectionInfo linked
            lists for each window until it finds one corresponding
            to the section record. It returns a pointer to the
            window containing the section.) */
        wp = DoFindSectionWindow( mySectionHndl );

        /* DoRemoveSectionInfo removes the sectionInfo record
            for the section from the linked list. */
```

Listing 5-14. The source code for Skeleton's handlers for the Apple events used by the Edition Manager (continued)

```
        if ( wp ) DoRemoveSectionInfo( wp, mySectionHndl );

        /* dispose of the section's alias record */
        DisposHandle( (Handle)(**mySectionHndl).alias );

        /* dispose of the section record */
        DisposHandle( (Handle)mySectionHndl );
    }
    InitCursor();        /* restore normal cursor */
    return( myErr );
}


/* The following routine is called when a 'Read Section' event occurs */
pascal OSErr DoReadEdition( AppleEvent *theAppleEvent, AppleEvent *reply,
                                      long myRefCon )
{
    WindowPtr        wp;          /* pointer to section's window */
    winPrivateHndl   myPrivHndl;  /* handle to wp's private data stash */
    SectionHandle    mySectionHndl;
    OSErr            myErr, regErr;
    DescType         typeCode;
    Size             actualSize;
    Size             myBuffLength;/* numer of chars to read */
    EditionRefNum    myEdRefNum;   /* refuNum for edition container */
    CharsHandle      tempCharsHndl;/* handle to text in TE field */
    char             theMark;   /* Stop All Editions mark character */

    myErr = noErr;   /* default response */
    /* handle event only if the Stop All Editions item is not marked */
    /* mEdit is the menu ID; iStopEditions is the item number */
    GetItemMark( GetMHandle( mEdit ), iStopEditions, &theMark );
    if ( theMark == noMark ) {

        SetCursor( *GetCursor( watchCursor ) ); /* wristwatch cursor */

        /* extract the section handle from the direct parameter */
        myErr = AEGetKeyPtr( theAppleEvent, keyDirectObject, typeSectionH,
                            &typeCode, (Ptr)&mySectionHndl,
                            sizeof( mySectionHndl ), &actualSize );

    if ( !myErr ) {
        /* is section registered? (may have been unregistered while
                event was in queue) */
            regErr = IsRegisteredSection( mySectionHndl );
            if ( !regErr ) { /* if it's registered, read it in */
                DoReadContents( mySectionHndl );
            }
        }
        InitCursor();    /* restore normal cursor */
    }
    return( myErr );
```

Listing 5-14. The source code for Skeleton's handlers for the Apple events used by the Edition Manager (continued)

```
}


/* This routine is responsible for opening, reading, and closing
    an edition file in order to extract the contents of a subscriber.
    The data that is read is put directly into the document
    that owns the subscriber whose contents are are being read. */
void DoReadContents( SectionHandle mySectionHndl )
{
    WindowPtr         wp;              /* pointer to section's window */
    winPrivateHndl    myPrivHndl;      /* handle to private data area */
    OSErr             myErr;
    Size              myBuffLength;    /* number of chars to read */
    EditionRefNum     myEdRefNum;      /* refuNum for edition container */
    CharsHandle       tempCharsHndl;   /* handle to text in TE field */

    /* open the edition file */
    myErr = OpenEdition( mySectionHndl, &myEdRefNum );

    if ( !myErr ) {  /* if it opened, keep going */
        /* make room to hold data being read */
        tempCharsHndl = (CharsHandle)NewHandle( 32000 * sizeof( char ) );
        HLock( (Handle)tempCharsHndl );

        /* read the TEXT from the edition container */
        /* (we're not expecting more than 32000 characters) */
        myBuffLength = 32000;
        myErr = ReadEdition( myEdRefNum, 'TEXT', *tempCharsHndl,
                                    &myBuffLength );

        if ( !myErr ) {

            /* Find the window associated with this section.
                (DoFindSectionWindow scans the sectionInfo linked
                lists for each window until it finds one corresponding
                to the section record. It returns a pointer to the
                window containing the section.) */
            wp = DoFindSectionWindow( mySectionHndl ); /* Find section's owner */
            myPrivHndl = (winPrivateHndl)GetWRefCon( wp );
            HLock( (Handle)myPrivHndl );

            /* stuff TEXT we just read into TE field */
            TEInsert( *tempCharsHndl, myBuffLength, (**myPrivHndl).winTEHndl );

            HUnlock( (Handle)myPrivHndl );
        }

        DisposHandle( (Handle)tempCharsHndl );

        if ( myErr ) {
            myErr = CloseEdition( myEdRefNum, false );    /* read failed */
```

Listing 5-14. The source code for Skeleton's handlers for the Apple
events used by the Edition Manager (continued)

```
        } else {
           myErr = CloseEdition( myEdRefNum, true );      /* read succeeded */
        }
    }
}


/* The following routine is called when a 'Scroll Section' event occurs */
pascal OSErr DoScrollEdition( AppleEvent *theAppleEvent, AppleEvent *reply,
                                                long myRefCon )
{
    WindowPtr             wp;                /* pointer to section's window */
    OSErr                 myErr;
    SectionHandle         mySectionHndl;
    DescType              typeCode;
    Size                  actualSize;
    ProcessSerialNumbermy SerialNum;         /* serial number for this app */
    Rect                  tempRect;          /* section's bounding rect */
    WindowPtr             wpTemp;

    SetCursor( *GetCursor( watchCursor ) ); /* wristwatch cursor */

    /* extract the section handle from the direct parameter */
    myErr = AEGetKeyPtr( theAppleEvent, keyDirectObject, typeSectionH,
                    &typeCode, (Ptr)&mySectionHndl,
                    sizeof( mySectionHndl ), &actualSize );

    if ( !myErr ) {
        /* We could have been in background or foreground when this event */
        /* was received. If we weren't even launched, Finder launched us */
        /* and we're just waking up. So, make sure we're in front of all */
        /* other applications. */
        GetCurrentProcess( &mySerialNum ); /* get serial number for this app */
        SetFrontProcess( &mySerialNum );   /* force us to front */

        /* Find the window associated with this section.
            (DoFindSectionWindow scans the sectionInfo linked
            lists for each window until it finds one corresponding
            to the section record. It returns a pointer to the
            window containing the section.) */
        wp = DoFindSectionWindow( mySectionHndl );
        if ( wp ) {
            DoForceWindowToFront( wp );/* force to front of all my windows */

            /* make this window the current grafPort */
            GetPort( &wpTemp );
            SetPort( wp );

            /* Scroll the document so that the section is visible.
                (DoShowSection is a routine that you provide.) */
            DoShowSection( wp, mySectionHndl );

            /* Draw a border around the publisher.
```

Listing 5-14. The source code for Skeleton's handlers for the Apple events used by the Edition Manager (continued)

```
                    (DrawPubBorder is a routine that you provide.) */
                DrawPubBorder( wp, mySectionHndl );
                SetPort( wpTemp );
        }
    }
    InitCursor();    /* restore normal cursor */
    return( myErr );
}


/* The following routine is called when a 'Write Section' event occurs */
pascal OSErr DoWriteEdition( AppleEvent *theAppleEvent, AppleEvent *reply,
                                            long myRefCon )
{
    WindowPtr        wp;                  /* pointer to section's window */
    winPrivateHndl   myPrivHndl;          /* handle to wp's private data stash */
    OSErr            myErr;
    Boolean          aliasChanged;
    SectionHandle    mySectionHndl;
    DescType         typeCode;
    Size             actualSize;
    TEHandle         tempTEHndl;          /* TEHandle for wp's window */
    Handle           myData;              /* publisher's contents go here */
    char             theMark;             /* Stop All Editions mark character */

    myErr = noErr;    /* default response */
    /* handle event only if the Stop All Editions item is not marked */
    /* mEdit is the menu ID; iStopEditions is the item number */
    GetItemMark( GetMHandle( mEdit ), iStopEditions, &theMark );
    if ( theMark == noMark ) {

        SetCursor( *GetCursor( watchCursor ) ); /* wristwatch cursor */

        /* extract the section handle from the direct parameter */
        myErr = AEGetKeyPtr( theAppleEvent, keyDirectObject, typeSectionH,
                            &typeCode, (Ptr)&mySectionHndl,
                            sizeof( mySectionHndl ), &actualSize );

        if ( !myErr ) {
            /* Find the window associated with this section.
                (DoFindSectionWindow scans the sectionInfo linked
                lists for each window until it finds one corresponding
                to the section record. It returns a pointer to the
                window containing the section.) */
            wp = DoFindSectionWindow( mySectionHndl );

            if ( wp ) {

                /* get handle to wp's TextEdit record */
                myPrivHndl = (winPrivateHndl)GetWRefCon( wp );
                HLock( (Handle)myPrivHndl );
```

Listing 5-14. The source code for Skeleton's handlers for the Apple events used by the Edition Manager (continued)

```
        tempTEHndl = (**myPrivHndl).winTEHndl;

        /* Get data that should be written.
            (DoGetThePublisher retrieves the data from the publisher
            and stores a handle to it in the myData variable.) */
        DoGetThePublisher( wp, mySectionHndl, &myData );
        HLock( myData );

        /* open, write, close requested edition */
        /* See Listing 5-8 for the DoWriteContents source code */
        myErr = DoWriteContents( mySectionHndl,
                                 &(**myPrivHndl).winFSSpec, myData);

        HUnlock( (Handle)myData );
        HUnlock( (Handle)myPrivHndl );
        /* free memory allocated by DoGetThePublisher() */
        DisposHandle( myData );
      }
    }
    InitCursor();    /* restore normal cursor */
  }
  return( myErr );
}
```

▶ Summary

In this chapter you learned about the publish and subscribe mechanism and examined sample source code showing how your application can support the Edition Manager. Application developers have some work to do to implement Edition Manager support, but the functionality it provides is well worth the effort! Publish and subscribe is clearly the next generation of the copy and paste capability that once seemed so novel. Soon, all System 7 customers will come to expect it, so don't let them down.

In Chapter 6, we continue our exploration of System 7 by navigating through the Communications Toolbox. Along the way, we'll provide important information that will allow all types of applications to easily communicate with other computers, even if they are not on the same local area network.

6 ▶ Communications Toolbox

Although System 7's advanced interapplication communication capabilities—provided by the PPC Toolbox, Apple Event Manager, and Edition Manager—enable you to add useful new functionality to an application, they allow your application to communicate with another application only across a local-area network. System 7 also contains a Communications Toolbox that addresses the problem of connecting Macintoshes to remote computers, such as mainframes and minicomputers, using a variety of standard protocols. The toolbox is flexible enough to handle network communications as well. The Communications Toolbox is ideal for quickly designing a terminal emulator, a general-purpose communications program, or an interactive multi-player game that requires management of one or more communications channels.

The Communications Toolbox uses three types of tools to manage different aspects of the communications environment:

- terminal emulation tools (such as VT102 and TTY)
- connection tools (such as modem, serial, and ADSP)
- file transfer tools (such as text and Xmodem)

System 7 does not include any tools for the Communications Toolbox—tools must be purchased separately from the Apple Programmers and Developers Association (see Appendix C) and installed by putting them in the Extensions folder (inside the System folder). The product that includes the tools referred to in parentheses above is called the Macintosh

Communications Tools Basic Connectivity Set. You can also purchase a Local Access Transport (LAT) connection tool and a VT320 terminal emulation tool from APDA. If you want to distribute any of these tools with your application, you need a license from Apple Software Licensing.

This chapter explores the following areas of the Communications Toolbox:

- Communications Toolbox managers
- connection tools
- terminal emulation tools
- configuring the Communications Toolbox tools

One interesting topic not covered here is how to use file transfer tools. Refer to the definitive reference for the Communications Toolbox, *Inside the Macintosh Communications Toolbox*, for information on file transfer tools. That book also covers how to write your own Communications Toolbox tools.

▶ Communications Toolbox Managers

The Communications Toolbox is made up of four managers and some utilities that implement a variety of connection-related services for applications—data communications, terminal emulations, and protocol transfers. The application program makes high-level calls to the Communications Toolbox to gain access to these services; it is not concerned about which emulations and file transfer protocols are available, which have been selected, or how they work.

The three main managers inside the Communications Toolbox are the Terminal Manager, the Connection Manager, and the File Transfer Manager. (Two other managers, the Communications Resource Manager and the Communications Toolbox Utilities, manage communications-related resources and devices.) Each of these managers encompasses the basic functions of one aspect of connectivity and its routines implement the specific protocols of that connectivity. The Terminal Manager's tools implement various terminal emulations, the Connection Manager's tools implement various data connection protocols, and the File Transfer Manager's tools implement various file transfer protocols.

Before using the Communications Toolbox, its managers must be initialized in a particular order by calling five **Init** routines. The required order is as follows:

- **InitCRM**—Initializes the Communications Resource Manager
- **InitCTBUtilities**—Initializes the Communications Toolbox utilities
- **InitTM, InitCM, InitFT** (in any order)—Initializes the Terminal Manager, Connection Manager, and File Transfer Manager

The function prototypes for these five initialization routines are as follows:

```
pascal CRMErr  InitCRM( void );
pascal CTBUErr InitCTBUtilities( void );
pascal TMErr   InitTM( void );
pascal CMErr   InitCM( void );
pascal FTErr   InitFT( void );
```

The data types CRMErr, CTBUErr, TMErr, CMErr, FTErr represent error codes and are equivalent to the data type OSErr. If either **InitCRM** or **InitCTBUtilities** returns an error, the other initialization routines must not be called, and you won't be able to use the Communications Toolbox.

Adding communications capabilities to your application using the Communications Toolbox is remarkably straightforward. The basic steps to be performed are as follows:

- When the application first starts up, initialize the Communications Toolbox and set up connection and terminal records for the default connection and terminal emulation tools. These records are used if the user tries to open a connection without first configuring the tools and are described in the "Connection Tools" and "Terminal Emulation Tools" sections.
- Modify your **WaitNextEvent** event handler so that you react to Communications Toolbox-related events properly. See the "Event Handling" section in this chapter for instructions on how to do this.
- Add menu items for selecting and configuring a connection tool, a terminal emulation tool, and a file transfer tool. These menu items are usually called Connection..., Terminal..., and File Transfer..., respectively. See the "Configuring the Communications Toolbox

Tools" section in this chapter for instructions on how to handle the selection of these items.

- Add menu items for opening a new or existing terminal emulation window and for closing a terminal emulation window. These menu items are usually called New Terminal, Open Terminal..., and Close Terminal.

- Add menu items for opening and closing a connection. These menu items are usually called Open Connection and Close Connection.

▶ Connection Tools

Connection tools manage the transport of data between the Macintosh and other computer systems. The user needs to select and configure a connection tool before a communications session can begin.

The fundamental data structure for a connection tool is the connection record. This data structure is of type ConnRecord and defines the type of connection (serial, modem, and so on) being used, which communications channels are available (data, attention, or control), whether the tool's custom menus should appear, the configuration settings for the tool, and pointers to the buffers for reading and writing the channels.

All connection tools support a data channel which is the primary channel for data exchange. They may or may not support attention and control channels which are used for specialized handshaking services.

▶ The ConnRecord Structure

The Connection Manager uses the data in a ConnRecord to manage and maintain the underlying communications channel. Your application creates this record by calling **CMNew**—it does not have to understand how to maintain the connection or be concerned about which connection the user has selected. The structure of a ConnRecord is shown in Listing 6-1.

Listing 6-1. The structure of a ConnRecord record

```
struct ConnRecord {
    short        procID;
    CMRecFlags   flags;
    CMErr        errCode;
    long         refCon;
    long         userData;
    ProcPtr      defProc;
    Ptr          config;
```

Listing 6-1. The structure of a ConnRecord record

```
        Ptr             oldConfig;
        long            asyncEOM;
        long            reserved1;
        long            reserved2;
        Ptr             cmPrivate;
        CMBuffers       bufferArray;
        CMBufferSizes   bufSizes;
        long            mluField;
        CMBufferSizes   asyncCount;
    };
```

The meanings of the fields in ConnRecord are as follows:

procID—The ID of the connection tool associated with the ConnRecord. You normally use the **CMNew** routine, described below, to put the appropriate value in this field.

flags—Reflects the general attributes of the connection tool. The Connections.h interface file defines the following constants for the bits in this field:

```
#define cmData (1<<0)          /* data channel exists */
#define cmCntl (1<<1)          /* control channel exists */
#define cmAttn (1<<2)          /* attention channel exists */
#define cmDataClean (1<<8)     /* data channel is error-free */
#define cmCntlClean (1<<9)     /* control channel is error-free */
#define cmAttnClean (1<<10)    /* attention channel is error-free */
#define cmNoMenus (1L<<16)     /* don't insert tool's custom menus */
#define cmQuiet (1L<<17)       /* don't display status/error msgs */
```

To specify more than one attribute, simply add together the constants for the desired attributes.

| Important ▶ | Only the last two bits (cmNoMenus and cmQuiet) should be set directly by your application (when it calls the **CMNew** routine). The others are set by the connection tool. By specifying cmNoMenus, the tool's custom menus are suppressed, thus preserving valuable menu bar real estate and minimizing the changes you have to make to your application to support the Communications Toolbox. |

errCode—Set by the Connection Manager to reflect the last error encountered

refCon—Can hold whatever data the application wants and is initialized by the **CMNew** routine. Use the **CMGetRefCon** and **CMSetRefCon** routines to read and write this field. **CMGetRefCon** takes a handle to a ConnRecord as its only parameter and returns a long value representing the data stored in the refCon field. **CMSetRefCon** returns nothing, but requires both a handle to a ConnRecord and the long value that is to be put into the refCon field of the ConnRecord.

userData—Can hold whatever data the application wants and is initialized by the **CMNew** routine. Use the **CMGetUserData** and **CMSetUserData** routines to read and write this field. **CMGetUserData** takes a handle to a ConnRecord as its only parameter and returns a long value representing the data stored in the userData field. **CMSetUserData** returns nothing, but requires both a handle to a ConnRecord and the long value that is to be put into the userData field of the ConnRecord.

defProc—Set by the Connection Manager

config— The Connection Manager stores here a pointer to a private data space the connection tool uses to hold its configuration information. This field should not be read or written directly. Use the **CMGetConfig** and **CMSetConfig** routines instead (described in this chapter).

oldConfig—Store a pointer to the last saved configuration for the connection tool here. Since the Connection Manager provides no routines to read or write this field, you must access it directly.

asyncEOM—If your application makes an asynchronous call to the **CMRead** routine, the cmFlagsEOM bit of this field is set if an end-of-message indicator was received before your completion routine was called.

reserved1—Reserved by Apple Computer, Inc. It should not be used by your application.

reserved2—Reserved by Apple Computer, Inc. It should not be used by your application.

cmPrivate—Set by the Connection Manager to the address of another private data space used by the connection tool

bufferArray—Set by the Connection Manager. It is an array of pointers to the buffers used by the data, control, attention, and reserved channels. Separate buffers are used for reading and writing, meaning there is a total of eight buffer pointers in the array. The Connections.h interface file defines symbolic constants to represent the array indices of the six channels your application can use (if the selected connection tool supports all six). The constants, listed in the order the buffer pointers appear in the array (the reserved channel's input and output buffer pointers appear after the attention channel's buffers), are as follows:

```
#define cmDataIn  0    /* data channel's input buffer */
#define cmDataOut 1    /* data channel's output buffer */
#define cmCntlIn  2    /* control channel's input buffer */
#define cmCntlOut 3    /* control channel's output buffer */
#define cmAttnIn  4    /* attention channel's input buffer */
#define cmAttnOut 5    /* attention channel's output buffer */
```

bufSizes—The sizes of the data buffers referred to in **bufferArray**.

mluField—A private field that should not be used by your application.

asyncCount—The number of bytes that were read or written by the last asynchronous call to **CMRead** or **CMWrite**. (Both these routines are covered later in this section.) Completion routines will be interested in accessing this information.

▶ Determining a Connection Tool's Name

Applications can convert a connection tool's name into the correct value to put in the **procID** field of a ConnRecord by calling **CMGetProcID**. Pass the tool's name as the sole parameter to **CMGetProcID** and use the returned value as the **procID**. The function prototype for **CMGetProcID** is as follows:

```
pascal short CMGetProcID( ConstStr255Param name );
```

If no connection tool is found with the specified name, **CMGetProcID** returns -1.

If you don't know the name of a tool to pass to **CMGetProcID**, obtain the name of the first connection tool installed in the system by calling the Communications Resource Manager routine **CRMGetIndToolName** with the **index** parameter set to 1.

The function prototype for **CRMGetIndToolName** is as follows:

```
pascal OSErr CRMGetIndToolName( OSType bundleType,
                                short index,
                                Str255 toolName );
```

The parameters to **CRMGetIndToolName** are as follows:

bundleType—Describes the type of tool (terminal emulation, connection, or file transfer) being requested. Use `classCM` to specify a connection tool. The possible values for this field are the following:

```
#define classCM 'cbnd'/* connection tool */
#define classFT 'fbnd'/* file transfer tool */
#define classTM 'tbnd'/* terminal emulation tool */
```

index—Indicates which tool within the class of tools (described by `bundleType`) is to have its name returned. Set this parameter to 1 to obtain the name of the first tool; keep incrementing this parameter and calling **CRMGetIndToolName** for a complete list of tool names. When the value in `index` exceeds the number of installed tools, an empty string is returned for the tool's name.

toolName—The name of the requested tool is returned as a Pascal string in the space to which this parameter points.

▶ Creating a ConnRecord

In practice, your application will implement a connection in response to the selection of an Open Connection menu item. To create a connection record (`ConnRecord`), call the **CMNew** routine. Your application passes much of the data needed to complete the `ConnRecord`, the Terminal Manager supplies the rest. The function prototype for **CMNew** is as follows:

```
pascal ConnHandle CMNew( short procID, CMRecFlags flags,
                         const CMBufferSizes desiredSizes,
                         long refCon, long userData );
```

The purposes of the parameters for **CMNew** are the following:

procID—The ID of the requested connection tool. Use **CMGetProcID** to obtain the `procID` from the tool's name. Use **CRMGetIndToolName** to determine the name of the tool. If the user has not yet selected a connection tool, use the tool whose name is returned by **CRMGetIndToolName** when you pass it an index of 1.

flags—Indicates the general attributes of the connection tool. Refer to the discussion of the **flags** field in a **ConnRecord** earlier in this section for more information.

desiredSizes—Points to an array of buffer sizes (each element is a long value). This array contains the requested sizes of the read and write buffers for each communications channel (data input, data output, control input, control output, attention input, and attention output, in that order) maintained by the connection tool. The connection tool may not provide buffers of the requested size, depending on the amount of available memory—the actual buffer sizes used are stored in the **bufSizes** field of the **ConnRecord**. Pass zeros for the requested sizes to allow the connection tool to use whatever buffer size it considers appropriate. The constants **cmDataIn**, **cmDataOut**, **cmCntlIn**, **cmCntlOut**, **cmAttnIn**, and **cmAttnOut** are the indices for the elements of this array.

refCon—Available for your application to use as needed. It is put into the **ConnRecord's** **refCon** field and thereafter should be read or changed only by calling **CMGetRefCon** and **CMSetRefCon**.

userData—Available for your application to use as needed. It is put into the **ConnRecord's** **userData** field and thereafter should be read or changed only by calling **CMGetUserData** and **CMSetUserData**.

CMNew returns a handle to the connection record if it was successfully created; otherwise, it returns **0L**.

▶ Opening a Connection

After creating a connection record, you should allow the user to configure it by calling either **CMChoose** or **CMSetConfig** (both of which are discussed at the end of this chapter) or simply use the defaults set up by **CMNew**. Once configuration has been completed, initiate a connection by calling **CMOpen**. This dials the phone (if you're using the modem connection tool) or simply opens a direct channel through the selected serial port (if you're using the serial tool). The function prototype for **CMOpen** is as follows:

```
pascal CMErr CMOpen( ConnHandle hConn, Boolean async,
                     ProcPtr completor, long timeout );
```

The parameters passed to **CMOpen** are the following:

hConn—The handle to your connection record.

async—Set to true if your application is making an asynchronous call to open the connection (this would allow your application to perform other tasks while waiting for the modem to dial, the called system to answer, and so on). Set it to false if the connection is being opened synchronously.

completor—If the async parameter is set to true, this parameter must contain the address of the completion procedure that your application wants called when the connection is completed or when **CMOpen** times out. If your application is opening the connection synchronously, set this field to 0L.

timeout—Set to the maximum number of ticks your application is willing to wait for the connection to be completed. If the connection is not completed within this period, **CMOpen** returns a cmTimeOut error. Some connection tools attempt to complete a connection more than once if the first attempt failed (because of a busy signal, line noise, and so on). If only one connection attempt is permitted, set this field to 0. Set this field to -1 if no time-out period is to be used.

Note ▶

Only call **CMOpen** if the connection is not already open or opening—use **CMStatus** (see the following section) to determine this information.

▶ Writing to the Connection

Data can be sent out over the connection by calling **CMWrite**. Only one write request at a time can be processed since queuing is not supported. The function prototype for **CMWrite** is as follows:

```
pascal CMErr CMWrite( ConnHandle hConn, Ptr theBuffer,
                      long *toWrite, CMChannel theChannel,
                      Boolean async, ProcPtr completor,
                      long timeout, CMFlags flags );
```

The purposes of the parameters passed to **CMWrite** are the following:

hConn—A handle to the connection record.

theBuffer—The address of the buffer containing the data to be written through the connection.

toWrite—Set this variable to the number of bytes in theBuffer to be written. If **CMWrite** is called synchronously, the connection tool returns here the actual number of bytes written. If the call is made asynchronously, the connection record's asyncCount field will contain the actual number of bytes that were written.

theChannel—Set to the channel to which the data should be written. Use one of the following constants (defined in Connections.h):

```
#define cmData (1<<0) /* use data channel */
#define cmCntl (1<<1) /* use control channel */
#define cmAttn (1<<2) /* use attention channel */
```

async—Set it to true if your application is making an asynchronous call to write to the connection. Set it to false if the write is being made synchronously. When writing asynchronously, your application must first verify that an earlier write command is not pending—see the discussion of the **CMStatus** routine, in this chapter.

completor—If the async parameter is set to true, this parameter must be set to the address of the completion procedure to be called when the write operation completes or when it times out. If your application is writing the data synchronously, set this field to 0L.

timeout—Set to the maximum number of ticks your application will wait for the writing to be completed. If the writing is not completed within this period, **CMWrite** returns a cmTimeOut error. If your application sets this field to 0, only one attempt to write the data is made and as many bytes as possible (not exceeding toWrite) are written on this single attempt. Set this field to -1 if no time-out period is to be used.

flags—Set this parameter to indicate whether an end-of-message indicator should be sent after each write. Some communication protocols require an end-of-message indicator to signal that the complete message has been transferred.

Important ▶

Only one asynchronous write command and one asynchronous read command can be pending at a time because there is only one buffer for outgoing data and one buffer for incoming data. Therefore, your application must check for a pending command before sending another. Calling **CMStatus** lets your application quickly determine whether a write command is already pending.

The function prototype for **CMStatus** is as follows:

```
pascal CMErr CMStatus( ConnHandle hConn,
                       CMBufferSizes sizes,
                       CMStatFlags *flags );
```

The meanings of the parameters passed to **CMStatus** are:

hConn—The handle to your connection record.

sizes—The address of a space for an array of buffer sizes. On return, **CMStatus** completes the array to indicate the amount of data waiting to be read and written for each channel. For more information on this array, refer to the description of the buffSizes field of the ConnRecord earlier in this section.

flags—This value, returned by the **CMStatus**, reflects the current status of the connection. The bit numbers of interest to programmers are defined by the following constants:

```
#define cmStatusOpening (1<<0)          /* channel is being opened */
#define cmStatusOpen (1<<1)             /* connection is currently open */
#define cmStatusClosing (1<<2)          /* channel is being closed */
#define cmStatusDataAvail (1<<3)        /* data waiting on data channel */
#define cmStatusCntlAvail (1<<4)        /* data waiting on cntl channel */
#define cmStatusAttnAvail (1<<5)        /* data waiting on attn channel */
#define cmStatusDRPend (1<<6)           /* async data read pending */
#define cmStatusDWPend (1<<7)           /* async data write pending */
#define cmStatusCRPend (1<<8)           /* async control read pending */
#define cmStatusCWPend (1<<9)           /* async control write pending */
#define cmStatusARPend (1<<10)          /* async attention read pending */
#define cmStatusAWPend (1<<11)          /* async attention write pending */
#define cmStatusBreakPend (1<<12)       /* async break is pending */
#define cmStatusListenPend (1<<13)      /* tool listening for call */
#define cmStatusIncomingCallPresent (1<<14) /* incoming call waiting */
```

▶ Reading from the Connection

The data coming in from the connection can be read by calling **CMRead**. Once read, it can be passed to the Terminal Manager for display to the user by calling **TMStream**, which is discussed later in this chapter. The read operation can be performed either synchronously or asynchronously, but only one asynchronous read can be pending at a time because there is only one input buffer for a particular channel. Call **CMStatus** to determine whether or not an asynchronous read is pending before calling **CMRead**. The function prototype for **CMRead** is as follows:

```
pascal CMErr CMRead( ConnHandle hConn, Ptr theBuffer,
                     long *toRead, CMChannel theChannel,
                     Boolean async, ProcPtr completor,
                     long timeout, CMFlags *flags );
```

The parameters passed to **CMRead** are as follows:

hConn—The handle to your connection record.

theBuffer—The address of the buffer into which the data being read should be placed.

toRead—The number of bytes that should be read into **theBuffer**. If **CMRead** is being called synchronously, the connection tool returns here the actual number of bytes read. If the call is made asynchronously, the connection record's **asyncCount** field will contain the actual number of bytes that were read.

theChannel—The channel from which the data should be read. Use one of the following constants to specify the channel:

```
#define cmData (1<<0)        /* use data channel */
#define cmCntl (1<<1)        /* use control channel */
#define cmAttn (1<<2)        /* use attention channel */
```

async—Set to true if your application is making an asynchronous call to read data from the connection. Set this parameter to false if the read is being made synchronously. When reading asynchronously, your application must first verify that an earlier read command is not pending—see the discussion of the **CMStatus** routine, in this chapter.

completor—If the async parameter is set to true, this parameter *must* be set to the address of the completion procedure to be called when the read is completed or when it times out. If your application is reading the data synchronously, set this field to 0L.

timeout—Set to the maximum number of ticks your application will wait for the reading to be completed. If the reading is not completed within this period, **CMRead** returns a cmTimeOut error. If your application sets this field to 0, only one attempt to read the data is made and as many bytes as possible (not exceeding toRead) are read on this single attempt. Set this field to -1 if no time-out period is to be used.

flags—Set to the address of your end-of-message flag variable. If you call **CMRead** synchronously, it sets the cmFlagsEOM bit of this variable if an end-of-message indicator was received. If called asynchronously, the cmFlagsEOM bit of the asyncEOM field of the ConnRecord is set if an end-of-message indicator was received.

▶ Closing and Disposing of the Connection

When no longer needed, an active connection should be closed by calling **CMClose**. An application normally does this when the user selects a Close Connection menu item. Like many other Connection Manager calls, **CMClose** can be made synchronously or asynchronously. If the call is being made asynchronously, call **CMStatus** first to verify that the connection is open or opening. The function prototype for **CMClose** is as follows:

```
pascal CMErr CMClose( ConnHandle hConn, Boolean async,
                      ProcPtr completor, long timeout,
                      Boolean now );
```

The parameters for **CMClose** are the following:

hConn—The handle to the ConnRecord for the connection being closed.

async—True if the close operation should be performed asynchronously. Set it to false to close synchronously.

completor—set to the address of the procedure that should be called once an asynchronous close has completed. Set it to 0L if closing synchronously.

`timeout`—Set to the maximum number of ticks that your application will wait for the close operation to be completed. If the close operation does not complete within this period, **CMClose** returns a cmTimeOut error. If this field is set to 0, the connection tool makes only one attempt to close the connection. Set this field to -1 if no time-out period is to be used.

`now`—Set to false if the connection should be closed *after* all pending read/write operations have completed. To force the connection to be closed immediately, set it to true.

When the connection record is no longer needed, the memory it uses should be released by calling **CMDispose**. The sole parameter to **CMDispose** is a handle to the affected ConnRecord. The function prototype for **CMDispose** is as follows:

```
pascal void CMDispose( ConnHandle hConn );
```

Note ▶	Just because a connection has been closed doesn't mean its connection record is no longer needed. The user may want to quickly reestablish the connection using the same settings as before, for example. As a result, you may want to dispose of the connection record only when your application is quitting.

▶ Terminal Emulation Tools

Terminal emulation tools are used to manage the display of information on a "screen" that appears in a window. These tools emulate standard terminals that are commonly used with systems with which the Macintosh might communicate—a DEC VT102 terminal or a TeleType, for example.

▶ The TermRecord Structure

The fundamental data structure for a terminal emulation tool is the terminal record. This data structure, shown in Listing 6-2, is of type `TermRecord` and defines which type of terminal emulation tool is being used, whether the tool's custom menus should appear in the menu bar, and the configuration settings for the tool.

The Terminal Manager uses the data in a `TermRecord` to manage all aspects of the terminal emulation. Your application creates this record with the **TMNew** routine—it does not have to understand how the terminal emulation works or which emulation the user has selected.

Listing 6-2. The structure of a TermRecord record

```
struct TermRecord {
    short          procID;
    TMFlags        flags;
    TMErr          errCode;
    long           refCon;
    long           userData;
    ProcPtr        defProc;
    Ptr            config;
    Ptr            oldConfig;
    ProcPtr        environsProc;
    long           reserved1;
    long           reserved2;
    Ptr            tmPrivate;
    ProcPtr        sendProc;
    ProcPtr        breakProc;
    ProcPtr        cacheProc;
    ProcPtr        clikLoop;
    WindowPtr      owner;
    Rect           termRect;
    Rect           viewRect;
    Rect           visRect;
    long           lastIdle;
    TMSelection    selection;
    TMSelTypes     selType;
    long           mluField;
};
```

The fields in `TermRecord` are as follows:

procID—The ID of the terminal emulation tool associated with the `TermRecord`. You normally use the **TMNew** routine described in this chapter to put the appropriate value in this field.

flags—Reflects the general attributes of the terminal emulation tool. The Terminals.h interface file defines the following constants for the bits in this field:

```
#define tmInvisible (1<<0)          /* don't display emulation */
#define tmSaveBeforeClear (1<<1)    /* cache screen before clear */
#define tmNoMenus (1<<2)            /* don't insert tool's own menu */
#define tmAutoScroll (1<<3)         /* scroll while selecting */
```

To specify more than one attribute, simply add the constants for the desired attributes together. By specifying tmNoMenus, the tool's custom menus are suppressed, thus preserving valuable menu bar real estate and minimizing the changes you must make to your application to support the Communications Toolbox.

You normally use the **TMNew** routine, described in this chapter, to put the appropriate value in this field.

errCode—Not currently used, but reserved.

refCon—Can hold whatever information the application wants and is initialized by the **TMNew** routine. Use the **TMGetRefCon** and **TMSetRefCon** routines to read and write this field. **TMGetRefCon** takes a handle to a TermRecord as its only parameter and returns a long value representing the data stored in the TermRecord's refCon field. **TMSetRefCon** returns nothing, but requires both a handle to a TermRecord and the long value that is to be put into the refCon field of the TermRecord.

userData—Can hold whatever information the application wants and is initialized by the **TMNew** routine. Use the **TMGetUserData** and **TMSetUserData** routines to read and write this field. **TMGetUserData** takes a handle to a TermRecord as its only parameter and returns a long value representing the data stored in the TermRecord's userData field. **TMSetUserData** returns nothing, but requires both a handle to a TermRecord and the long value that is to be put into the userData field of the TermRecord.

defProc—Set and maintained by the Terminal Manager. Your application should not touch it.

config—The Terminal Manager stores a pointer here to the private data space the terminal emulation tool uses to hold its configuration information. This field should not be read or written directly. Use the **TMGetConfig** and **TMSetConfig** routines instead (they are described in this chapter).

oldConfig—Store a pointer to the last saved configuration for the terminal emulation tool here. Since the Terminal Manager provides no routines to read or write this field, you must set and read its contents directly.

environsProc—Set by the Terminal Manager to the address of a procedure within your application that the terminal emulation tool calls to learn about the connection environment. This pointer is set up when you call **TMNew** to create a `TermRecord`. See the Required Procedures for Terminal Emulation Tools subsection later in this section for instructions on how to write an `environsProc`.

reserved1—Reserved by Apple Computer, Inc. It should not be used by your application.

reserved2—Reserved by Apple Computer, Inc. It should not be used by your application.

tmPrivate—Set by the Terminal Manager to point to another private data space used by the terminal emulation tool.

sendProc—Set by the Terminal Manager to the address of a procedure within your application that the terminal emulation tool calls when it needs to send data. This pointer is set up when you call **TMNew** to create a `TermRecord`. See the "Required Procedures for Terminal Emulation Tools" subsection later in this section for instructions on how to write a `sendProc`.

breakProc—Set by the Terminal Manager to the address of a procedure within your application that the terminal emulation tool calls when it needs to send a break signal. See the "Required Procedures for Terminal Emulation Tools" subsection later in this section for more instructions on how to write a `breakProc`.

cacheProc—Set by the Terminal Manager to the address of a procedure within your application that the terminal emulation tool calls to save lines of text that are about to scroll off the top of the emulation screen. See the "Optional Terminal Emulation Tool Procedures" subsection later in this section for instructions on how to write a `cacheProc`.

clikLoop—Set by the Terminal Manager to the address of a procedure within your application that the terminal emulation tool calls when the user clicks the mouse in the terminal window. See the "Optional Terminal Emulation Tool Procedures" subsection later in this section for more instructions on how to write a `clikLoop`.

owner—The address of the `grafPort` for the window with which the terminal emulation tool is associated.

termRect—The `portRect` of the window with which the terminal emulation screen is associated (adjusted to exclude the scroll bar rectangles).

viewRect—The rectangle that surrounds the terminal emulation screen itself.

visRect—While this field is of type `Rect`, its contents are not a standard QuickDraw rectangle. Instead, the fields represent the first row, first column, last row, and last column in the terminal emulation window that are currently visible. The window itself may be resized, but the emulated screen represented by `visRect` is often a fixed size, leaving some portions of the emulated screen no longer visible. Columns and rows are numbered starting with 1, not 0. This field is maintained by the Connection Manager.

lastIdle—Holds the time, in ticks, when the terminal emulation tool's `idleProc` was last called. Call **TMIdle** once for each active terminal emulation each time through your application's main event loop so that the terminal emulation tool has the opportunity to perform idling tasks (such as blinking the cursor). **TMIdle** returns nothing and takes a handle to the `TermRecord` for which it is to perform idle processing.

selection—Either a rectangle or a region handle describing the data within the terminal emulation window that the user has selected. Several selection methods are supported (see the description of the `selType` field)—`Selection` contains a region handle when the `selType` is `selGraphicsLasso`. For the other methods, `selection` contains a rectangle whose coordinates describe row and column positions on a text terminal or pixel coordinates on a graphics terminal.

selType—Terminal emulation tools support four different selection methods but only one can be used at a time. These methods are represented by the following constants:

```
#define selTextNormal (1<<0)      /* standard TextEdit selection */
#define selTextBoxed (1<<1)       /* rectangular selection */
#define selGraphicsMarquee (1<<2) /* marquee selection */
#define selGraphicsLasso (1<<3)   /* lasso selection */
```

mluField—This field is private and should be ignored by your application.

▶ The TermDataBlock Structure

The Terminal Manager uses another important data structure, called a `TermDataBlock`, as its conduit for sharing the contents of a terminal emulation window with your application. The `TermDataBlock` contains a flag describing the type of emulation in effect (text or graphics) and a handle to the data it uses to update the terminal emulation window. Listing 6-3 presents the definition of the `TermDataBlock` structure.

Listing 6-3. The structure of the TermDataBlock record

```
struct TermDataBlock {
    TMTermTypes   flags;
    Handle        theData;
    Handle        auxData;
    long          reserved;
};
```

The fields in `TermDataBlock` are as follows:

flags—Indicates whether the terminal being emulated is a text or a graphics terminal. Use the constants defined in Terminals.h when setting or comparing this field:

```
#define tmTextTerminal (1<<0)       /* text terminal */
#define tmGraphicsTerminal (1<<1)   /* graphics terminal */
```

theData—A handle to the data which defines the emulated terminal's screen display. If `flags` is set to `tmTextTerminal`, `theData` is a handle to text; if `flags` is set to `tmGraphicsTerminal`, `theData` is a handle to a QuickDraw picture.

The remaining two fields, `auxData` and `reserved`, are not currently used and are reserved. Your application should not use them.

▶ Determining a Terminal Emulation Tool's Name

Applications can convert a terminal emulation tool's name into the correct value to put in the `procID` field of a `TermRecord` by calling **TMGetProcID**.

Pass the tool's name as the sole parameter to **TMGetProcID** and use the returned value as the procID. The function prototype for **TMGetProcID** is as follows:

```
pascal short TMGetProcID( ConstStr255Param name );
```

If no terminal emulation tool is found with the specified name, **TMGetProcID** returns -1.

If you don't know the name of a tool to pass to **TMGetProcID**, obtain the name of the first terminal emulation tool installed on the user's system by calling the Communications Resource Manager routine **CRMGetIndToolName** with the index parameter set to 1. Other tool names can be obtained by incrementing index and calling **CRMGetIndToolName**— see the Connection Tools section for information on **CRMGetIndToolName**.

▶ Caring for the Environment

A terminal emulation tool occasionally needs to know about the communications channel it is working with, so your application must provide a procedure, called an environsProc, that the tool can call to learn about the characteristics of the channel. The terminal emulation tool requires information be returned in the form of a ConnEnvironRec record shown in Listing 6-4.

Listing 6-4. The structure of the ConnEnvironRec record

```
struct ConnEnvironRec {
          short              version;
          long               baudRate;
          short              dataBits;
          CMChannel          channels;
          Boolean            swFlowControl;
          Boolean            hwFlowControl;
          CMFlags            flags;
};
```

The fields in ConnEnvironRec are as follows:

version—The version of the data structure. Under System 7, this equals curConnEnvRecVers (defined in Connections.h).

baudRate—The current baud rate being used by the selected connection tool.

dataBits—The number of significant bits per byte that are being used by the selected connection tool.

channels—A bit pattern indicating which channels are available. The constants defined in the Connections.h interface file can be used to interpret the contents of this field:

```
#define cmData     (1<<0)     /* data channel exists */
#define cmCntl     (1<<1)     /* control channel exists */
#define cmAttn     (1<<2)     /* attention channel exists */
#define cmDataClean (1<<8)    /* data channel is error-free */
#define cmCntlClean (1<<9)    /* control channel is error-free */
#define cmAttnClean (1<<10)   /* attention channel is error-free */
```

swFlowControl—Set to true if some form of software flow control (such as the Control-S/Control-Q start-stop protocol) is being used.

hwFlowControl—Set to true if some form of hardware flow control is being used.

flags—If the connection tool needs an end-of-message flag at the end of each message, set the cmFlagsEOM bit of this field.

In the next section, you will see how to write an environsProc that returns a completed ConnEnvironRec when the Terminal Manager calls it.

▶ Required Procedures for Terminal Emulation Tools

Your application must provide certain procedures—such as sending data through the connection, sending break signals, and so on—that the terminal emulation tools call to perform actions that are not implemented by the terminal emulation tools themselves. The procedures you provide will often call Connection Manager routines to perform the required action, but this is not a requirement.

Writing an environsProc

The first of the required routines provides the terminal emulation tool with an updated ConnEnvironRec (described in the "Caring for the Environment" subsection). Known as an environsProc, its function prototype is as follows:

```
pascal CMErr yourEnvironsProc( long refCon,
                      ConnEnvironRecPtr theEnvPtr );
```

The parameters passed to `yourEnvironsProc` are as follows:

refCon—The value stored in the `refCon` field of the `TermRecord` for the terminal emulation tool that called `yourEnvironsProc`.

theEnvPtr—A pointer to the space for a `ConnEnvironRec`. Your procedure should return the environment information in this space.

yourEnvironsProc—Should return an error code for any error that occurred while getting the environment, or `noErr` if no error occurred.

If your application is using a connection tool, an appropriate `ConnEnvironRec` can be obtained by calling **CMGetConnEnvirons** (pass it a handle to the connection record and a pointer to the space for the `ConnEnvironRec`). This is the technique used in Listing 6-5. If your application is maintaining a connection without using the services of the Connection Manager, it must fill in the fields of the `ConnEnvironRec` on its own.

Listing 6-5. Minimalist implementation of yourEnvironsProc

```
/* The following routine is responsible for determining the current */
/* connection environment and returning it via "theEnvironsPtr". This */
/* routine is called by terminal emulation tools. */
pascal CMErr yourEnvironsProc(long refCon, ConnEnvironRecPtr theEnvPtr)
{
    /* We're using the Connection Manager to manage our */
    /* connection, so let it figure out the environment. */
    return(CMGetConnEnvirons(gConnRecHndl, theEnvironsPtr));
}
```

Writing a sendProc

Your application must provide a procedure that the terminal emulation tool calls when it needs to send out data. In most cases, your procedure will call a Connection Manager routine (**CMWrite**), but other processing of the data could be performed as well. Known as a `sendProc`, its function prototype is as follows:

```
pascal long yourSendProc( Ptr buffPtr, long howMany,
                          long refCon, CMFlags flags );
```

The parameters passed to yourSendProc are as follows:

buffPtr—The address of a buffer containing the data to be sent.

howMany—The number of bytes in the buffer that should be sent.

refCon—The value of the refCon field of the TermRecord for the terminal emulation tool that called yourSendProc.

flags—Indicates whether the connection tool should send an end-of-message indicator—some communication protocols require an end-of-message indicator and others do not. If your application uses the Connection Manager to maintain the connection, simply pass the value in this parameter along to the Connection Manager by putting the value of this parameter into the flags parameter passed to **CMWrite**.

yourSendProc—Returns a long value describing how many characters were actually sent.

The easiest way to implement a sendProc is shown in Listing 6-6. This procedure simply calls the Connection Manager's **CMWrite** routine.

Listing 6-6. Minimalist implementation of yourSendProc

```
/* The following routine is called by the terminal emulation tool when */
/* it wants to send data out. We're doing no filtering, so just pass */
/* the buck to the connection tool. */
pascal long yourSendProc(Ptr buffPtr, long howMany, long refCon,
                         CMFlags flags)
{
    OSErr            myErr;

    if (gConnRecHndl) {      /* only send if there's a connection record */
        /* make the Connection Manager do the work */
        myErr = CMWrite(gConnRecHndl, buffPtr, &howMany, cmData, false, nil,
                        15, flags);
        if (!myErr) { howMany = 0; } /* if error, claim nothing was sent */
    } else {
        howMany = 0;   /* no connection record, so nothing sent */
    }
    return(howMany); /* tell caller how many we really sent */
}
```

Writing a breakProc

If the terminal emulation tool needs to send a modem break signal, instead of data, it calls a different procedure provided by your application. Known as a breakProc, its function prototype is as follows:

```
pascal void yourBreakProc( long duration, long refCon );
```

The parameters passed to yourBreakProc are as follows:

duration—The duration of the break signal, in ticks.

refCon—The value of the refCon field of the TermRecord for the terminal emulation tool that called yourBreakProc.

The easiest way to implement yourBreakProc is to call the Connection Manager's **CMBreak** routine, as shown in Listing 6-7. The function prototype for **CMBreak** is as follows:

```
pascal void CMBreak( ConnHandle hConn, long duration,
                     Boolean async, ProcPtr completor );
```

The parameters passed to **CMBreak** are as follows:

hConn—A handle to your connection record.

duration—The duration of the break signal, in ticks. Store here the value of the duration parameter passed to the breakProc.

async—True if the call to **CMBreak** is to be made asynchronously. Set to false if the call is to be made synchronously.

completor—Set this parameter to the address of your completion routine if the call to **CMBreak** is being made asynchronously. It will be called once the break signal has been sent. If the call is being made synchronously, set this parameter to 0L.

Listing 6-7. Minimalist implementation of yourBreakProc

```
/* The following routine is responsible for sending a 'break' that */
/* lasts for 'duration' ticks through the connection. Since our */
/* connection is being managed by the Connection Manager, pass the */
/* buck to it.... */
pascal void yourBreakProc(long duration, long refCon)
{
    /* Send it synchronously, so no completion routine will be needed. */
    CMBreak(gConnRecHndl, duration, false, 0L);
}
```

▶ Optional Procedures for Terminal Emulation Tools

You can add two optional terminal emulation tool procedures, a `cacheProc` and a `clikLoopProc`, to enhance your application. These procedures enable you to manage the storage and selection of lines of data that scroll off the top of a terminal emulation screen.

Writing a cacheProc

The first optional procedure is called by a terminal emulation tool just before a line scrolls off the top of the emulated screen. By providing an appropriate procedure, your application can easily cache these lines (perhaps by saving them to disk) and implement a scroll-back buffer. The function prototype of this `cacheProc` is as follows:

```
pascal long yourCacheProc( long refCon,
                        TermDataBlock *tdbPtr );
```

The parameters passed to `yourCacheProc` are as follows:

refCon—The value of the `refCon` field of the `TermRecord` for the terminal emulation tool that called `yourCacheProc`.

tdbPtr—A pointer to a `TermDataBlock` record. The `theData` field of the `TermDataBlock` contains a handle to the data that should be cached and is owned by the terminal emulation tool—make a copy of it (using **HandToHand**) if you need to retain a copy for your own use. Examine the `flags` field in the `TermDataBlock` to determine whether `theData` is a handle to text or to a QuickDraw picture.

Your cache procedure should return an appropriate error code, or `tmNoErr` if no error occurred. The sample source code in this chapter does not support caching. See *Inside the Macintosh Communications Toolbox* for more information on writing `cacheProc` procedures.

Writing a clikLoop

If your application intends to allow users to select text from the emulation screen or the scroll-back buffer and copy it to the clipboard, you need to provide a `clikLoop` procedure.

If the target window for a `mouseDown` event is a terminal emulation window, your application should call **TMClick** which, in turn, calls the procedure specified in the `clikLoop` field of the `TermRecord`. The function prototype for **TMClick** is as follows:

```
pascal void TMClick( TermHandle hTerm,
                        const EventRecord *theEvent );
```

The purposes of the parameters to **TMClick** are the following:

hTerm—The handle to your terminal record.

theEvent—A pointer to the event record describing the `mouseDown` event.

TMClick repeatedly calls the procedure specified in the `clikLoop` field while the mouse is held down. When called, your procedure receives the value of the `refCon` field of the `TermRecord` for the terminal emulation tool that called it. The function prototype for this procedure is as follows:

```
Boolean yourClickLoop( long refCon );
```

`yourClickLoop` should return true if the mouse was clicked within the cached region and false if the mouse was clicked outside of the cached region. The cached region is the area of the screen maintained by the `yourCache` procedure to support the scroll-back feature.

Since the sample source code in this chapter doesn't support caching and doesn't allow text on the emulated screen to be copied to the clipboard, it has no need for a `clikLoop` procedure. See *Inside the Macintosh Communications Toolbox* for more information on writing a `clikLoop` procedure.

▶ Creating a TermRecord

In practice, your application will implement a terminal emulation in response to the selection of an Open Terminal or New Terminal menu item. It should first open a standard window which acts as the terminal emulation screen and then use **SetPort** to ensure it is the active **grafPort**. Provide a name for the window that identifies it as a terminal emulation screen.

To create a terminal record (`TermRecord`) and call the **TMNew** routine. Your application passes much of the data needed to complete the

TermRecord, the Terminal Manager supplies the rest. The function prototype for **TMNew** is as follows:

```
pascal TermHandle TMNew( const Rect *termRect,
                         const Rect *viewRect,
                         TMFlags flags, short procID,
                         WindowPtr owner, ProcPtr sendProc,
                         ProcPtr cacheProc,
                         ProcPtr breakProc, ProcPtr clikLoop,
                         ProcPtr environsProc, long refCon,
                         long userData );
```

The parameters passed to **TMNew** are the following:

termRect—Set this parameter to the rectangle that bounds the terminal emulation region.

viewRect—Set this parameter to the rectangle within the termRect
that bounds the area in which the terminal emulation tool can write.
This parameter may be changed later by the terminal emulation tool.

flags—The general attributes of the terminal emulation tool. The
Terminals.h interface file defines the following constants for the bits of
this parameter:

```
#define tmInvisible (1<<0)        /* don't display emulation */
#define tmSaveBeforeClear (1<<1) /* cache screen before clear */
#define tmNoMenus (1<<2)          /* don't insert tool's own menu */
#define tmAutoScroll (1<<3)       /* scroll while selecting */
```

To specify more than one attribute, simply add the constants for the
desired attributes together. By specifying tmNoMenus, the tool's menus are
suppressed.

procID—The ID of the requested terminal emulation tool. Use
TMGetProcID to obtain the procID from the tool's name. Use
CRMGetIndToolName to determine the name of the tool. If the user has
not yet selected a terminal emulation tool, use the tool whose name is
returned by **CRMGetIndToolName** when you pass it an index of 1.

owner—A pointer to the window record for the window in which the
terminal emulation is to appear. If tmInvisible attribute was not
specified in the flags field, the terminal emulation tool assumes complete control over the window. See the "Event Handling" section in

this chapter for information on how to handle events that relate to a terminal emulation window.

sendProc—The address of your SendProc.

cacheProc—The address of your CacheProc. If your application is not providing a cacheProc procedure, pass 0L instead.

breakProc— The address of your BreakProc.

clikLoop—The address of your ClikLoop. If your application is not providing a clikLoop procedure, pass 0L instead.

environsProc—The address of your EnvironsProc.

refCon—Available for your application to use as needed. The value stored here is put into the TermRecord's refCon field where it can be read or set by calling **TMGetRefCon** and **TMSetRefCon**.

userData—Available for your application to use as needed. The value stored here is put into the TermRecord's userData field where it can be read or set by calling **TMGetUserData** and **TMSetUserData**.

TMNew returns a handle to the terminal record if it was able to successfully create one; otherwise, it returns 0L.

| Note ▶ |

After calling **TMNew**, it's convenient to store a unique constant in the windowKind field of the window record associated with the terminal. (Use (WindowPeek)wp->windowKind to access this field.) This provides an easy way for the application to determine whether the window is one that the Communications Toolbox knows about—it needs to know this information when processing events retrieved by **WaitNextEvent**. See the "Event Handling" section later in this chapter for more information.

▶ Writing Data to the Terminal

Sending text data to the terminal's screen requires only a simple call to **TMStream**. This data typically comes from the computer to which the application is connected via the Connection Manager. The function prototype for **TMStream** is as follows:

```
pascal long TMStream( TermHandle hTerm, void *theBuffer,
                      long theLength, CMFlags flags );
```

The purposes of the parameters for **TMStream** are the following:

hTerm—The handle to the `TermRecord` for the terminal to which the data is being written.

theBuffer—The address of the buffer containing the data to be written to the terminal's screen.

theLength—The number of bytes to be written from `theBuffer`

flags—Set the `cmFlagsEOM` bit of this parameter if the data stream includes an end-of-message indicator. If you're streaming data received by calling the **CMRead** routine, set this parameter to the value returned in the `flags` variable passed to **CMRead**.

TMStream returns the number of bytes that were actually written to the terminal.

Graphics data can be written on the terminal's screen by calling **TMPaint**. The function prototype for **TMPaint** is as follows:

```
pascal void TMPaint( TermHandle hTerm,
                     const TermDataBlock *theTermData,
                     const Rect *theRect );
```

The parameters for **TMPaint** are the following:

hTerm—A handle to the `TermRecord` for the terminal to which the data is being written.

theTermData—The address of the `TermDataBlock` that defines the graphics data to be painted. The graphics data should be held in a handle allocated on the heap and the handle should be put into the `theData` field of the `TermDataBlock` before calling **TMPaint**.

theRect—The rectangle in which `theTermData` should be drawn. Specify this rectangle in the local coordinates of the terminal emulation window.

▶ Reading Data from the Terminal

If the user has selected a range of data on the emulated terminal's screen, your application can obtain a copy of the data by calling **TMGetSelect**. The function prototype for **TMGetSelect** is as follows:

```
pascal long TMGetSelect( TermHandle hTerm, Handle theData,
                         ResType *theType );
```

The parameters passed to **TMGetSelect** are the following:

hTerm—A handle to the `TermRecord` for the terminal that contains the data being retrieved.

theData—Pass a handle to a block of size 0 in this parameter. The terminal emulation tool resizes the handle before putting a copy of the selected data into it. Your application is responsible for disposing of the handle when it is no longer needed.

theType—On return, this variable contains the data type for the selection—`'TEXT'` for text or `'PICT'` for a QuickDraw picture.

TMGetSelect returns the number of bytes retrieved—this will be 0 if there was no selection range in the terminal window. When the call completes, you can use `theData` and `theType` to put the returned information on the clipboard (by calling **PutScrap**).

If your application needs to obtain a specific line of text but the line is not selected, the application can retrieve the line by calling **TMGetLine**. The function prototype for **TMGetLine** is as follows:

```
pascal void TMGetLine( TermHandle hTerm, short lineNo,
                        TermDataBlock *theTermData );
```

The purposes of the parameters passed to **TMGetLine** are the following:

hTerm—A handle to the `TermRecord` for the terminal containing the line being retrieved.

lineNo—The line number that your application wants to retrieve from the emulation buffer. Lines are numbered starting at 1.

theTermData—The address of a `TermDataBlock` record that is to hold the retrieved line. The `theData` field of the `TermDataBlock` should be a handle to a block of size 0 that the application owns. The terminal emulation tool resizes the handle before putting the contents of the line into it.

▶ Disposing of the Terminal Emulation

When the terminal emulation is no longer needed—perhaps because the user selected a Close Terminal menu item or clicked in the window's close box—the terminal record and its associated data structures need to be disposed. To do this, call **TMDispose**, which has the following function prototype:

```
pascal void TMDispose( TermHandle hTerm );
```

The hTerm parameter is a handle to the TermRecord of the terminal you're disposing.

▶ Event Handling

Some Communications Toolbox managers may, from time-to-time, display private status windows or dialog boxes on the screen. (The window used for the emulation screen is not considered private.) The Communications Toolbox provides routines you must use to process events that relate to these windows: **CMEvent** (for Connection Manager windows) and **TMEvent** (for Terminal Manager windows). (There is also a similar routine for File Transfer windows.) The four window-related events you have to handle with these routines are as follows:

- a mouseDown event in the menu bar when the front window (returned by **FrontWindow**) is a private Communications Toolbox window

- a keyDown or autoKey event when the front window (returned by **FrontWindow**) is a private Communications Toolbox window

- an updateEvt when the message field of the event record contains a pointer to a private Communications Toolbox window

- an activateEvt when the message field of the event record contains a pointer to a private Communications Toolbox window

To determine if one of these window-related events relates to a private Communications Toolbox window, first use **GetWRefCon** to obtain the value stored in the window's refCon field. If this value is a handle to an active TermRecord or ConnRecord (or file transfer record), it is a private window and you should call **TMEvent** or **CMEvent**, as the case may be, to handle the event. You will have to maintain a list of handles to active terminal records and connection records to determine whether the window is owned by the Communications Toolbox.

The function prototypes for **TMEvent** and **CMEvent** are as follows:

```
pascal void TMEvent( TermHandle hTerm,
                         const EventRecord *theEvent );

pascal void CMEvent( ConnHandle hConn,
                         const EventRecord *theEvent );
```

The first parameter passed to these routines is a handle to a `TermRecord` or a `ConnRecord`. The second parameter is the address of the event record.

If the window associated with one of the four window-related events just described is *not* a private Communications Toolbox window, but it is a terminal emulation window (one you passed as a parameter to the **TMNew** routine), there are other Communications Toolbox routines you must call to handle the event properly. These are covered in separate subsections of this chapter. There are also special routines to call for handling suspend and resume events.

There are two common methods for determining whether a window is a terminal emulation window. One method is to maintain a list of the windows you've passed to **TMNew** and check to see whether the window in which you're interested is in the list. The other method, mentioned previously in the discussion of **TMNew**, is to store a unique value in the `windowKind` field of the window record after calling **TMNew**. If you use this method, you simply have to check whether the `windowKind` field of the window in which you are interested contains this value.

▶ Activate Events

For `activateEvt` events, call **TMActivate** with a handle to the `TermRecord` associated with the window and a Boolean set to true if the window is being activated or false if it is being deactivated. Also call **CMActivate** for the connection record you're using to handle data transmission to and from the terminal.

The function prototypes for these routines are as follows:

```
pascal void TMActivate( TermHandle hTerm,
                           Boolean activate );

pascal void CMActivate( ConnHandle hConn,
                           Boolean activate );
```

244 Chapter 6 Communications Toolbox

▶ Update Events

For updateEvt events, call **BeginUpdate**, **TMUpdate**, and then **EndUpdate**. For **TMUpdate**, pass a handle to the TermRecord being affected along with a handle to the region to be updated. The function prototype for **TMUpdate** is as follows:

```
pascal void TMUpdate( TermHandle hTerm, RgnHandle visRgn );
```

▶ Keyboard Events

For keyDown and autoKey events, call the **TMKey** routine. It requires a handle to the TermRecord being affected and a pointer to the event record describing the event.

The function prototype for **TMKey** is as follows:

```
pascal void TMKey( TermHandle hTerm,
                   const EventRecord *theEvent );
```

▶ Mouse-Down Events

For mouseDown events in the content region of a terminal emulation window, call **TMClick** with a handle to the TermRecord affected and a pointer to the event record. The function prototype for **TMClick** is as follows:

```
pascal void TMClick( TermHandle hTerm,
                     const EventRecord *theEvent );
```

For mouseDown events in the grow box area of a terminal emulation window, first call **GrowWindow** and **SizeWindow** as you would when resizing a standard window. Then call **TMResize** with a handle to the TermRecord affected and the address of a rectangle describing the dimensions of the new terminal rectangle (this is usually set to the portRect of the resized window). The function prototype for **TMResize** is as follows:

```
pascal void TMResize( TermHandle hTerm,
                      const Rect *newViewRect );
```

▶ Suspend/Resume Events

For `osEvt` events caused by suspend or resume operations, call the **TMResume** routine once for each active terminal emulation session and the **CMResume** routine once for each active connection. The function prototype these routines are as follows:

```
pascal void TMResume( TermHandle hTerm, Boolean resume );
pascal void CMResume( ConnHandle hConn, Boolean resume );
```

The first parameter in each routine is a handle to the `TermRecord` or `ConnRecord`, as the case may be. The second parameter is a Boolean indicating whether the application is being resumed (true) or suspended (false).

▶ Configuring the Communications Toolbox Tools

An important aspect of the Communications Toolbox is that its tools can be easily configured by the user through the use of standard dialog boxes. These dialog boxes allow the user to change the values of the parameters that tools use to perform their tasks—the serial connection tool, for example, uses baud rate and data format parameters to set the data transmission speed and the format of the serial data stream.

This section focuses on the routines you can use to display the dialog boxes that enable the user to change the settings of tool options. These dialogs are typically brought up in response to the selection of a related menu item.

Although there are several techniques for configuring the tools used by the Terminal, Connection, and File Transfer Managers use, only two will be examined here. The first technique involves displaying a standard configuration dialog box for each class of tools—terminal tools, connection tools, and file transfer tools. Every Communications Toolbox tool provides routines for handling user input in this dialog. This is the technique you will likely implement in your applications.

The second technique relies on the fact that, once configured, you can query a tool for a text string that describes the tool's current configuration. The configuration string can be saved in the document's resource fork so that it can be retrieved and used to restore the configuration the next time the document is opened.

You can also obtain configuration settings using custom configuration dialogs, but this technique is far more complex and is not needed in most circumstances. For more information on this technique, refer to *Inside the Macintosh Communications Toolbox*.

Many of the standard Communications Toolbox tools also support their own menus for allowing individual tool settings to be changed directly. You can easily suppress these menus, requiring the user to make all configuration changes by bringing up a configuration dialog box, if you wish. The sample source code presented in this chapter does suppress the tool menus. If you choose to use the tool menus, refer to *Inside the Macintosh Communications Toolbox* for instructions on how to handle them properly.

▶ Configuring Terminal Emulation Tools

The simplest way for an application to allow a user to select and configure a terminal emulation tool is to use the standard configuration dialog for the tool. Bring up the configuration dialog by calling **TMChoose**. The function prototype for **TMChoose** is as follows:

```
pascal short TMChoose( TermHandle *hTerm, Point where,
                       ProcPtr idleProc );
```

The purposes of the parameters passed to **TMChoose** are as follows:

hTerm—The address of the handle to your terminal record (`TermRecord`).

where—The location of the dialog's top left corner (in global coordinates). This point should be kept close to the top left corner of the screen since the dialog's height and width can differ for each terminal emulation tool and both can be quite large.

idleProc—The address of the procedure the Terminal Manager is to call during idle time while the dialog is being displayed. No parameters are passed to the idle procedure. Specify `0L` if your application is not providing an idle procedure.

TMChoose returns a result indicating which of several possible actions your application should take. These results are defined by the following constants in the CTBUtilities.h interface file:

```
#define chooseCancel 3
#define chooseOKMajor 2
#define chooseOKMinor 1
#define chooseFailed -1
#define chooseDisaster -2
```

The appropriate actions your application should take in response to these results are as follows:

chooseCancel—The Cancel button was clicked. No special action is required by your application in response to this return code.

chooseOKMajor—The OK button was clicked and the user changed at least one configuration setting for the tool. The Terminal Manager returns in hTerm a handle that refers to the new TermRecord; you should save the new terminal record the next time the user saves the document.

chooseOKMinor—The OK button was clicked, but no changes were made to the configuration settings.

chooseFailed—The configuration failed, but the terminal record is still intact. The application should inform the user of the problem and offer to try again.

chooseDisaster—The configuration failed and the terminal record was destroyed in the process. The Terminal Manager sets hTerm to 0L and the application should inform the user of the problem and offer to try again.

Your application will typically call **TMChoose** when the user selects the Terminal . . . item (or similarly named item) from a Communications menu you've put in the menu bar.

The configuration dialogs for the TTY and VT102 terminal emulation tools are shown in Figures 6-1 and 6-2. Notice the Emulation pop-up menu near the upper left corner in both dialogs. This pop-up menu allows the user to change the type of terminal emulation desired. By imbedding this tool-selection function in the configuration dialog (under the control of the Communications Toolbox), the application can support all terminal emulation tools without source code changes. If each type of terminal emulation had to be understood and handled specially by the application, writing your application would be much harder.

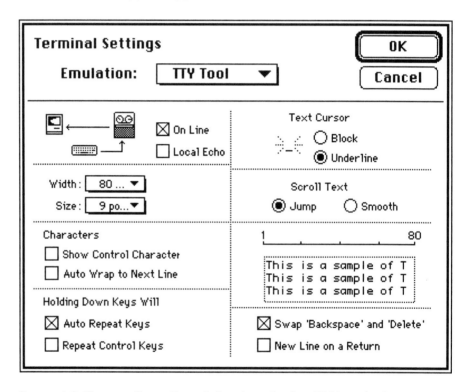

Figure 6-1. The configuration dialog box for the TTY terminal emulation tool

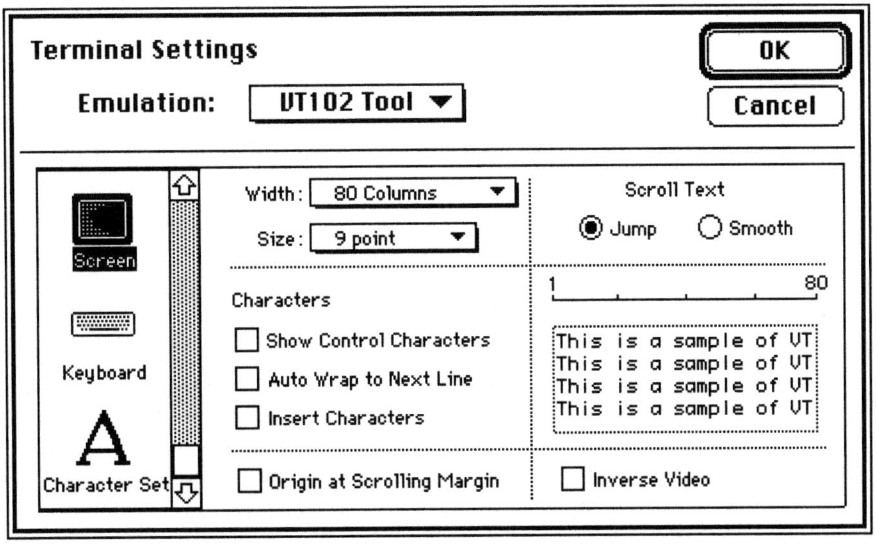

```
┌─────────────────────────────────────────────────────────────┐
│ Terminal Settings                              ╔══════════╗   │
│                                                ║    OK    ║   │
│      Emulation:   │ VT102 Tool ▼ │             ╚══════════╝   │
│                                                ┌──────────┐   │
│                                                │  Cancel  │   │
│                                                └──────────┘   │
├─────────────────────────────────────────────────────────────┤
│  ┌───────┐⬆  Width: │ 80 Columns  ▼│      Scroll Text        │
│  │ ▣     │▒   Size : │ 9 point     ▼│   ◉ Jump   ○ Smooth     │
│  │Screen │▒                                                   │
│  │       │▒  ······················   1                   80  │
│  ┌───────┐▒  Characters              └───────────────────┘    │
│  │▭▭▭▭▭▭▭│▒   ☐ Show Control Characters  This is a sample of VT│
│  Keyboard │▒   ☐ Auto Wrap to Next Line   This is a sample of VT│
│           │▒   ☐ Insert Characters        This is a sample of VT│
│    A      │▒                              This is a sample of VT│
│ Character Set⬇ ☐ Origin at Scrolling Margin  ☐ Inverse Video  │
└─────────────────────────────────────────────────────────────┘
```

Figure 6-2. The configuration dialog box for the VT102 terminal emulation tool

The configuration settings the user selects can be retrieved from the terminal emulation tool by calling **TMGetConfig**. The function prototype for **TMGetConfig** is as follows:

```
pascal Ptr TMGetConfig( TermHandle hTerm );
```

TMGetConfig requires a handle to a terminal record (`TermRecord`) as its only input.

This routine returns a pointer to the configuration string for the tool. This string is null-terminated, can be of any length, and should be disposed of by calling **DisposPtr** when no longer needed. The format of a configuration string is unique to each tool.

A configuration you've previously saved can be easily invoked by calling **TMSetConfig**. The function prototype for **TMSetConfig** is as follows:

```
pascal short TMSetConfig( TermHandle hTerm,
                          const void *thePtr );
```

The parameters to **TMSetConfig** are as follows:

hTerm—The handle to the terminal record (`TermRecord`).

thePtr—The address of the null-terminated configuration string (obtained earlier from **TMGetConfig** or read from a resource).

<table>
<tr><td>**Note** ▶</td><td>If **TMSetConfig** is unable to configure the terminal emulation tool, it returns an error code. If the error was caused by an unrecognized command in the configuration string, a positive value, representing the position within the string where the error occurred, is returned. If the cause of the problem was a system error, a negative value, indicating which system error occurred, is returned (-1 represents an error of unknown type). If the configuration request was successful, the return value is equal to the constant `tmNoErr` (defined in the Terminals.h interface file).</td></tr>
</table>

▶ Configuring Connection Tools

Configuring a connection tool is similar to configuring a terminal emulation tool. In fact, the routines your application needs to call seem almost identical to those made when configuring a terminal emulation tool. The main differences are the type of handle passed and the structure of data referred to by the handle.

Bring up the configuration dialog for a connection tool by calling **CMChoose**. The function prototype for **CMChoose** is as follows:

```
pascal short CMChoose( ConnHandle *hConn, Point where,
                                ProcPtr idleProc );
```

The purposes of the parameters passed to **CMChoose** are as follows:

hConn—The address of the handle to your connection record (`ConnRecord`).

where—The location of the dialog's top left corner (in global coordinates). This point should be kept close to the top left corner of the screen since the dialog's height and width can differ for each connection tool and both can be quite large.

idleProc—The address of the procedure the Terminal Manager is to call during idle time while the dialog is being displayed. No parameters are passed to the idle procedure. Specify 0L if your application is not providing an idle procedure.

CMChoose returns a result indicating which of several possible actions your application should take. These results are defined by the following constants in the CTBUtilities.h interface file:

```
#define chooseCancel 3
#define chooseOKMajor 2
#define chooseOKMinor 1
#define chooseAborted 0
#define chooseFailed -1
#define chooseDisaster -2
```

The appropriate actions your application should take in response to these results are as follows:

chooseCancel—The Cancel button was clicked. No special action is required by your application in response to this return code.

chooseOKMajor—The OK button was clicked and the user changed at least one configuration setting for the tool. The Connection Manager returns in hConn a handle that refers to the new connection ConnRecord; you should save the new connection record the next time the user saves the document.

chooseOKMinor—The OK button was clicked, but no changes were made to the configuration settings.

chooseDisaster—The configuration failed and the connection record was destroyed in the process. The Connection Manager sets hConn to 0L and the application should inform the user of the problem and offer to try again.

chooseAborted—If the user changes the connection settings while a connection is open and clicks the OK button, the Connection Manager displays a dialog asking for confirmation. If the user clicks that dialog's Cancel button, **CMChoose** returns chooseAborted.

chooseFailed—The configuration failed, but the connection record is still intact. The application should inform the user of the problem and offer to try again.

Your application will typically call **CMChoose** when the user selects the Connection... item (or similarly named item) from a Communications menu you've put in the menu bar.

The configuration dialog for the serial and Apple modem connection tools are shown in Figures 6-3 and 6-4. Notice the Method pop-up menu near the upper left corner in both dialogs. This pop-up menu allows the user to change the type of connection desired. By imbedding this tool-selection function in the configuration dialog (under the control of the Communications Toolbox), the application can support all connection tools without source code changes. If each type of connection had to be understood and handled specially by the application, writing your application would be much harder.

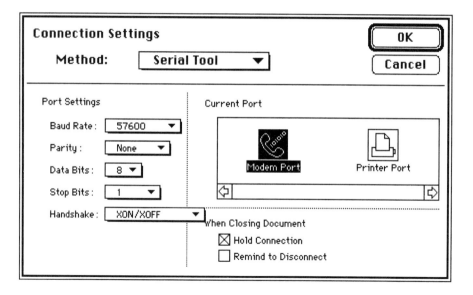

Figure 6-3. The configuration dialog box for the serial connection tool

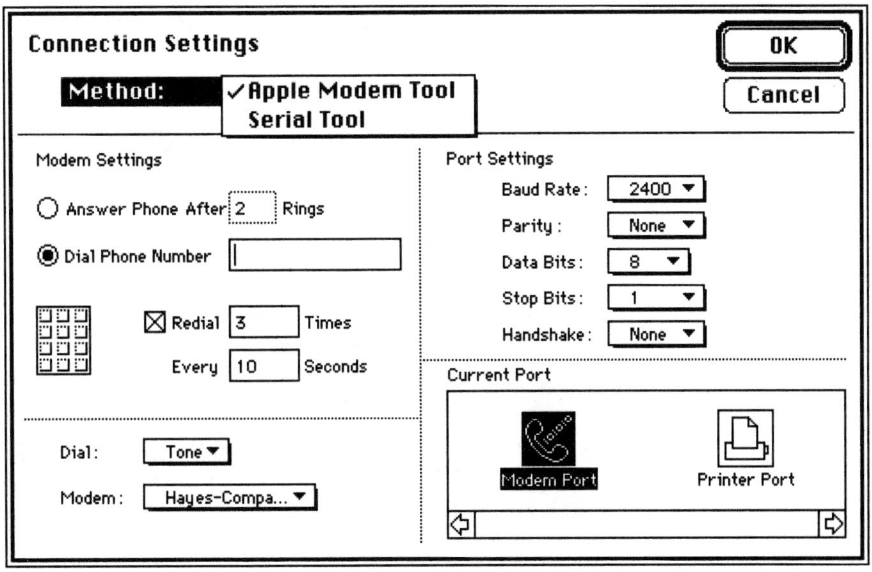

Figure 6-4. The configuration dialog box for the Apple modem connection tool

The configuration settings the user selects can be retrieved from the connection tool by calling **CMGetConfig**. The function prototype for **CMGetConfig** is as follows:

```
pascal Ptr CMGetConfig( ConnHandle hConn );
```

CMGetConfig requires a handle to a connection record (ConnRecord) as its only input.

This routine returns a pointer to the configuration string for the tool. This string is null-terminated, can be of any length, and should be disposed of by calling **DisposPtr** when no longer needed. The format of a configuration string is unique to each tool.

A configuration you've previously saved can be easily invoked by calling **CMSetConfig**. The function prototype for **CMSetConfig** is as follows:

```
pascal short CMSetConfig( ConnHandle hConn, Ptr thePtr );
```

The parameters to **CMSetConfig** are as follows:

hConn—The handle to the connection record (ConnRecord).

thePtr—The address of the null-terminated configuration string (obtained earlier from **CMGetConfig** or read from a resource).

<table>
<tr><td>Note ▶</td><td>If **CMSetConfig** is unable to configure the connection tool, it returns an error code. If the error was caused by an unrecognized command in the configuration string, a positive value, representing the position within the string where the error occurred, is returned. If the cause of the problem was a system error, a negative value, indicating which system error occurred, is returned (-1 represents an error of unknown type). If the configuration request was successful, the return value is equal to the constant cmNoErr (defined in the Connections.h interface file).</td></tr>
</table>

▶ Putting the Pieces Together

Now that you are familiar with the groundwork and have seen how to implement the features of the Communications Toolbox, it's time to put all the pieces together to provide the Skeleton application with telecommunications capabilities.

First, you'll need to define menu items to configure a terminal emulation tool, to configure a connection tool, to open the connection, and to close the connection. You'll also need a window for the terminal emulation tool to use as its screen (it could be created in response to a New or Open... item in the File menu) and a set of required procedures (breakProc, sendProc, and environsProc) that the selected terminal emulation tool can use.

Listing 6-8 shows the procedure that is called when Skeleton's Connection... menu item is selected. Listing 6-9 shows the procedure called when Skeleton's Terminal... menu item is selected.

Listing 6-8. Skeleton's Connection... routine

```
/* The following routine is responsible for displaying a configuration */
/* dialog for the connection tools or using a configuration string to */
/* configure the connection. If the "configString" is nil, use the */
/* dialog, otherwise use the passed-in configuration string... */
void DoCMConfiguration(Ptr configString)
{
    short    junkErr;
    short    myCode;        /* holds the code returned by CMChoose */
    Point    myTopLeft;     /* top, left corner of configuration dialog */

    if (configString) { /* non-nil means use configuration string */
        junkErr = CMSetConfig(gConnRecHndl, configString);
    } else {
        SetPt(&myTopLeft, 20, 40); /* keep it high and left on screen */
        if (gConnRecHndl) {    /* global ConnRecord */
            myCode = CMChoose(&gConnRecHndl, myTopLeft, 0L);
        }
    }
}
```

Listing 6-9. Skeleton's Terminal... routine

```
/* The following routine is responsible for displaying a configuration */
/* dialog for the terminal emulation tools or using a configuration */
/* string to configure the terminal. If the "configString" is nil, */
/* use the dialog, otherwise use the passed-in configuration string... */
void DoTMConfiguration(Ptr configString)
{
    short    junkErr;
    short    myCode;        /* holds the code returned by TMChoose */
    Point    myTopLeft;     /* top, left corner of configuration dialog */

    if (configString) {    /* non-nil means use configuration string */
        junkErr = TMSetConfig(gTermRecHndl, &configString);
    } else {
        SetPt(&myTopLeft, 20, 40); /* keep it high and left on screen */
        if (gTermRecHndl) {    /* global TermRecord */
            myCode = TMChoose(&gTermRecHndl, myTopLeft, 0L);
        }
    }
}
```

Listing 6-10 shows the procedure called when Skeleton's Open Connection menu item is selected. Listing 6-11 shows the procedure called when Skeleton's Close Connection menu item is selected.

Skeleton's implementation of the required procedures needed to support the terminal emulation tools can be found in Listings 6-5, 6-6, and 6-7.

Listing 6-10. Skeleton's Open Connection routine

```
/* The following routine is responsible for opening the connection. */
void DoOpenConnection(void)
{
    OSErr              myErr;
    CMStatFlags        myFlags;
    CMBufferSizes      myCMBufSizes;

    SetCursor(*GetCursor(watchCursor)); /* set cursor to watch */

    /* Check to see if connection is already open, or is being opened */
    myErr = CMStatus(gConnRecHndl, myCMBufSizes, &myFlags);

    if (!myErr) { /* if status check worked, keep going */
        /* only open connection if it's not already open or being opened */
            if (!((myFlags & cmStatusOpen) || (myFlags & cmStatusOpening))) {
                myErr = CMOpen(gConnRecHndl, false, 0L, 2400);
        }
    }
    InitCursor(); /* restore normal cursor */

}
```

Listing 6-11. Skeleton's Close Connection routine

```
/* The following routine is responsible for shutting down connections. */
void DoCloseConnection(void)
{
    OSErr                myErr;
    CMStatFlags        myFlags;
    CMBufferSizes      myCMBufSizes;

    SetCursor(*GetCursor(watchCursor)); /* set cursor to watch */

    /* Check to see if connection is already closed, or is being closed */
    myErr = CMStatus(gConnRecHndl, myCMBufSizes, &myFlags);

    if (!myErr) { /* if status check worked, keep going */
        /* only close it if it's open or being opened */
        if (((myFlags & cmStatusOpen)) || (myFlags & cmStatusOpening)) {
            myErr = CMClose(gConnRecHndl, false, 0L, 1200, true);
        }
    }
    InitCursor(); /* restore normal cursor */

}
```

▶ Summary

This chapter described the services and functions that System 7 offers all applications through the Communications Toolbox. The basic operation of the Communications Toolbox and the ease with which you can harness its power were demonstrated. The major routines in both the Terminal Manager and the Connection Manager were described.

While not discussed, the File Transfer Manager's routines are similar to those of the Terminal and Connection Managers, making file transfers as easy as establishing a connection or emulating a terminal. For more information on all the capabilities of the Communications Toolbox, refer to *Inside the Macintosh Communications Toolbox*.

The next chapter moves away from the communications area and discusses Apple's new font technology, TrueType, and how it affects the way you develop applications.

7 ▶ Font Manager

The Macintosh has worked with bit-mapped fonts since day one. With the release of System 7, however, a powerful new font technology is available—TrueType. TrueType fonts offer several advantages over their bit-mapped cousins, stemming from the fact that by installing just one file containing the TrueType definition for a particular font, the System can truly render the font in almost any point size.

This chapter will explore the following topics:

- the scaling characteristics of TrueType fonts
- what a System 7 application has to do to work seamlessly with both TrueType and bit-mapped fonts
- designing a Size menu that makes sense in a TrueType world

▶ TrueType Scaling

The problem with a bit-mapped font is that if you haven't installed the font definition for the point size you want to use, the font has to be scaled, and scaling, particularly to unusual point sizes, can result in very jagged and very unattractive glyphs. (A glyph is the visual representation of a character.) To be fair, scaling from a font that is twice as big or twice as small works fairly well, but the result still looks a bit rough. This poor scalability is due to the fact that bit-mapped fonts are defined as a simple array of pixels at 72 pixels per inch; a resolution this coarse isn't particularly conducive to effective scaling.

Each glyph in a TrueType font is stored as a set of points, not an array of pixels. But don't confuse these points with a font's point size or a QuickDraw point, the points that define the glyph are expressed in terms of a grid with far finer resolution than the pixels on a screen or the dots on a printer's page.

The points for a particular glyph definition can either be on the curve of the glyph or off of it. Glyphs are rendered by connecting consecutive on-curve points with a line. This line is usually straight, but can be bent by intervening off-curve points that behave like magnets, bending the line towards the off-curve points. The result is a glyph with the curved shapes it needs to be clearly represented.

The set of points for a glyph is used as the input to a mathematical curve-fitting algorithm (known as a *parametric Bézier equation*). The Font Manager uses this algorithm to render the font perfectly at any arbitrary point size. The result is a much better representation at a given point size than would be possible if you had to scale a bit-mapped font to the same point size.

Another advantage of TrueType fonts is that they don't eat up a lot of disk space. One TrueType font file per typeface can be scaled to produce beautiful looking output at any point size. If you're using bit-mapped fonts and you want to avoid scaling, you have to provide definitions in all point sizes of interest to your customers. This is clearly impractical.

▶ Living with Bit-Mapped and TrueType Fonts

The user may install both bit-mapped and TrueType fonts in System 7, so your application should be prepared to handle both font types in a sensible way. As you will see, there's actually not much the application has to do since much of the hard work is done transparently by the operating system.

The Font Manager is responsible, for example, for determining which type of font to display if a font is available in both a bit-mapped and a TrueType version. The default behavior is to choose the bit-mapped font if it exists in the exact point size desired, otherwise the TrueType font is chosen. This is because presumably the bit-mapped font has been fine-tuned to look just right at the point size for which it was designed; a TrueType font, on the other hand, scales much better to an arbitrary point size. Obviously, if only a bit-mapped font is installed, that font is always used; the same goes for TrueType fonts.

You can override the default font type selection using the **SetOutlinePreferred** routine. The function prototype for

`SetOutlinePreferred` is the following:

```
pascal void SetOutlinePreferred( Boolean outlinePreferred );
```

The `outlinePreferred` parameter controls whether a TrueType font will be used even if a bit-mapped font exists at the desired size. Set this field to true to use TrueType fonts and set it to false to use bit-mapped fonts.

You can determine the current font selection behavior by calling `GetOutlinePreferred`:

```
pascal Boolean GetOutlinePreferred( void );
```

This routine returns true if the Font Manager prefers to use TrueType fonts or false if it uses bit-mapped fonts that are available in the desired size.

Using TrueType fonts in a document does not impair the user's ability to view the document on systems that have only bit-mapped versions of the same fonts. The Font Manager does not insist that the TrueType fonts be present. Off course if you're using unusual point sizes, the document will not look as good when viewed on a system that does not have TrueType fonts.

TrueType fonts scaled to a specific point size for display on the screen will look almost as good as hand-tuned bit-mapped fonts of the same size. In general, however, TrueType fonts look much better than bit-mapped fonts when drawn on the printed page by a high-resolution printer like one of Apple's LaserWriters. The exception is where a PostScript version of the bit-mapped font exists in the printer; in this case, the quality is about the same as when the TrueType font is used.

Perhaps the best strategy for managing fonts is to use `SetOutlinePreferred` to set the Font Manager's preferred font technology to TrueType so that you get nice looking output both on the screen and on paper. If the desired font is available only as a bit map, the Font Manager will still use it. The fact that you indicate a preference for TrueType technology does not foreclose the use of bit-mapped fonts.

▶ TrueType's Impact on Applications

Since the Font Manager can scale TrueType fonts to any point size and the result will look attractive, a System 7 application should provide the user with more control over the choice of point size than was the case in older applications. In particular, the application should include menu items for increasing and decreasing the current point size by one point at a time as well as a menu item for allowing the selection of any arbitrary point size.

The established convention for pre-System 7 applications is to draw, in outline styling, the menu item name of any point size for which an exact font description is available. This convention still applies to System 7 applications, but for TrueType fonts, nearly all font sizes will need to be outlined. However, a TrueType font can have a minimum size embedded in its definition by its designer indicating the smallest size at which the designer feels the font looks appropriate. Menu item names for sizes below the minimum size should not be in outline styling.

Use the **RealFont** routine to determine if the font size you're interested in is available (for bit-mapped fonts) or above the limit (for TrueType fonts). The function prototype for **RealFont** is the following:

```
pascal Boolean RealFont( short fontNum, short size );
```

Here are the meanings of the two parameters to **RealFont**:

fontNum—The font number for the font family in question. Each font family has a unique number assigned by the system when it is first installed. Since this number can vary from system to system, but font names are unique, the best strategy for determining the font number is to use the **GetFNum** routine (described below) to convert the font name to a font number.

size—The point size in which you're interested.

RealFont returns true if the font specified by fontNum exists in the size specified by size. If the requested size is not available, **RealFont** returns false.

The function prototype for **GetFNum** is the following:

```
pascal void GetFNum(ConstStr255Param name, short *familyID);
```

Here are the meanings of the parameters to **GetFNum**:

name—The font whose font number you want to determine.

familyID—The family ID for the specified font is returned in this variable. Use this value as the font number input to **RealFont**.

Note ▶

All fonts have a family ID and a unique family name assigned by Apple's Developer Technical Support group. The family ID is always between 0 and 255, obviously not enough to accommodate the hundreds of commercial fonts available. As a result, family ID conflicts may occur when a font family is installed in the system. When the system detects a conflict, it changes the family ID of the font being installed to a family ID that is not in use on that system. This is why the fonts a document uses should be recorded by family name rather than by family ID.

Figure 7-1 shows a sample Size menu that you should use in applications that allow users to change point sizes for text selections. The following sections discuss how to implement such a menu.

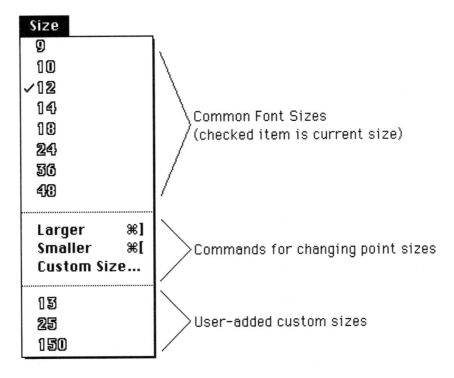

Figure 7-1. A typical Size menu for managing TrueType font size changes

▶ Incremental Font Size Adjustments

The menu item named Larger in Figure 7-1 increases the current point size by one, while the item named Smaller decreases the current point size by one. These are provided to allow the user to quickly adjust the size of a TrueType font to one that looks just right.

Listing 7-1 shows a single routine you can use to increase or decrease the point size of the currently selected text by one point. Pass 1 to the DoNudgeFontSize routine to increase the point size by one and pass -1 to decrease it by one.

Listing 7-1. A routine for increasing or decreasing the type size by one point

```
/* put this short chunk into DoMenuCommand() */
    case mSpecial:
        switch ( menuItem ) {
            case iLarger:
                DoNudgeFontSize( 1 );      /* increase size by 1 point */
                break;
            case iSmaller:
                DoNudgeFontSize( -1 );     /* decrease size by 1 point */
                break;
        }
    break;



/* put this chunk anywhere */
  void DoNudgeFontSize(short nudgeBy)
  /* add 'nudgeBy' to current selection's font size */
  {
      TextStyle       myStyle;
      winPrivateHndl  myPrivHndl;

      /* should buffer current style so UNDO works */

      myStyle.tsSize = nudgeBy;  /* amount to nudge font size by */

      /* get handle to data stashed in front window's refCon */
      myPrivHndl = (winPrivateHndl)GetWRefCon( FrontWindow() );

      if (myPrivHndl) { /* ignore front window if nothing is stashed */
          /* force selected text to new size */
          TESetStyle(addSize, &myStyle, true, (**myPrivHndl).winTEHndl);
      }
  }
```

To adjust the point size, call the **TESetStyle** routine and tell it to add (or subtract) one point to (or from) the point size of the selected text. The function prototype for **TESetStyle** is the following:

```
pascal void TESetStyle( short mode, const TextStyle
            *newStyle, Boolean redraw, TEHandle hTE );
```

The meanings of the parameters are as follows:

mode—Controls which style attributes are affected by the newStyle parameter. Possible values for mode are:

```
#define doFont    1    /* set font (family) number */
#define doFace    2    /* set character style */
#define doSize    4    /* set type size */
#define doColor   8    /* set color */
#define doAll    15    /* set all attributes */
#define addSize  16    /* adjust type size */
```

newStyle—Contains the style information to be imposed on the selected text, based on the mode specified in the mode parameter. To increase the font's size by a specific number of points, set mode to addSize and set the newStyle->tsSize field to the number of points that should be added to the selected text's point size. Use a negative value for newStyle->tsSize to decrease the selected text's point size by a specific number of points.

redraw—If true, TextEdit immediately redraws the TextEdit field to reflect the style changes. If false, the TextEdit field is not redrawn; style changes are hidden until something else forces the TextEdit field to be redrawn.

hTE—A handle to the TextEdit record containing the text to which the new style is being applied.

If the selection range includes fonts of different sizes, each font will be increased or decreased by the amount specified in newStyle->tsSize. Thus, if the user selects a range of text that includes 10-point, 12-point, and 18-point text, then selects Larger from the Size menu, the 10-point text becomes 11-point, the 12 becomes 13, and the 18 becomes 19.

When shrinking text, the Font Manager prevents font sizes from going below 1 point. The same selected text (10-, 12-, and 18-point mixed together), if decreased (with Smaller) 13 times, will convert the 10- and 12-point text into 1 point. When the text size is increased (with Larger), all of what used to be 10-point text will be the same size as the text that used to be 12-point (the Font Manager loses the information that these two subranges are supposed to be a different size).

▶ Custom Font Size Selection

Providing a method for users to enter any arbitrary font size takes a little more thought. Perhaps the easiest implementation is to bring up a modal dialog that prompts for a new size, as shown in Figure 7-2. If the user dismisses the dialog by clicking the OK button, the custom size entered is applied to the selected text.

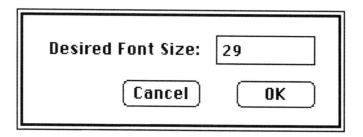

Figure 7-2. A simple modal dialog for changing the point size

Another alternative is to include within the dialog a text sample drawn in the point size the user selects (see Figure 7-3). This technique isn't appropriate when dealing with large point sizes because the dialog has to be very large or most of the text sample won't show up. As with the previous example, if the user dismisses the dialog by clicking the OK button, the custom size is applied to the selected text.

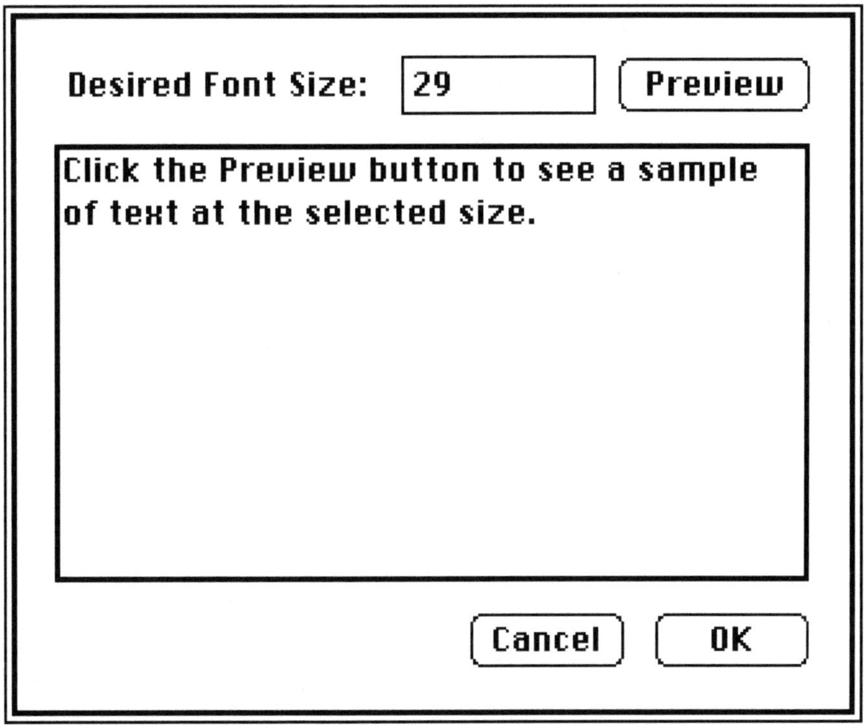

```
┌─────────────────────────────────────────────────────┐
│  ┌───────────────────────────────────────────────┐  │
│  │                                                 │  │
│  │  Desired Font Size:  ┌──────────┐  ┌─────────┐ │  │
│  │                      │ 29       │  │ Preview │ │  │
│  │                      └──────────┘  └─────────┘ │  │
│  │  ┌─────────────────────────────────────────┐  │  │
│  │  │ Click the Preview button to see a sample │  │  │
│  │  │ of text at the selected size.             │  │  │
│  │  │                                           │  │  │
│  │  │                                           │  │  │
│  │  │                                           │  │  │
│  │  │                                           │  │  │
│  │  └─────────────────────────────────────────┘  │  │
│  │                         ┌────────┐  ┌────────┐ │  │
│  │                         │ Cancel │  │   OK   │ │  │
│  │                         └────────┘  └────────┘ │  │
│  └───────────────────────────────────────────────┘  │
└─────────────────────────────────────────────────────┘
```

Figure 7-3. A better method for changing the point size

Using a non-modal point size control window is probably the best solution (see Figure 7-4). Such a strategy allows users to quickly switch back and forth between the document window and the size control window until the desired size is entered. This approach also makes it possible to quickly see new sizes, using the actual selected text in the context of its surrounding text, without having to first dismiss the font size dialog. The next section describes a routine you can use to implement such a window.

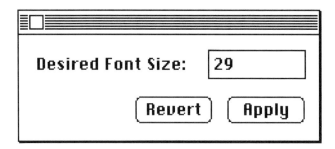

Figure 7-4. A modeless dialog for allowing custom font size entry

You should also consider providing the ability for the user to append custom font sizes to the Size menu so they can be quickly selected. The names of these custom sizes should have outline styling if **RealFont** returns true for the font at that point size. Figure 7-1 shows where custom fonts would be installed in the sample Size menu.

▶ Implementing Custom Size Control

The ability to allow a change in the point size of selected text in a background window (using a non-modal dialog like the one shown in Figure 7-4) was available in TextEdit prior to System 7 (through the use of the **GetStylScrap**, **SetStylScrap**, and **TESetStyle** routines), but is particularly helpful for demonstrating TrueType's flexibility. Prior to System 7, only bit-mapped fonts were available and there was little point in allowing the user to choose any possible font size because the scaled fonts looked so unattractive. Thus, this feature in TextEdit was generally untapped.

Applying a new size to the selected text is similar to the Larger and Smaller menu items discussed earlier in this chapter. The desired size is extracted from the data entry field of the modeless dialog and that number is passed to **TESetStyle**; the mode field should be set to doSize instead of addSize since we want all of the selected text to be forced to the custom size selected by the user.

Reverting to the original sizes is trickier than applying a new size since the text being restored could easily be of several different sizes. (Apply makes them all one size, but Revert has to restore their original, possibly mixed, sizes). The best way to accomplish this is to save the current styles of the selected text before applying the user's custom size. The saved styles can be stored in the window's private data area (accessed via the handle stored in the window's refCon field) and retrieved later if the user selects Revert.

The easiest way to save the current styles of the selected text is to use the **GetStylScrap** routine. The function prototype for **GetStylScrap** is the following:

```
pascal StScrpHandle GetStylScrap( TEHandle hTE );
```

The hTE parameter is a handle to the TextEdit record containing the selected text. **GetStylScrap** returns a handle to the styles used for the selected text. Up to 1,601 styles can be mixed in the selected range.

GetStylScrap is similar to a Copy command, except that the clipboard and TextEdit's scrap are unaffected by the routine (which prevents their contents from being trampled). The handle that **GetStylScrap** returns reflects the styles for only the text that was selected by the user. If no text was selected, the handle reflects the style associated with the insertion point.

Restoring the styles requires only that the saved styling information be retrieved from the window's private structure and passed to **SetStylScrap**. The function prototype for **SetStylScrap** is the following:

```
pascal void SetStylScrap( long rangeStart,
             long rangeEnd, StScrpHandle newStyles,
             Boolean redraw, TEHandle hTE );
```

The meanings of the parameters to **SetStylScrap** are as follows:

rangeStart—The offset into the TextEdit field of the first character to which the style information should be applied. This value should be saved in the window's private data area before the user's new size is applied.

rangeEnd—The offset into the TextEdit field of the last character to which the style information should be applied. This value should be saved in the window's private data area before the user's new size is applied.

newStyles—The handle returned by **GetStylScrap** and saved in the window's private data area. This handle reflects up to 1,601 styles to be applied to the selection range specified by rangeStart and rangeEnd.

redraw—If true, TextEdit immediately redraws the TextEdit field to reflect the style changes. If false, redrawing occurs when the next update event is handled.

hTE—A handle to the TextEdit record in which the selected text is included.

SetStylScrap applies the styles specified in newStyles to the text within the TextEdit record without disturbing the user's current selection. One range of text could be selected, a new size applied, another range selected, and Revert would still be able to restore the original sizes for the first range of text while leaving the new range still selected.

| Important ▶ | Care should be taken to monitor when the text in the TextEdit field has changed and Revert should be disabled. Revert is only meaningful after a new size has been applied and before the text has changed in any other way. |

Controlling the TextEdit record for a window that is not at the front is fairly simple. All that's needed is a handle to the TextEdit record for that window. The sample code in Listing 7-2 assumes that this handle has been stored in the private data structure whose handle is stored in the window's refCon field (an old trick). Before making calls to TextEdit that affect the window behind a modeless dialog, the TextEdit field should be made active by calling **TEActivate**. Then, after adjusting the size of the selected text, restore the TextEdit field to its inactive state by calling **TEDeactivate**.

The function prototypes for **TEActivate** and **TEDeactivate** are as follows:

```
pascal void TEActivate( TEHandle hTE );

pascal void TEDeactivate( TEHandle hTE );
```

The hTE parameter is a handle to the TextEdit record containing the selected text that you want to resize.

Listing 7-2 shows a routine you can use to implement the custom font size entry shown in Figure 7-4. It provides support for an Apply button (for applying the entered point size to the text selection in the window behind it) and a Revert button (for undoing the result of the previous Apply operation).

Listing 7-2. A routine to implement the modeless dialog shown in Figure 7-4 for changing type sizes

```
#define rFontSize          150 /* resource ID of our modeless dialog */
#define rCustomSizeNum      2   /* second item in DITL is editText field */
#define rCustomSizeRevert   3   /* third item in DITL is 'Revert' button */

#define rCustomSizeApply    4   /* fourth item in DITL is 'Apply' button */

extern DialogPtr  gCustomFontSizeDlgPtr;

/* The following routine creates the Custom Font Size modeless dialog. */
void ShowFontSize(WindowPtr wp)
{
    short           itemsType;
    Handle          itemsHndl;
    Rect            itemsRect;
    winPrivateHndl  myPrivHndl;

    if (gCustomFontSizeDlgPtr == nil) {
        gCustomFontSizeDlgPtr = GetNewDialog(rFontSize, nil, (WindowPtr) -1);

        /* disable Revert button - enabled when Apply is pressed */
        GetDItem(gCustomFontSizeDlgPtr, rCustomSizeRevert, &itemsType,
                &itemsHndl, &itemsRect);
        HiliteControl( (ControlHandle) itemsHndl, 255); /* 255 = disable */

        /* select all text in data entry field */
        SelIText(gCustomFontSizeDlgPtr, rCustomSizeNum, 0, 32767);

        myPrivHndl = (winPrivateHndl)GetWRefCon( wp ); /* get stashed info */

        /* activate the TextEdit field we're working with */
        TEActivate((**myPrivHndl).winTEHndl);

        /* buffer currently selected text */
        (**myPrivHndl).winScrapHndl = GetStylScrap((**myPrivHndl).winTEHndl);

        /* buffer selection range as well */
        (**myPrivHndl).winSelStart = (**((**myPrivHndl).winTEHndl)).selStart;
        (**myPrivHndl).winSelEnd = (**((**myPrivHndl).winTEHndl)).selEnd;

        /* deactivate the TextEdit field we're working with */
        TEDeactivate((**myPrivHndl).winTEHndl);

    } else {    /* already exists, so bring it to the front */
        SelectWindow( gCustomFontSizeDlgPtr );
        /* Check flag to see if text has changed since Apply button was */
        /* last pressed. If it has changed, disable Revert button. */
    }
}


/* The following routine handles item hits in modeless dialog. */
void DoHandleHit(short hitItemsNum)
{
```

Listing 7-2. A routine to implement the modeless dialog shown in
Figure 7-4 for changing type sizes (continued)

```
short           itemsType;
Handle          itemsHndl;
Rect            itemsRect;
Str255          itemsText;
long            applySize;
TextStyle       myStyle;
winPrivateHndl  myPrivHndl;
WindowPtr       wpUs;    /* window ptr to modeless dialog */
WindowPtr       wpThem;  /* window ptr to window behind modeless dialog */

/* We need a pointer to the window immediately behind this dialog, so */
/* call FrontWindow to get a pointer to ourselves, then peek into the */
/* WindowRecord and grab the pointer to the next window in the list. */
wpUs = FrontWindow();
wpThem = (WindowPtr) ((*((WindowPeek) wpUs)).nextWindow);

switch (hitItemsNum) {
    case rCustomSizeNum:    /* key was pressed */
        PrintString((ConstStr255Param) "\pTim Swihart was here");
        break;
    case rCustomSizeApply: /* APPLY button was clicked */
        /* get stashed info */
        myPrivHndl = (winPrivateHndl)GetWRefCon( wpThem );

        /* extract requested font size */
        GetDItem(wpUs, rCustomSizeNum, &itemsType, &itemsHndl,
                        &itemsRect);

        /* get text out of data entry field */
        GetIText(itemsHndl, itemsText);
        StringToNum( (ConstStr255Param) itemsText, &applySize );
        myStyle.tsSize = applySize; /* put the number in new font's size */

        /* activate TE field before setting new font size */
        TEActivate((**myPrivHndl).winTEHndl);

        /* buffer currently selected text */
        (**myPrivHndl).winScrapHndl =
                    GetStylScrap((**myPrivHndl).winTEHndl);

        /* buffer selection range as well */
        (**myPrivHndl).winSelStart =
                            (**((**myPrivHndl).winTEHndl)).selStart;
        (**myPrivHndl).winSelEnd = (**((**myPrivHndl).winTEHndl)).selEnd;

        /* set new size for the selected text */
        TESetStyle(doSize, &myStyle, true, (**myPrivHndl).winTEHndl);

        /* deactivate TE field now that we're done */
        TEDeactivate((**myPrivHndl).winTEHndl);
```

Listing 7-2. A routine to implement the modeless dialog shown in Figure 7-4 for changing type sizes (continued)

```
                    /* enable the Revert button - disabled by typing & reverting */
                    GetDItem(wpUs, rCustomSizeRevert, &itemsType, &itemsHndl,
                            &itemsRect);
                    HiliteControl((ControlHandle) itemsHndl, 0);  /* 0 = enable */
                    break;
            case rCustomSizeRevert:/* Revert button was clicked */
                    /* get stashed info */
                    myPrivHndl = (winPrivateHndl)GetWRefCon( wpThem );

                    /* activate TE field before setting new font size */
                    TEActivate((**myPrivHndl).winTEHndl);

                    /* restore original style */
                    SetStylScrap((**myPrivHndl).winSelStart, (**myPrivHndl).winSelEnd,
                                (**myPrivHndl).winScrapHndl, true,
                                (**myPrivHndl).winTEHndl);

                    /* deactivate TE field now that we're done */
                    TEDeactivate((**myPrivHndl).winTEHndl);

                    /* disable Revert button - enabled when Apply is pressed */
                    GetDItem(wpUs, rCustomSizeRevert, &itemsType, &itemsHndl,
                            &itemsRect);
                    HiliteControl((ControlHandle) itemsHndl, 255); /* 255 = inactive */
                    break;
        }
    }
```

▶ User Interface Tip

TextEdit supports outline highlighting for inactive TextEdit records. Outline highlighting surrounds the selected text with an open rectangle when the window containing the TextEdit record is inactive. Few applications make use of this feature—they provide no inactive highlighting at all. When using a modeless dialog which affects the text selection in another (inactive) window, you should use outline highlighting to remind the user what text will be affected by the Apply button.

You can turn on outline highlighting using the **TEFeatureFlag** routine. The function prototype for **TEFeatureFlag** is as follows:

```
pascal short TEFeatureFlag( short feature,
                short action, TEHandle hTE );
```

Here are the meanings of the parameters to **TEFeatureFlag**:

feature—Specifies which features should be turned on, turned off, or have their current settings returned to the caller. Values for this parameter are the following:

```
#define teFTextBuffering    1    /* text buffering—speeds TE up */
#define teFOutlineHilite    2    /* outline highlighting */
#define teFInlineInput      3    /* inline input features */
#define teFUseTextServices  4    /* use inline input services */
```

action—Tells TextEdit whether to turn on the requested feature, turn off the requested feature, or return its value. Values for this parameter are the following:

```
#define TEBitSet     1    /* turn feature on */
#define TEBitClear   0    /* turn feature off */
#define TEBitTest   -1    /* return current setting */
```

hTE—The handle to the TextEdit record being affected by this routine.

Specify teFOutlineHilite for feature and TEBitSet for action to turn outline highlighting on for the TextEdit record given by hTE.

Note ▶

TextEdit's original design did not support styled text. The routines in this section assume that the TextEdit records they're acting on do support styled text. Styled text will be supported if you use **TEStylNew** instead of **TENew** to create the TextEdit record (the parameters are the same, only the name of the routine is different). TextEdit calls dealing with style will have no effect (good, bad, or otherwise) if made on old-style TextEdit records.

▶ Special Characters

Bit-mapped fonts are designed to have a fixed maximum height for a given point size, a height that is sufficient to accommodate the placement of accent marks (like the first 'e' in 'Bézier') above the tallest characters. TrueType fonts, however, do not share this feature. TrueType fonts are designed to be closer to the original (non-computer-based) typeface's design and certain glyphs within some typefaces extend further above the normal top (ascent line) or below the normal bottom (descent line) for those typefaces. Examples of special characters like this include the integral sign used in calculus or a capital letter that has an accent mark above it.

Most applications set the spacing between lines of text to the sum of the `ascent`, `descent`, and `leading` fields in the `FontInfo` record. Since a TrueType font may have glyphs that extend beyond the ascent or descent line, collisions will occur with an adjacent line of text unless precautions are taken.

The Font Manager's default strategy for avoiding such a collision is to automatically scale oversized TrueType characters to be no higher than the ascent line and no lower than the descent line. Your System 7 application can prevent this scaling, thus preserving the full size of the character, by calling **SetPreserveGlyph**. The function prototype for **SetPreserveGlyph** is the following:

```
pascal void SetPreserveGlyph( Boolean preserveGlyph );
```

The Boolean passed to **SetPreserveGlyph** tells the Font Manager whether it should scale oversized characters (false) or preserve their sizes (true).

When saving a document to disk, it's good practice to save the state of the `preserveGlyph` flag in the resource fork of the document. If you do this, the flag can be retrieved the next time the document is loaded and used to set the proper state of `preserveGlyph`.

If you don't know the current setting of `preserveGlyph`, you can call **GetPreserveGlyph**. The function prototype for **GetPreserveGlyph** is the following:

```
pascal Boolean GetPreserveGlyph( void );
```

GetPreserveGlyph returns false if oversized characters are to be scaled; otherwise, it returns true.

If you choose not to scale oversized characters, take care to ensure that they do not interfere with the text above or below. The easiest way to avoid interference is to increase the spacing between the lines. You can use the **OutlineMetrics** routine, described in *Inside Macintosh*, Volume VI, to quickly determine the actual height of a line to see if you need to increase the line spacing beyond the value given by `ascent+descent+leading`.

▶ Summary

In this chapter you learned about the benefits of TrueType fonts and saw how easy it is to exploit, not just support, the TrueType font technology. You also saw how easy it is to write an application that works properly with both TrueType and bit-mapped fonts.

In Chapter 8 we continue our exploration of System 7 by showing how to use the Help Manager to provide online help for your application. You will learn the different aspects of balloon help, aided by numerous source code samples.

8 ▶ Balloon Help

Over the years, Macintosh applications have grown increasingly sophisticated and complex. As a result, the need to include on-line user assistance in applications has grown. Today, the best applications frequently include Help... menu items and on-line tutorials.

System 7 simplifies the user support issue by providing an easy, yet effective, means of on-screen help for practically every aspect of an application. Called *balloon help*, this system lets users turn help on and off via a Help menu on the right side of the menu bar, next to the Application menu (see Figure 8-1).

Figure 8-1. A typical menu bar showing the location of the Help menu

When balloon help is on, System 7's Help Manager draws comic-book-style balloons for various items of interest on the screen as the user passes the mouse pointer over them. The balloons contain information that tells the user more about the item and how to use it. Balloons cover small portions of the screen until the user moves the mouse away from an item's hot area, but do not otherwise interfere with normal operation of the application.

This chapter covers the following topics:

- what help balloons look like
- providing help balloons for menu items
- adding items to the standard Help menu
- providing help balloons for dialog and alert boxes
- providing help balloons for windows and their contents

Note ▶

Chapter 11 of *Inside Macintosh,*Volume VI, contains a style guide for writing the the text that goes into help balloons. Refer to it for useful tips on how to write help messages that are concise and useful.

▶ What Help Balloons Look Like

Balloon help is available for menu titles and items, dialogs and alerts, window frames and contents, and the application's icon itself. Balloon help for application icons that the Finder displays is covered in Chapter 9. Figure 8-2 shows a typical desktop with various types of balloons superimposed on it—on an actual desktop, only one balloon appears at a time.

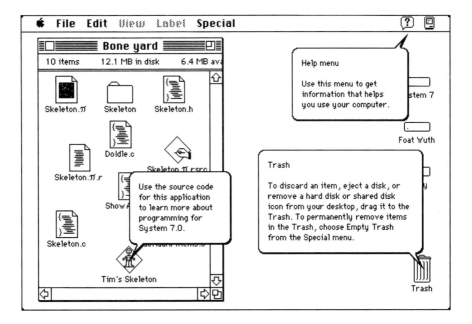

Figure 8-2. Desktop showing many different types of balloons

Most techniques for adding balloon help to applications do not require you to add any code to your application. They generally involve only adding sets of resources to the application. The techniques discussed in this chapter are summarized in Table 8-1.

Table 8-1. Summary of the techniques used for adding help balloons to an application

For adding help balloons to...	*Use these techniques....*
Menus and menu items	`'hmnu'` resource
Dialog and alert boxes	`'DITL'` HelpItem + `'hdlg'` resource
	or
	`'DITL'` HelpItem + `'hrct'` resource
	or
	`'hwin'` + `'hdlg'` resources
	or
	`'hwin'` + `'hrct'` resources

Table 8-1. Summary of the techniques used for adding help
balloons to an application (continued)

For adding help balloons to...	Use these techniques...
Windows (with static items)	`'hwin'` + `'hrct'` resources
Windows (with movable items)	use **HMShowBalloon** routine
Application icon in Finder	`'hfdr'` resource

▶ Balloon Help Resources

Most of the resource types that support balloon help include a header
that contains the following four fields:

- the version number of the Help Manager (`HelpMgrVersion`)
- an options field
- a pointer to a balloon definition procedure
- a balloon variation code

The Rez template file that defines the formats of all the Help Manager
resources is BalloonTypes.r. Read it carefully to learn about resource
formats and the symbolic names you can use for values in resource fields
(such as `HelpMgrVersion` for the version number).

The number you store in the options field of a header will vary from
one type of help resource to another and will be discussed throughout
this chapter as the need arises. When in doubt, set this field to
`hmDefaultOptions`; this tells the Help Manager to use its default values
for all options.

If you want to override the shape of the standard balloons, pass the
resource ID of your own balloon definition procedure in the third field
(balloon definition procedures are `'WDEF'` resources). In most circumstances, the standard balloon definition function is adequate, so put 0 in
this field.

The Help Manager has eight built-in balloon shapes, each with the tip
in a different location, which you can select using the balloon variation
codes shown in Figure 8-3. This provides a great deal of versatility to the
Help Manager in its quest to make the entire balloon fit on the screen.
The Help Manager checks to see if the balloon with the variation code
you specify fits on the screen—if it doesn't, the Help Manager uses a
more appropriate variation code instead.

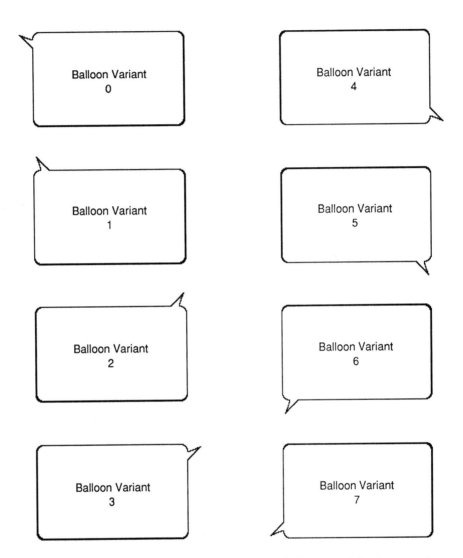

Figure 8-3. The eight standard balloon variations and their numeric codes

Balloons for menus, windows, and dialogs can be created using a general resource development tool such as Rez or using Apple's BalloonWriter program. BalloonWriter is essentially a "balloon processor" that simplifies the task of connecting help messages to the more common instances of balloons. BalloonWriter cannot currently define a help balloon for the application icon itself—for that you must use Rez, as you will see in Chapter 9.

▶ Balloon Help for Menus and Menu Items

Balloon help for each menu and its menu items is provided by a single resource of type 'hmnu'. This resource specifies a different message for each of several states for a menu title and for each of the items it contains. The three states of a menu title are as follows:

- enabled
- disabled (dimmed)
- modal dialog is present, forcing menu title to be disabled

The five states of a menu item are the following:

- enabled, but not checked or marked
- disabled (dimmed)
- marked by a check mark and enabled
- marked by a character other than a check mark and enabled
- modal dialog is present, forcing the menu item to be disabled

The resource ID of an 'hmnu' resource should be the same as the menu with which it is associated. An 'hmnu' for a menu with a resource ID of 133, for example, would use 133 as its own resource ID.

The 'hmnu' resource begins with the standard help header, messages for any item that lacks its own balloon message, messages for each state of the menu title, and messages for each state of each item. (The sets of messages for the menu items appear in the same order as the menu items appear in the menu.) The message for a menu item that is disabled due to the presence of a modal dialog is actually part of the set of messages for a menu title. This means each message section contains four messages.

Balloon messages can be specified in one of five different ways in the Rez source for the 'hmnu' definition (or in any other Help Manager resource):

- as an imbedded Pascal string—Use the HMStringItem keyword.
- as a picture ('PICT' resource)—Use the HMPictItem keyword.
- as a Pascal string ('STR ' resource)—Use the HMSTRResItem keyword.

- as a Pascal string and index ('STR#' resource)—Use the HMStringResItem keyword.
- as styled text (a 'TEXT' and a 'styl' resource)—Use the HMTEResItem keyword.

It is easiest to put embedded Pascal strings in an 'hmnu' resource since you only need to define a single long resource instead of several smaller resources. Localization may be a bit more difficult, however, since strings will be imbedded in the 'hmnu' resource itself.

Listing 8-1 shows the Rez source used to create menu help balloons for the Special menu in the Skeleton application. Figure 8-4 shows Skeleton's Special menu with some of its possible help balloons.

Listing 8-1. Rez source for Skeleton's balloon help messages for the Special menu

```
// Balloon help for the Special menu
// resource ID must match that of the 'Special' menu
resource 'hmnu' (mSpecial, "Special menu's Balloons", purgeable) {
    // Standard header block comes first
    HelpMgrVersion,
    hmDefaultOptions, // use defaults
    0,                 // use std balloon def function
    0,                 // use balloon position 0
    // Now we do the messages for items without messages
    HMSkipItem {       // no items will be missing, so skip this section
        },
    {
    // Now we do the messages for the menu title
    HMStringItem {                              // use embedded pstrings
            "Special Menu\n\nUse the item in this "
            "menu to call your test routine.", // 'enabled' message
            "Special Menu\n\nUse the item in this "
            "menu to call your test routine.\n\n"
            "Unavailable right now.",        // 'disabled' message
            "This menu is unavailable until you "
            "dismiss the dialog/alert.",     // 'dimmed title' due to dialog
            "This item is unavailable until you "
            "dismiss the dialog/alert.",     // 'dimmed item' due to dialog
        },
    // Now we do the first menu item's messages
    HMStringItem {                              // use embedded pstrings
            "Calls your test routine.",      // enabled message
            "Not available until a window "
            "has been opened.",              // disabled message
            "",                              // item is never checked
            "",                              // item is never marked
        },
    // Additional items would go here...
    // No more items, so wrap it up.
    }
};
```

Figure 8-4. Skeleton's Special menu and some of its balloons

If you specify an empty string for an item's balloon message and the Help Manager needs a message for that item, the Help Manager uses the corresponding message in the "missing item" section of the resource (the first section after the help header). Since all possible cases are covered in the example, you don't need to provide any "missing item" messages. If you prefer not to provide a series of empty strings for the four "missing item" messages, specify the item HMSkipItem after the help header so that the Help Manager will skip over the "missing" section. If an item lacks a message, and you provide no "missing item" message, the Help Manager does not display a balloon for that item.

Listing 8-2 shows how to define help balloon messages using each of the other techniques the Help Manager understands. You can use any of these techniques instead of the HMStringItem technique used in the Rez source in Listing 8-1.

Listing 8-2. Different ways to implement balloon messages

```
// Use 'STR#' resource
// Each entry is a 'STR#' resource ID and an index
// into that 'STR#' resource.
HMStringResItem { // use "0,0" for no message
    mSpecial, 1, // enabled message
    mSpecial, 2, // disabled message
    0, 0,        // item is never checked
    0, 0,        // item is never marked
},
```

Listing 8-2. Different ways to implement balloon messages
(continued)

```
// Use 'STR ' resource
// Each entry is the ID of a 'STR ' resource
HMSTRResItem {     // use "0" for no message
    2362,          // enabled message
    2363,          // disabled message
    0,             // items is never checked
    0,             // items is never marked
},


// Use 'PICT' resource
// Each entry is the ID of a 'PICT' resource
HMPictItem {                 // use "0" for no message
    2362,          // enabled message
    2363,          // disabled message
    0,             // items is never checked
    0,             // items is never marked
},


// Use styled text ('TEXT' + 'styl' resource)
// Each entry is the ID of a 'TEXT' and 'styl' resource
// 'TEXT' & 'styl' resource IDs MUST be identical
// for each item
HMTEResItem {                // use "0" for no message
    2362,          // enabled message
    2363,          // disabled message
    0,             // items is never checked
    0,             // items is never marked
},
```

▶ Dynamic Menu Items

It is quite common for a menu item to change its name when selected—a
Show Palette item could be renamed Hide Palette after it is selected and
vice versa. As explained earlier, sets of balloon messages for menu items
are specified in an 'hmnu' resource in the order the items appear in the
menu, with each item having one message for each of its four possible
states (enabled, disabled, checked, and marked). However, none of these

states relate to the situation where an item changes its name, even though a new set of messages is clearly needed for such an item.

Instead of including a single `HMStringItem` entry for this kind of menu item, include a `HMCompareItem` entry for each name the item may assume. Each `HMCompareItem` includes one of the item names and an `HMStringItem` defining the set of four help messages to be used when that item name is active.

Listing 8-3 shows the Rez source for a fictitious menu whose second item's name toggles between two values.

Listing 8-3. Rez source for a menu with a dynamic item

```
#define SystemSevenOrLater 1
#include "Types.r"
#include "SysTypes.r"
#include "BalloonTypes.r"
#define mFictitious 132 /* three items. second items has two
                           possible names */

// Balloon help for the 'Fictitious' menu
resource 'hmnu' (mFictitious, "Fictitious help", purgeable) {
   // Standard header block comes first
   HelpMgrVersion,
   hmDefaultOptions, // use defaults
   0,                     // use std balloon def function
   3,                     // use balloon position 3
   // Now we do the messages for items without messages
   HMSkipItem {           // no missing items, so skip this section
   },
   {
   // Now we do the messages for the menu title
   HMStringItem {         // use embedded pstrings
     "Fictitious Menu\n\nUse the items in this "
     "menu to do various things.", // 'enabled' message
     "Fictitious Menu\n\nUse the items in this "
     "menu to do various things.\n\n"
     "Unavailable right now.",    // 'disabled' message
     "This menu is unavailable until you "
     "dismiss the dialog/alert.",
     "This item is unavailable until you "
     "dismiss the dialog/alert.",
     },
   // Now we do the first menu item's messages
   HMStringItem {         // use embedded pstrings
     "Sends information to the Debug Window",   // enabled
     "Sends information to the Debug Window"
     "\n\nNot available until the Debug "
     "Window is visible.",            // disabled
```

Listing 8-3. Rez source for a menu with a dynamic item
(continued)

```
      "",                          // item is never checked
      "",                          // item is never marked
    },
// Now we do the second menu item's messages
HMCompareItem { /* second item, first name */
  "Show Debug Window",   /* the item's name */
  HMStringItem {    // use embedded pstrings
    "Makes the Debug window appear.", // enabled message
    "",             // item is never disabled
    "",             // item is never checked
    "",             // item is never marked
  },
},
HMCompareItem { /* second item, second name */
  "Hide Debug Window",   /* the item's name */
  HMStringItem {          // use embedded pstrings
    "Makes the Debug window disappear.",    // enabled
    "",              // item is never disabled
    "",              // item is never checked
    "",              // item is never marked
  },
},
// Now we do the third menu item's messages
HMStringItem {          // use embedded pstrings
  "Drops into MacsBug.", // enabled message
  "Drops into MacsBug.\n\nNot available "
  "since MacsBug is not installed.", // disabled message
  "",              // item is never checked
  "",              // item is never marked
},
  }
};
```

▶ Adding Items to the Help Menu

With System 7's introduction of a Help menu that's always available, you no longer need an application to add its own help menu items to the Apple menu or to include a Help button in its About box. Instead, your application should append its help menu items to the Help menu, the standard place System 7 users will look for help.

Items appended to the system's Help menu are available only to the application that appended them, since every application has its own copy of the Help menu. This prevents overcrowding of the Help menu when many applications are running at once. Still, added items should include the name of the application to emphasize that they are specific to a particular application and are not system help items.

| Warning ▶ |

Do not call **GetMHandle** to obtain a handle to the Help menu because that routine gives you a handle to the *system's* Help menu. Installing items into the system's Help menu causes your item to appear under all applications and provides no way for your application to detect a hit on the item when your application is in the background.

The proper technique is to call the **HMGetHelpMenuHandle** routine to obtain a handle to the Help menu that is specific to your application. Then use the handle returned by **HMGetHelpMenuHandle** as an input to the standard **AppendMenu** routine in order to add your help items to the Help menu. The function prototype for **HMGetHelpMenuHandle** is as follows:

```
pascal OSErr HMGetHelpMenuHandle( MenuHandle *mh );
```

When a user selects an application-specific item from the Help menu, the menu item number is returned in the low word and the menu ID is returned in the high word of the result returned by **MenuSelect** and **MenuKey**. The Help menu's ID is represented by the constant kHMHelpMenuID in the interface file Balloons.h.

Care should be taken to determine which item in the Help menu belongs to the application. At present, System 7 uses the first four positions (two of which are dividing lines) for its own needs, but that number could climb in the future, so don't assume the item ID for your custom help item will be 5. Instead, call **CountMItems** to find the ID of the last item in the menu, which is the help item you added.

Naturally, you should also provide help balloons for the items you append to the Help menu. To do this, you use a slightly different 'hmnu' resource, with an ID of kHMHelpMenuID, to attach balloons to the appended items. The menu title section of this 'hmnu' resource is omitted; you provide only the header, missing items, and menu items sections. The Help Manager provides messages of its own for the standard items in the Help menu.

Listing 8-4 shows the source code for adding two items to the Help menu and Listing 8-5 shows how to handle the selection of those items. Listing 8-6 shows the Rez source for attaching help messages to the two extra items in the Help menu.

Listing 8-4. Source code for adding items to the Help menu

```
/* The following routine is responsible for appending */
/* application-specific help items to the 'Help' menu.*/
/* It's called from "Initialize()", just before */
/* "DrawMenuBar()" is called.*/
void DoAddHMItems(void)
{
    MenuHandle      myHelpMenuHndl;
    OSErr               myErr;

    myErr = HMGetHelpMenuHandle(&myHelpMenuHndl);
    if ((!myErr) && (myHelpMenuHndl != nil)) {
        AppendMenu(myHelpMenuHndl,
                (ConstStr255Param) "\pSkeleton Tutorial");
        AppendMenu(myHelpMenuHndl,
                (ConstStr255Param) "\pPizza Help");
    }
}
```

Listing 8-5. Source code for detecting hits on the appended items

```
/* add the following to the variables in 'DoMenuCommand()' */
    short               tutHelpID;
    short               pizHelpID;
    MenuHandle      myHelpMenuHndl;
    OSErr               myErr;


/* add to the end of 'switch' statement in 'DoMenuCommand()' */
    case kHMHelpMenuID:
        myErr = HMGetHelpMenuHandle(&myHelpMenuHndl);
        if ((!myErr) && (myHelpMenuHndl != nil)) {
            pizHelpID = CountMItems(myHelpMenuHndl);
            tutHelpID = pizHelpID - 1;
            if ( menuItem == tutHelpID) {
                /* put code here to provide quick tutorial on app */
            }
            else {
            if (menuItem == pizHelpID) {
                /* put code here to provide list of pizza places */
            }
        }
    }
    break;
```

Listing 8-6. Rez source for help messages for items added to the Help menu

```
resource 'hmnu' (kHMHelpMenuID, "Help Menu balloons", purgeable) {
    // Standard header block comes first
    HelpMgrVersion,
    hmDefaultOptions,  // use defaults
    0,              // use std balloon def function
    0,              // use balloon position 0
    // Now we do the messages for items without messages
    HMSkipItem {      // no missing items
        },
    {
    // Now we do the first appended item's messages
    HMStringItem {
        "Provides a quick tutorial for this application.",
        "",          // never disabled by app
        "",          // never checked by app
        "",          // never marked by app
        },
    // Now we do the second appended item's messages
    HMStringItem {
        "Provides a list of the author's favorite pizza vendors.",
        "",          // never disabled by app
        "",          // never checked by app
        "",          // never marked by app
        },
    }
};
```

▶ Balloon Help for Dialogs and Alerts

The Help menu is always enabled, even if a modal dialog or alert box is on the screen. Users puzzled by items in a dialog or alert box can use the standard help system to learn more before selecting an option from the dialog. Generally, each item in a dialog or alert should have its own balloon help message, but some items, such as a set of radio buttons, can be grouped together for clarity so that they all share the same message.

System 7's Help Manager provides two basic methods for applications to add balloon help to dialog and alert boxes. One method involves the use of 'hwin' resources and may require changes to the application's source code. This approach will be covered in the "Using 'hwin' Resources with Dialogs and Alerts" section of this chapter.

The other method for adding balloon help to a dialog or alert box is to include a HelpItem at the end of the dialog's 'DITL' resource that refers to either a dialog help resource ('hdlg') or a help rectangle resource ('hrct').

▶ Using 'hdlg' Resources

A dialog help resource contains a slightly modified balloon help header, messages to be displayed for items lacking a specific message, and messages for each item in the dialog's 'DITL' list. The Help Manager automatically displays and removes the help balloons for each item in the 'DITL' based on the information it finds in the 'hdlg' resource.

The help entries in an 'hdlg' resource can be specified using the same Rez keywords used for an 'hmnu' resource: HMStringItem, HMPictItem, HMStringResItem, HMTEResItem, and HMSTRResItem. The structures of these 'hdlg' entries are different, however, in that they begin with a balloon tip point and a hot rectangle.

The tip point indicates where the tip of the balloon is to appear and is expressed relative to the top left corner of the rectangle of the 'DITL' item to which it corresponds. Specify a point of {0, 0} to select the default tip location (the middle right edge of the item's rectangle).

The hot rectangle, also expressed relative to the 'DITL' item rectangle, is the area of the screen for which you want to provide balloon help; when the mouse cursor enters this area, and balloon help is on, the help balloon appears. If you specify the default rectangle of {0, 0, 0, 0}, the Help Manager uses the rectangle of the 'DITL' item to which the 'hdlg' entry corresponds.

The help header for an 'hdlg' resource has an extra field inserted between the standard help header's first and second fields. This extra field tells the Help Manager which item is the first one for which help balloons are defined. By arranging dialog items carefully and adjusting the starting number in the 'hdlg' header, minor items that need no balloons can be easily skipped. Just put the items that don't need balloons first in the 'DITL' resource and set the "first item to get a balloon" field of the 'hdlg' resource appropriately. Items are numbered starting from zero, so if you want to skip the first two items in a 'DITL', for example, put a 2 in this field.

There are two other ways to prevent a balloon message from appearing for an individual dialog item. The first is to define all 'DITL' items that should not have messages at the end of the 'DITL' resource and then provide balloon messages in the 'hdlg' resource only for the items that need them (that is, provide fewer messages than there are items). Since messages within the 'hdlg' resource match up with consecutive 'DITL' items, the last items will have no messages—if no message is available, no balloon is displayed.

The second method is to use the constant HMSkipItem instead of HMStringItem in the 'hdlg' resource for the items that are to have no balloon messages—this way, individual items can be skipped without juggling them to the beginning or end of the 'DITL' resource.

For the Help Manager to know whether a dialog has help balloons associated with it, you must add a hidden item, known as a HelpItem, to the dialog's 'DITL' resource. The presence of the help item tells the Help Manager to scan the dialog's 'DITL' resource and match the messages in an 'hdlg' resource with the items in the 'DITL'.

The last field of the help item's resource definition determines whether an 'hdlg' or an 'hrct' resource (explained later in this section) is used. Specify HMScanhdlg to use an 'hdlg' resource or HMScanhrct to use an 'hrct' resource. The ID of the matching 'hdlg' or 'hrct' resource is given just after the HMScanhdlg keyword in the Rez source for the help item's definition.

Listing 8-7 shows the Rez source for the help balloon item (HelpItem) that should be added, just like any other item, to the 'DITL' resource for the About box. The Skeleton application's About box is an alert and Listing 8-8 shows the Rez source for the 'hdlg' resource that provides the balloons for it. If you forget to include the HelpItem in the 'DITL', the 'hdlg' resource is ignored and no balloons will appear for the dialog!

Figure 8-5 shows Skeleton's About box along with all of its balloons.

Listing 8-7. Rez source for the About box's help item

```
// Use this one for 'hdlg'
    {0, 0, 0, 0},              // the rect for the help item
    HelpItem {                 // HelpItem defined in Types.r
        disabled,              // disable it
        HMScanhdlg {rAboutBox}   // use 'hdlg', ID = rAboutBox
        },


// Use this one for 'hrct'
    {0, 0, 0, 0},
    HelpItem {
        disabled,
        HMScanhrct {rAboutBox}   // use 'hrct', ID = rAboutBox
    },
```

Listing 8-8. Rez source for the About box's 'hdlg' resource

```
// Balloon help for the About box (which is an alert)
resource 'hdlg' (rAboutBox, "About box's help", purgeable) {
    // Standard header block comes first
    HelpMgrVersion,
    0,                        // provide help starting with first item
    hmSaveBitsNoWindow,       // makes alert cleaner
    0,                        // use std balloon def function
```

Listing 8-8. Rez source for the About box's 'hdlg' resource (continued)

```
0,                                // use balloon position 0
      // Now we do the messages for items without messages
      HMSkipItem {               // all items are given their own message

            },
      // Now we do the messages for the items
      {
            // the OK button comes first in our DITL
            HMStringItem {        // use embedded pstrings
                  {0,0},          // tip at default location
                  {0,0,0,0},      // use item's rect
                  "Click this button to "  // the enabled OK button
                  "hide the About box.",
                  "",             // OK btn never disabled
                  "",             // OK btn never has check mark
                  "",             // or any other marking
            },
            // the application name and version number comes second
            HMStringItem {        // use embedded pstrings
                  {5,80},         // put tip on top right
                  {0,0,0,0},        // use item's rect
                  "",             // static text never enabled
                  "Shows the name of this "     // msg for dimmed item
                  "application and its version number.",
                  "",             // never has a check
                  ""              // or any other marking
            },
            // the text of our copyright message comes third
            HMStringItem {        // use embedded pstrings
                  {5,115},        // put tip along top right
                  {0,0,0,0},        // use item's rect
                  "",             // static text never enabled
                  "Explains who wrote this application "  // msg for this
                  "and when it was copyrighted.",         // dimmed item
                  "",             // never has a check
                  ""              // or any other marking
            }
      }
};
```

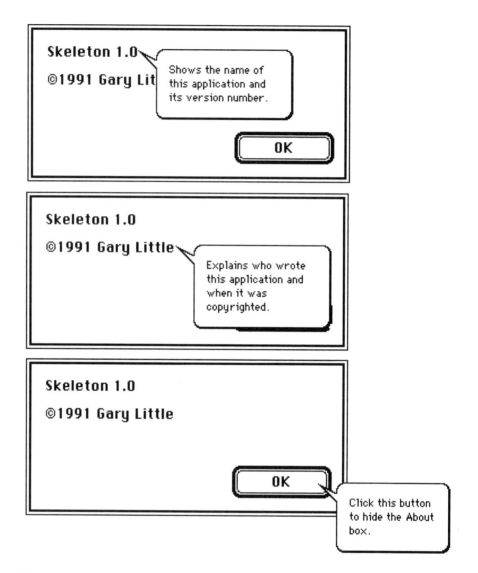

Figure 8-5. Skeleton's About box and its balloons

The bold outline surrounding the default button in an alert or dialog box is not redrawn properly when a help balloon covering it disappears. To avoid this problem, use the pre-defined constant hmSaveBitsNoWindow in the options field of the balloon header. This option causes the Help Manager to buffer the pixels on the screen prior to drawing the balloon and to replace those pixels after the balloon is removed.

Warning ▶

Since some applications use a dialog filter procedure to provide simple animation in their dialogs, the technique of replacing the existing pixels on the screen can cause problems—the image being replaced on the screen might no longer match what should be there. Therefore, use the hmSaveBitsNoWindow option with care.

▶ Using 'hrct' Resources

An 'hrct' resource is a series of rectangles and messages associated with those rectangles. You can use it, instead of an 'hdlg' resource, to provide balloon messages for items within dialogs and alerts.

When told to use an 'hrct' resource, the Help Manager uses the rectangles specified within the 'hrct' resource to determine whether the mouse cursor is in a hot area—item rectangles in a 'DITL' resource are not used as they usually are for 'hdlg' resources. This means you can easily arrange for a group of related items to share the same help balloon by providing one rectangle that surrounds all the items. This strategy makes sense where a single message is clearer than individual messages for each item.

The 'hrct' format is somewhat simpler than 'hdlg' since it provides only one message for each item, regardless of whether that item is enabled or disabled. The 'hdlg' resource, on the other hand, permits four different messages (enabled, disabled, checked, and marked) for each item. Another difference is that the 'hrct' resource does not include messages for missing items since the resource deals with rectangles, not items.

Specifying where the balloon's tip should be placed is handled differently in an 'hrct' resource than it is in an 'hdlg' resource. Balloon tip locations in an 'hrct' resource are relative to the dialog's frame, with the top left corner of the dialog being considered 0,0. Tip locations in an 'hdlg' resource are relative to the item's rectangle given in the 'DITL' resource, with the top left corner of the item's rectangle being considered 0,0.

Listing 8-9 shows the Rez source for the 'hrct' resource you could use to accomplish the same task as the 'hdlg' resource in Listing 8-8.

Listing 8-9. Rez source for the About box's 'hrct' resource

```
// Balloon help for the About box - using hrct's
resource 'hrct' (rAboutBox, "About box's help", purgeable) {
    HelpMgrVersion,
    hmSaveBitsNoWindow,            // makes Alert look cleaner
    0,                             // use std balloon def function
    0,                             // use balloon position 0
      {
      // the OK button comes first in our 'DITL'
      HMStringItem {               // use embedded pstrings
          {98,186},                   // tip on left side
          {88, 180, 108, 260},     // must provide the rect
          "Click this button to "
          "hide the About box.",
      },
      // the application name and version number comes second
      HMStringItem {               // use embedded pstrings
          {13,6},                  // place balloon tip along left side
          {8, 8, 24, 214},     // must provide item's rect
          "Shows the name of this application "
          "and its version number.",
      },
      // the text of our copyright message comes third
      HMStringItem {               // use embedded pstrings
          {37,6},                  // place balloon tip along left side
          {32, 8, 48, 237},    // rect around the collar
          "Explains who wrote this application "
          "and when it was copyrighted.",
      }
    }
};
```

▶ Testing Help Balloons

Testing your attempts to provide balloon help for dialogs and alerts can be simplified considerably by the **HMSetBalloons** routine that lets you force balloons to be shown or hidden. **HMSetBalloons** takes a Boolean as its only input—true turns balloon help on, false turns it off.

The function prototype for **HMSetBalloons** is the following:

```
pascal OSErr HMSetBalloons( Boolean flag );
```

Before forcing balloon help on with **HMSetBalloons**, the user's current setting should be saved so it can be restored later. Call **HMGetBalloons** to return this setting; it returns a Boolean true for on, or false for off.

Listing 8-10 shows the source code for a `ShowAlert` routine that saves the current status of balloon help, forces balloon help on, displays the same alert used for the About box (so the balloon messages for its items can be seen easily), and restores the user's setting for balloon help after the dialog is dismissed. The user can change the state of balloon help while the dialog is present, so you must call **HMGetBalloons** after the alert has been dismissed and use its return value to determine whether to restore the earlier setting. Otherwise, the user could have balloon help on going into the alert, turn it off before dismissing the alert, and the `ShowAlert` routine would erroneously turn it back on before exiting.

Listing 8-10. Source code to force balloon help on

```
void ShowAlert(void)
    {
        short         itemHit;
        Boolean       curHMStatus;
        Boolean       myHMStatus;
        OSErr         myErr;

        curHMStatus = HMGetBalloons();      /* buffer current status */
        myErr = HMSetBalloons( true );      /* force balloons on */
        itemHit = Alert( rAboutBox, 0L );   /* display About box */
        myHMStatus = HMGetBalloons();       /* check current status */
        if myHMStatus { /* did user leave Help on? */
            myErr = HMSetBalloons(curHMStatus);
        }

    }
```

▶ Balloon Help for Standard Windows

To define help balloons for a standard window—one not associated with a 'DITL' resource—use an 'hwin' resource. An 'hwin' resource ties an 'hrct' resource to all windows whose names match the name specified in the 'hwin' resource, or whose windowKind values match the windowKind specified in the 'hwin' resource. (You can also use an 'hwin' resource to tie an 'hdlg' resource to dialog and alert windows as you will read in the next section.)

An 'hwin' resource's header contains less information than the standard balloon header, using only the version and options fields. An 'hwin' resource also includes a series of items, each of which specifies the type of help resource to use ('hrct' or 'hdlg') and the matching window name or windowKind value.

The window name field consists of the number of characters of a window's name to use when checking for a match, followed by the actual name string. If your application opens all new documents as "Untitled1", "Untitled2", and so on, it could use "8" as the number of characters and "Untitled" as the string to check against. In this case, all "Untitledxxx" windows would have the same set of help messages.

To match based on windowKind, the third field (number of characters to match) should be a negative number. The absolute value of that negative number is the windowKind value to match and the negative sign tells the Help Manager to match by windowKind instead of by window title.

You may design your application so that each document window has the same windowKind value and other types of windows have a different windowKind value. This would allow you to attach one set of help messages for the common elements of all windows with a given windowKind (such as rulers in a word processor's document windows).

If the hmMatchInTitle bit is set in the options field of the 'hwin' resource, the Help Manager returns a match if any portion of the window name contains the string specified in the last field. Thus, a window named "I'm Untitled" would be considered a match for "Untitled" only if the hmMatchInTitle bit is set. Otherwise, only strings such as "Untitled1" or "Untitled and Loving It" would be considered matches.

Listing 8-11 shows the Rez source for an 'hwin' resource connecting the message window of the Skeleton application to its help message. Don't use this technique for Skeleton's main window because it can be resized. See the section "Windows with Dynamic Objects" for tips on how to add balloon help to a window like this.

Listing 8-11. Rez source for window help based on 'hwin' resources

```
// Balloon help for all windows - using 'hwin' resource
// 'hwin' connects to either 'hrct' or 'hdlg'
    resource 'hwin' (rWHelp, "Help for all wdnws", purgeable) {
        HelpMgrVersion,
        hmDefaultOptions,
        {
            rMainWindow, // resource ID of main window
            'hrct',      // resource type to connect with
            8,           // match 8 characters in name
            "Untitled",  // the 8 characters to match...

            rDebugWindow,// resource ID of message window
            'hrct',      // resource type to connect with
            7,           // match 7 characters in name
```

Listing 8-11. Rez source for window help based on `hwin` resources (continued)

```
            "Message",           // the 7 characters to match...
      },
};

   resource 'hrct' (rDebugWindow, "Msg wndw's help", purgeable) {
         HelpMgrVersion,
         hmDefaultOptions,     // use default options
         0,                    // use std balloon def function
         6,                    // use balloon position 6
         {
              HMStringItem {   // use embedded pstrings
              {15, 410},       // tip's location
              {0, 0, 30, 475}, // item's rect
              "Debugging messages are sent "
              "here during development.",
               },
         }
      };
```

▶ Using 'hwin' Resources with Dialogs and Alerts

As mentioned at the beginning of the previous section, you can add balloon messages to dialog and alert windows by including resources of type 'hwin' in the application. This is an alternative to the technique of adding a HelpItem to the dialog's 'DITL' resource which ties to an 'hdlg' or an 'hrct' resource.

The 'hwin' resource ties an 'hrct' or an 'hdlg' resource to a window by matching either the window's name or its windowKind value to information in the 'hwin' resource. For dialogs and alerts you will usually want to match the windowKind of 2, since modal dialogs aren't normally titled. The use of an 'hwin' resource for tying help messages to dialogs and alerts requires fewer resources (since all dialogs and alerts share the same 'hwin' resource), but results in less flexibility than using a 'DITL' HelpItem that allows each dialog or alert to have its own set of messages.

You can compensate for this lack of flexibility by dynamically attaching another set of help messages to a dialog or alert using the

HMSetDialogResID routine. The function prototype for **HMSetDialogResID** is the following:

```pascal
pascal OSErr HMSetDialogResID( short resID );
```

The sole parameter passed to **HMSetDialogResID** is the resource ID of an `'hdlg'` resource. The messages within this `'hdlg'` resource, in addition to any messages attached through an `'hwin'` resource (matched via the `windowKind` field), are used the next time a dialog or alert is displayed. You are responsible for defining no more than one balloon for the same item—if you do, the results are unpredictable.

If you define a single `'hwin'` resource for the common elements in all alerts and dialogs in an application (such as the OK and Cancel buttons), you can use **HMSetDialogResID** to attach additional messages to the rest of the items within each alert or dialog. This strategy reduces the redundancy within help messages by combining all common messages into one resource and still permits each item to have its own unique message by attaching the additional messages.

When using this strategy for a child dialog (one that is brought up by another dialog), you should save the resource ID of the current dialog's attached `'hdlg'` before calling **HMSetDialogResID** to attach a different set of messages to the child dialog. The resource ID of the currently-attached `'hdlg'` resource can be obtained by calling **HMGetDialogResID** and restored when the child dialog is closed by calling **HMSetDialogResID**.

The function prototype for **HMGetDialogResID** is as follows:

```pascal
pascal OSErr HMGetDialogResID( short *resID );
```

The current `'hdlg'` resource ID is returned in the `resID` variable passed to **HMGetDialogResID**.

Passing a -1 for the `resID` parameter when calling **HMSetDialogResID** removes the attached set of messages without attaching another set. This causes only those messages within the `'hwin'` resource's message block to be used, since passing -1 clears the additional messages.

▶ Windows with Dynamic Objects

As you've seen, the best way to attach help messages to windows that have a fixed size and static objects is to use `'hwin'` and `'hrct'` resources. You must use a different strategy to add help messages to windows that can be resized or that contain dynamic objects that move about because of scrolling or dragging operations. You cannot use 'hrct' resources because the rectangles in them are fixed and cannot be changed easily.

Showing the balloons associated with dynamic objects in a window is the application's responsibility. To do this properly, it must track the location of the dynamic objects and carefully maintain the rectangles surrounding them. When the mouse enters a help rectangle, it must call a routine to display the help balloon. You don't have to worry about explicitly removing the balloon when the mouse leaves the help rectangle because the Help Manager does this for you automatically in most cases.

Before an application displays a balloon, it should call **HMGetBalloons** to determine whether or not the user wants to see balloons. If **HMGetBalloons** returns true, a balloon can be displayed by calling **HMShowBalloon** and hidden (for those situations the Help Manager does not handle) by calling **HMRemoveBalloon**. The function prototypes for **HMShowBalloon** and **HMRemoveBalloon** are as follows:

```
pascal OSErr HMShowBalloon( HMMessageRecord *aHelpMsg,
            Point tip,
            RectPtr alternateRect,
            Ptr tipProc,
            short theProc,
            short variant,
            short method );

pascal OSErr HMRemoveBalloon( void );
```

The meaning of each of these parameters is as follows:

aHelpMsg—Contains a pointer to a help message record (HMMessageRecord) that ties a help message to a dynamic rectangle. The structure of an HMMessageRecord is shown in Listing 8-12.

Listing 8-12. The structure of an HMMessageRecord record

```
struct HMMessageRecord {
    short  hmmHelpType;
    union {
            char                hmmString[256];
            short               hmmPict;
            Handle              hmmTEHandle;
            HMStringResType     hmmStringRes;
            short               hmmPictRes;
            Handle              hmmPictHandle;
```

Listing 8-12. The structure of an HMMessageRecord record (continued)

```
            short                hmmTERes;
            short                hmmSTRRes;
    } u;
};
```

The `HMStringResType` data type is a structure composed of two words: `hmmResID` (the 'STR#' resource ID) and `hmmIndex` (the 'STR#' resource index).

The first field in a help message record, `hmmHelpType`, is an integer describing the type of balloon message referred to in the union that follows it. Use the following symbolic names in the Rez source to specify the balloon message type:

```
#define khmmString 1      /* a literal pstring */
#define khmmPict 2        /* a resource ID to a 'PICT' resource */
#define khmmStringRes 3   /* a resource ID and index to a 'STR#' rsrc */
#define khmmTEHandle 4    /* a TextEdit handle */
#define khmmPictHandle 5  /* a QuickDraw picture handle */
#define khmmTERes 6       /* a resource ID to 'TEXT' / 'styl' resources */
#define khmmSTRRes 7      /* a resource ID to a 'STR ' resource */
```

The next field contains the actual reference to the help message, which is either a resource ID or a handle, depending on what's in `hmmHelpType`.

tip—The point on the screen, in global coordinates, where the Help Manager should place the tip of the help balloon.

alternateRect—The rectangle, in global coordinates, in which the mouse should be tracked. If you provide a nonzero value and the mouse moves outside of this rectangle, the the Help Manager removes the balloon automatically. If you put zeros here, the application is responsible for determining when to remove a displayed help balloon—you remove it with the **HMRemoveBalloon** routine.

tipProc—Points to a routine that is called before the balloon is actually displayed. This gives the application a chance to modify the tip location and the `alternateRect` if needed. To use the standard `tipProc`, put `0L` in this field.

theProc—Specifies which balloon definition procedure the Help Manager is to use to draw the balloon. Balloon definition procedures are stored as 'WDEF' resources. Putting a 0 in this field tells the Help

Manager to use the standard balloon definition procedure. To use a different balloon definition procedure, store the resource ID of the desired 'WDEF' resource in this field.

variant—The variation code to use when drawing the balloon. Variation codes of 0 through 7 are standard to the Help Manager (see Figure 8-3). If you specify a custom balloon definition procedure in theProc, the value of variant is passed to the procedure.

method—Describes how the screen should be redrawn when a help balloon is removed—similar in concept to the options field of a standard balloon header. Only three values are supported and constants have been defined for each:

```
#define kHMRegularWindow 0        /* don't save bits behind balloon,
                                     generate update event when
                                     balloon is removed */
#define kHMSaveBitsNoWindow 1     /* save bits, no update event */
#define kHMSaveBitsWindow 2       /* save bits, generate update
                                     event when balloon is removed */
```

An array of rectangles, referenced by the refCon field of each window record, is perhaps the easiest way to keep track of the rectangles surrounding movable objects within a window. The mouse's position should be checked during null events to determine whether it is within one of the front window's dynamic rectangles. If the user has turned balloon help on and the mouse is within a dynamic rectangle, the application should call **HMShowBalloon**.

The routines within an application that move dynamic objects should also be responsible for adjusting that object's entry in the array of rectangles. The routines that add new movable objects should be responsible for adding a rectangle to the array and setting it to match the new object's location. This way, the rectangles always match the true location of dynamic objects and there's always a rectangle for each object.

Listing 8-13 contains the source code for a DoIdle routine that displays a different balloon message for each of three rectangles in a window when balloon help is on. Each rectangle represents one dynamic object in the main window. The outlines of the rectangles are drawn (by the window's content-drawing procedure) to make it easier to test the routine. Listing 8-14 shows the Rez source for the 'STR#' resource used by the **HMShowBalloon** routine.

Listing 8-13. Providing balloon help for dynamic objects

```
#define rDynamicBalloon 131

/* The following routine is responsible for implementing manual balloon help */
void DoIdle( EventRecord *event)
{
    extern Rect         gMyRect[]; /* defined in Skeleton.c — 3 elements */
    extern short        gMyBalloon; /* defined in Skeleton.c */
    extern Rect         gTempRect;

    WindowPtr           myWindow;
    GrafPtr             curPort;
    Point               myTip, myTL, myBR;
    short               i,j,k;
    OSErr               myErr;
    Rect                myTempRect;
    HMMessageRecord     myHelpMsg;
    Boolean             isBHelpOn;
    Boolean             ourBalloon;

    isBHelpOn = HMGetBalloons();
    if (isBHelpOn) { /* skip all this if help is off */
       ourBalloon = false; /* assume no balloon up */
       GetPort(&curPort);
       myWindow = FrontWindow();
       SetPort(myWindow);
       GetMouse(&myTip);/* get the current location of the mouse */
       if (PtInRect(myTip, &(myWindow->portRect))) { /* is the mouse in the
                                                      front window? */
          for (i = 0 ; i < 3 ; i++) {
             if (PtInRect(myTip, &gMyRect[i])) { /* is the mouse any a rect? */
                ourBalloon = true;
                if (i != gMyBalloon) { /* if no balloon on this rect yet */
                       /* convert the rect from local to global coords */
                       myTempRect = gMyRect[i];
                       SetPt(&myTL, myTempRect.left, myTempRect.top);
                       SetPt(&myBR, myTempRect.right, myTempRect.bottom);
                       LocalToGlobal(&myTL);
                       LocalToGlobal(&myBR);
                       SetRect(&myTempRect, myTL.h, myTL.v, myBR.h, myBR.v);

                       /* set the tip to the middle of the rect */
                       j = (myBR.h - myTL.h) >> 1;
                       k = (myBR.v - myTL.v) >> 1;
                       SetPt(&myTip, myTL.h + j , myTL.v + k );

                       /* set up the help message record */
                       myHelpMsg.hmmHelpType = khmmStringRes; /* 'STR#' */
                       myHelpMsg.u.hmmStringRes.hmmResID = rDynamicBalloon;
                       myHelpMsg.u.hmmStringRes.hmmIndex = i + 1;
```

Listing 8-13. Providing balloon help for dynamic objects
(continued)

```
                        /* show the balloon */
                        myErr = HMShowBalloon(&myHelpMsg, myTip,
                                        &myTempRect, nil, 0, 0,
                                        kHMRegularWindow);
                        if (!myErr) {
                          gMyBalloon = i; /* balloon for item #i is on */
                        }
                    }
                }
            }
        }
        if (!ourBalloon) {
            gMyBalloon = -1; /* no balloon is active */
        }
        SetPort(curPort);  /*restore original GrafPort */
    }
}
```

Listing 8-14. Rez source for the 'STR#' resource used by the routine
in Listing 8-13

```
#define rDynamicBalloon 131

resource 'STR#' (rDynamicBalloon, "Dynamic item messages", purgeable) {

    "Adjusts the TAB stops for this document.",
    "Adjusts the indentation of the current line.",
    "Adjusts the left edge of the current line.",
};
```

▶ Summary

In this chapter, you learned the benefits that balloon help offers users of
your applications, explained the major features of balloon help, and
presented several examples of how to implement balloon help. By adding
balloon help to your applications, your customers will enjoy the benefits
of an on-screen, context-sensitive help system—something they will quickly
come to expect from all Macintosh applications.

Chapter 9 completes our exploration of System 7 by focusing on new
capabilities provided by the System 7 Finder.

9 ▶ Fit and Finish

Macintosh applications are renowned for the fact that they all use the same consistent user interface. As a result, users can learn to use new applications more quickly than would otherwise be possible. Just as important as the user interface an application employs, however, is how the application and its documents interact with the user through the services of the Finder.

This chapter focuses on several techniques you can use to make your application fit seamlessly with the Finder, thereby enhancing the user experience. In particular, the following topics are covered:

- how to define icon families for your application and its documents
- how to associate file types with the icons you define
- how to tell the Finder to associate documents with your application
- how to define a Finder help balloon for your application
- how to define a custom message the Finder can display if it can't find the application associated with a given document
- how to add comments to a file that can be viewed with the Finder Get Info command

By studying these topics and implementing the features they describe, you'll make your application an excellent Finder citizen.

▶ Icons, Signatures, and Bundles

One of the most endearing features of the Finder is its ability to automatically launch the correct application when the user opens (from the desktop) a document. Another is the Finder's ability to display unique icons for each type of application and document it encounters.

However, the Finder needs help before it can implement these features for your application. In particular, your application must include the following types of resources:

- icons for the application itself and each unique document type it creates
- a file reference ('FREF') that maps document types to specific icons
- a signature that uniquely identifies the application
- a bundle ('BNDL') that ties the signature, file references, and icons together

Experienced Macintosh programmers will realize that the same general rules also apply to pre-System 7 applications. However, it is now possible to define these resources in such a way as to take advantage of Finder features that are unique to System 7.

▶ Icon Families

Prior to System 7, all standard Finder icons were simple monochrome 32x32-pixel bitmaps. When the Finder needed a smaller version of an icon, it scaled the 32x32-pixel image into a 16x16-pixel image (often resulting in fuzzy mush). System 7, however, works with icons with 1, 4, or 8 bits of color information in both large (32x32) and small (16x16) sizes. A complete set of icons, called an *icon family*, is made up of six icons—an 'ICN#' (32x32 pixels, 1-bit deep), an 'icl4' (32x32, 4-bits deep), an 'icl8' (32x32, 8-bits deep), an 'ics#' (16x16, 1-bit deep), an 'ics4' (16x16, 4-bits deep), and an 'ics8' (16x16, 8-bits deep).

The Finder always uses the deepest color icon available (not exceeding the current setting in the Monitors control panel) but will use a shallower icon if you fail to provide an icon that matches the specified monitor depth.

If an application does not provide an icon for a given type of file, the Finder is forced to use generic icons for files of that type. Figure 9-1 shows the Finder's generic icons for applications, documents, and stationery pads. Don't get caught using them!

Application   Document   Stationery

Figure 9-1. Generic icons the Finder uses when an application
doesn't define its own icon family

All resources within an icon family have the same resource ID. An
application icon traditionally has an ID of 128 and its document icons
have consecutively numbered IDs beginning at 129. You should define an
icon family for each type of document file your application supports.

Icon Editors

So how do you create an icon family? Rez is definitely *not* the appropriate
tool to use to create icon resources from scratch unless you enjoy staring
at hex digits. The best tool is a graphical resource editor like ResEdit or
Resorcerer. Figure 9-2 shows ResEdit's icon editor in action.

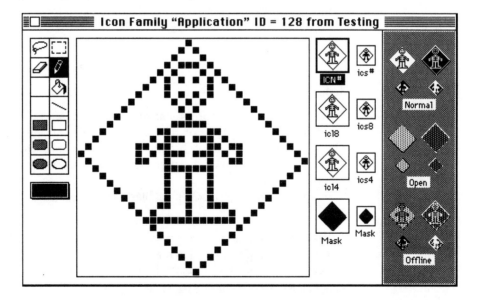

Figure 9-2. ResEdit's icon editor in action

When using ResEdit, begin creating a new icon family by requesting a new 'ICN#' resource for the application file. The best strategy is to define the 'icl8' icon first, then drag its image onto the 'icl4' image. ResEdit will automatically perform color substitution. Tweak the resulting image so that the 'icl4' icon looks just right, then drag it onto the 'ICN#' image and tweak it.

To quickly create small versions of the three large icons, drag their images to the corresponding small icon images. ResEdit will automatically scale your 32x32 images into 16x16 images. After tweaking the small icons, create masks by dragging the 'icl8' image to the 32x32 mask and the 'ics8' image to the 16x16 mask.

For complete information about how to use the ResEdit icon editor, refer to *ResEdit Reference*.

Note ▶

For consistency, color versions of your icons should be colorful examples of your black-and-white icon, not totally different. To help enforce this convention, the Finder uses only two masks for an icon family—one for large icons and one for small icons. With only one mask per icon size, you can't define radically different icons that look attractive when highlighted and unhighlighted on different screen depths.

Stationery Pad Icons

If your application supports stationery pad files, you should provide an icon family for each type of stationery pad. A stationery pad icon should follow the convention of having a "turned-up bottom corner" visual element but otherwise resemble the corresponding standard document icon.

Figure 9-3 shows the 32x32-pixel black-and-white icons defined for Skeleton.

Application   Document   Stationery

Figure 9-3. Skeleton's 32x32-pixel icons

Custom Icons

A new feature is that the System 7 Finder lets you define a *custom icon family* for any file. The Finder uses this family in preference to the one the application may have defined for all files of that file type. The custom icon family is stored in the *file's* resource fork and each icon in the family has an ID of -16455.

Take advantage of the custom icon feature to make all the document files that ship with your application look like they belong together even if they were created with different applications. For example, if you're including a HyperCard help stack with your product, include in the file a custom icon family that incorporates unique elements of your standard icon design. Preserving the look of the original icon helps the user remember what application will launch when the document is opened from the Finder.

▶ ## 'FREF' Resources

The Finder has always used 'FREF' (file reference) resources to associate document types the application supports with icons defined in the application's resource fork.

An 'FREF' resource consists of a file type, a *local icon ID* (which maps to a specific file type), and a file name field that should be left blank (see the definitions in Listing 9-1). Local IDs are used instead of actual IDs to prevent Finder conflicts from arising over use of the actual icon resource numbers. (Most applications use an icon with an ID of 128 for their application icon.)

The Finder translates local icon IDs into actual icon IDs using information in the 'BNDL' resource that you will learn about later in this section.

Stationery Pad Pseudo-File Types

A stationery pad document has the same file type as the corresponding standard document. (If a file is a stationery pad, the isStationery bit in its Finder information record will be set; see Chapter 2.) So how can we provide special icons for stationery pad documents? When the Finder tries to find an icon for a stationery pad document, it seeks an icon associated with the pseudo-file type 'sxxx' where xxx represents the last three characters of the stationery pad's file type. For example, if the stationery pad is a 'TEXT' file, the Finder looks for an icon associated with the 'sEXT' file type. Thus, to attach an icon family to a stationery pad document of a given type, include an 'FREF' resource for the appropriate pseudo-file type in the application's resource fork.

Opening with Foreign Documents

The System 7 Finder introduces the ability to open an application and pass it the name of a document created by *another* application. This occurs if the user drags a document icon on top of the application icon and the application includes an 'FREF' resource for the document's file type. A well-written application should therefore include an 'FREF' resource for itself, its documents, its stationery pads, and any foreign file type (created by another application) it can handle.

An application that supports all possible file types, as ResEdit does for example, should include an 'FREF' for the wildcard file type ('****'). If the application performs special operations with folders or disk volumes, it should also include 'FREF' resources for 'fold' and 'disk', respectively, so that the user can easily pass to it from the Finder a folder or disk name to act on.

Rez source for the 'FREF' resources in the Skeleton application are shown in Listing 9-1.

Listing 9-1. Rez source for Skeleton's 'FREF' resources

```
// 'FREF' resources map local ID's to file types
resource 'FREF' (rRefAPPL, "Application") {
    'APPL', 0, ""       // FREF for our app itself
};

resource 'FREF' (rRefTEXT, "TEXT Document") {
    'TEXT', 1, ""       // FREF for our document files
};

resource 'FREF' (rRefsEXT, "Our Stationery Files") {
    'sEXT', 2, ""       // FREF for our stationery files
};

resource 'FREF' (rRefttro, "TeachText Read-Only Files") {
    'ttro', 3, ""       // FREF for TeachText files
};
```

```
01011101
00101001
01101010
00011110
01000000
...
```

▶ SKEL Signature Resources

How does the Finder associate a document with the correct application? Each application has a unique *signature* and all files have a *file type* and a *creator type*. A signature is a special resource type that the Finder uses to identify each application. A file created by an application should have its creator type set to the signature of the creating application. This allows the Finder to determine the correct application to launch in response to a request to open or print a document.

A signature resource is just a 'STR ' resource whose type is four unique characters, in this case 'SKel'. The ID of a signature resource is generally 0, but this is a conventional choice, not a requirement. Listing 9-2 shows the Rez source for the signature resource used by the Skeleton application.

Listing 9-2. Signature resource example

```
// Signature resource - used by the Finder to map
// documents to application.

type 'SKel' as 'STR ';
resource 'SKel' (0, "Our John Hancock…") {
    "Skeleton v.1.0, © Copyright 1991 Gary Little, "
    "All Rights Reserved."
};
```

Note ▶

The signature for an application must be unique to prevent the Finder from launching the wrong application. To ensure uniqueness, apply to register the application signature you want to use with Apple's Developer Technical Support group. DTS compares your request with an internal list of previously-approved signatures; it gives you the go-ahead if your requested signature has not been allocated. You should also register with DTS any unique file types that your application creates.

▶ 'BNDL' Resources

Having your icon families tied (via 'FREF' resources) to their respective
file types isn't enough to make things work smoothly. The Finder has to
be able to match documents with applications as well as determine actual
icon numbers from local icon numbers. Icons are great for permitting
visual identification by users, but are a poor way for the Finder to match
applications to documents. Instead, the Finder looks at the signature
resource within the user's document and tries to match that unique, four-
character resource to an application with the same signature (comparing
four characters is much faster than trying to compare icons).

A 'BNDL' resource contains the type and ID of the application's signature resource, a mapping of local IDs to icon family IDs, and a mapping
of local IDs to file references ('FREF' resources). Think of a 'BNDL' as the
glue that ties everything together to make it possible for a user to double-
click on an icon and have the correct application launched.

The signature's resource ID is included in a 'BNDL' in case you decide
to buck tradition and use something other than 0 as its resource ID.

The 'FREF' resources maps file types to local icon IDs, and the 'BNDL'
maps local icon IDs to the actual resource IDs for the icons within an
application. Mapping within a 'BNDL' resource occurs in both its 'ICN#'
section (where each icon family within the application is assigned a local
ID) and in its 'FREF' section (where each 'FREF' resource is assigned a
local ID). The local ID is listed first, followed by the resource's actual ID.
Foreign file types (created by other applications, folders, disks, and so on)
are not mapped into an actual icon because you don't define an icon
family for them. This prevents foreign files from looking like your application created them (and confusing the user), but still allows your application to open those files if the user drags the foreign file icon on top of
your application's icon.

The Rez source for the Skeleton application's 'BNDL' resource is shown
in Listing 9-3.

Listing 9-3. Rez source for Skeleton's 'BNDL' resource

```
resource 'BNDL' (128) {
    'SKel',                   // signature's resource type
    0,                        // signature's resource ID
    {
        'ICN#',               // mapping of local IDs to icon
                              // families
        {
```

Listing 9-3. Rez source for Skeleton's 'BNDL' resource (continued)

```
            0, rIconAPPL,     // local ID 0 = app's icon family
            1, rIconTEXT,     // local ID 1 = document's ICN#
            2, rIconsEXT,     // local ID 2 = stationery ICN#
        },
        'FREF',               // mapping of local IDs to file
                              // references

        {
        0, rRefAPPL,          // local ID 0 = app
        1, rRefTEXT,          // local ID 1 = documents
        2, rRefsEXT,          // local ID 2 = stationery
        3, rRefttro,          // local ID 3 = TeachText's
                              // Read-Only files
        }
    }
};
```

Notice that the 'BNDL' resource in Listing 9-3 indicates that there is an 'FREF' resource in our application for TeachText files, but there is no corresponding icon family. This "stray" 'FREF' tells the Finder that it should pass a TeachText document to Skeleton if the user drags such a document on top of the Skeleton application icon. All such foreign file types that an application supports should have a corresponding 'FREF' resource and be listed in the 'FREF' section of the 'BNDL' resource. Do not include icon families for foreign files.

Note ▶

Normally once the Finder processes an application's 'BNDL' resource and retrieves your application's icons, it does not process the 'BNDL' again. This can pose problems during application development because changes you make to 'BNDL', and the resources to which it refers, are ignored—you won't observe changes you make to icons, for example. You can force the Finder to reprocess your application's 'BNDL', however, by telling the system to rebuild the desktop database where it stores bundle and icon information. To do this, hold down the Command and Option keys when a disk is mounted (do this when you boot the computer to rebuild a hard disk). When the system detects this secret handshake, it asks you to verify the operation before it actually performs it.

▶ Version Information

Since applications tend to take more than one compile to create and tend to be updated periodically after release, most applications include a version number. Prior to System 7, the Finder's Get Info window was the only place a user was likely to see version information without launching an application. Under System 7, users who check *Show Version* in the Views control panel will see version information in all non-icon views (that is, when viewing by name, size, kind, date, and so on) under the Finder.

Version information is kept in resources of type 'vers'—only resource IDs 1 and 2 are used at this time. Any application lacking these 'vers' resources will have the text from its signature resource displayed in the Finder's Get Info window and will have only a dash ("-") displayed in its version field when viewed by name, size, and so on.

Rez source for the 'vers' resources for the Skeleton application is shown in Listing 9-4. Figure 9-4 indicates where the various pieces of both the 'vers' 1 and 'vers' 2 resources are displayed in the Finder's Get Info window. Figure 9-5 indicates where the 'vers' 1 version number string is shown in a non-icon view under the Finder.

Listing 9-4. Expanded Rez source for Skeleton's 'vers' resources

```
resource 'vers' (1, purgeable) {
    0x1,            // first 'digit' of version#
    0x00,           // second & third 'digits'
    final,          // release level (alpha, beta, etc)
    0x0,            // pre-release level
    verUS,          // country code
    "1.0",          // version number pstring
    "1.0, © 1991 Gary Little" // version message pstring
};

resource 'vers' (2, purgeable) {
    0x1,            // first 'digit' of version#
    0x00,           // second & third 'digits'
    final,          // release level (alpha, beta, etc.)
    0x0,            // pre-release level
    verUS,          // country code
    "1.0",          // version number pstring
    "Skeleton 1.0"  // version message pstring
};
```

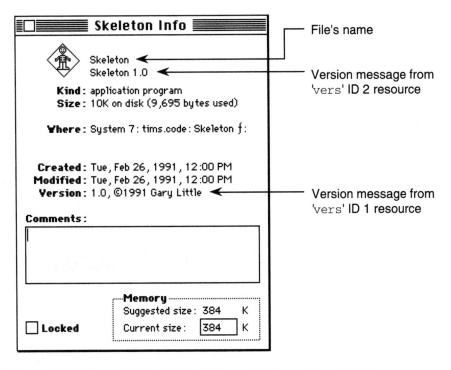

Figure 9-4. Where "Get Info" puts 'vers' ID 1 and 'vers' ID 2 information

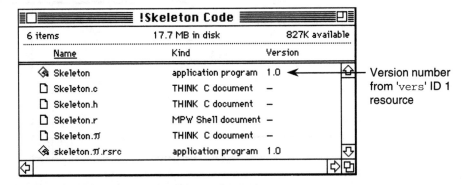

Figure 9-5. Version information in Finder folder windows

▶ Finder Help Balloons for Applications

In Chapter 8 you saw how to add help balloons to your application that will appear when the application is running. As you will see in this section, you can also define a special help balloon that appears when the application is not running. The balloon appears when the user is in the Finder with balloon help on and moves the mouse cursor over the application icon on the desktop or in a window. Such a balloon can explain what your application is or does without the user having to launch the application.

System 7 provides a default help balloon for all applications that lack a specific description, but the contents of this balloon are quite general and not particularly helpful (see Figure 9-6).

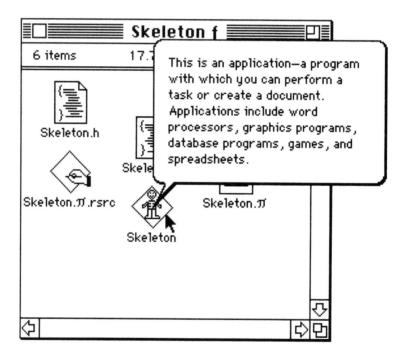

Figure 9-6. The Finder's default help balloon for an application

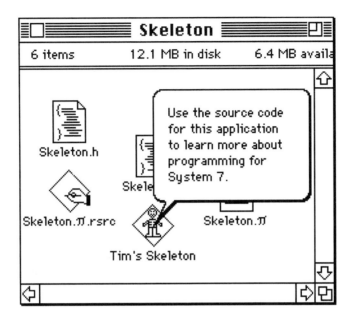

Figure 9-7. You can define a custom Finder help balloon for an application

Adding a custom balloon help resource enables the Finder to display a description of your application (see Figure 9-7). To do this, add a resource of type 'hfdr' with a resource ID of kHMHelpID to the resource fork of your application (see the Rez definition in Listing 9-5). A 'hfdr' resource can include the resource ID of a 'STR ', 'PICT', styled TextEdit string (a combination of a 'TEXT' and a 'styl' resource), or a 'STR#' (and an index). A standard Pascal string can also be imbedded directly in the 'hfdr' resource; this technique is shown in Listing 9-5. Examples of using 'STR ', 'PICT', styled TextEdit string, and 'STR#' resources for balloon messages can be found in Chapter 8.

Listing 9-5. A sample Finder help balloon resource for an application

```
// Balloon Help message for the app (when viewed by Finder)
// The resource ID must be kHMHelpID (defined in BalloonTypes.r)
// Finder help — using a pstring resource

resource 'hfdr' (kHMHelpID, "Balloon help for app's icon") {
    HelpMgrVersion,          // version of the Help Manager
    hmDefaultOptions,        // use defaults for Help Mgr resources
```

Listing 9-5. A sample Finder help balloon resource for an application (continued)

```
    0,                          // use standard Balloon Proc
    0,                          // Balloon position
    {
        HMStringItem {          // using a pstring
            "Use the source code for this application to "
            "learn more about programming for System 7."
        }
    }
};
```

▶ Leaving a Calling Card with Documents

Most applications you write will create document files of some type. As you saw at the beginning of this chapter, if you manage matters just right, the user can automatically launch your application by double-clicking on a document icon from the Finder. But what happens if a document created by your application is sent to another user who doesn't have your application? How can you tell this user to buy your application in order to view the file?

Under System 6.x, the Finder displays the rather unhelpful generic alert shown in Figure 9-8 when it can't find a document's application. You'll also see this alert under System 7 if you don't provide a helping hand to the Finder.

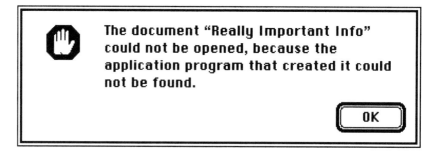

The document "Really Important Info" could not be opened, because the application program that created it could not be found.

OK

Figure 9-8. The default "application not found" dialog

How do you do that? Simple. Add either a *message string* resource or a *name string* resource ('STR ' resources with IDs of -16397 and -16396, respectively) to the resource fork of each document your application creates. When the Finder tries to open or print your document file, but can't find the application, it retrieves the string from the message string resource and displays it instead of the standard message. Figure 9-9 shows an alert defined by a message string resource.

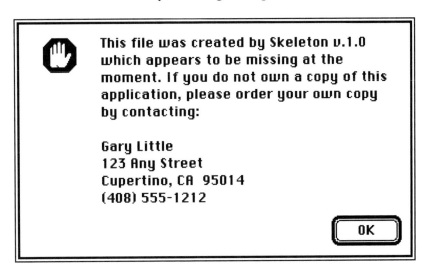

Figure 9-9. A message string resource (see Listing 9-6) added to a document enables the Finder to use your message as the text in the "application not found" dialog

If the Finder finds no message string resource in the document, it uses the contents of the name string resource instead of the phrase *program that created it* in the generic alert. Figure 9-10 shows an alert that incorporates a name string resource of "Skeleton v.1.0".

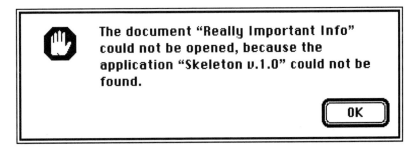

Figure 9-10. A name string resource (see Listing 9-7) in a document enables the Finder to include your application's name in the "application not found" dialog

Listing 9-6 is the Rez source for a sample message string. Listing 9-7 is the Rez source for a sample name string.

Listing 9-6. The Rez definition for a message string resource

```
// Message string resource - used by the Finder when a
// document's application can't be found.

resource 'STR ' (-16397, "Document's message") {
    "This file was created by Skeleton v.1.0 "
    "which appears to be missing at the moment."
    "If you do not own a copy of this application, "
    "please order your own copy by contacting:\n\n"
    "Gary Little\n"
    "123 Any Street\n"
    "Cupertino, CA  95014\n"
    "(408) 555-1212"
};
```

Listing 9-7. This is the Rez definition for a name string resource

```
// Name string resource - used by the Finder when
// a document's application can't be found instead of
// the standard "Application can't be found..." alert.

resource 'STR ' (-16396, "Application Not Found...") {
    "Skeleton v.1.0"
};
```

Keep name string resources short. As shown in Figure 9-10, the name string is part of a longer paragraph that appears in the alert and space is limited. So don't put your company's phone number, business hours, price list, and so on, in the name string resource! (Use a message string resource for that.) Stick with the application name, or, better yet, the application name and version number. Including the version number eliminates confusion in the event the user has an older version of your application that is not able to read new document types the newer version creates.

Note ▶	Files of type `'TEXT'` and `'PICT'` are not treated like other file types. The Finder offers to open these two types of files using TeachText if the creating application can't be found. As a result, you need not add message string and name string resources to these types of files. Figure 9-11 shows the dialog the Finder uses for a `'TEXT'` or `'PICT'` file when the application that created it is not available.

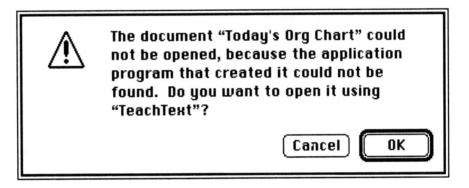

Figure 9-11. The dialog that appears when you double-click a 'TEXT' or 'PICT' file and the application that created it is not available

▶ File Comments

The Finder stores the information in `'BNDL'` resources in a *desktop database* file on any volume with a capacity of 2 Mb or more. Volumes with capacities under 2 Mb store their desktop information in the resource fork of the invisible Desktop file—as was done in earlier versions of system software.

Applications rarely need to access the information in the Finder's new desktop database, but the following five major types of information can be easily retrieved from the desktop database by applications:

- the size and parent directory of the desktop database
- the file name, parent directory ID, and creation date for the application with a given signature
- any icon type and its associated file type for a given application

- the bitmap for any member of an icon family stored in the database
- the user comments for files and volumes seen when using the Finder Get Info command

This section focuses on three routines: **PBDTGetPath**, **PBDTGetComment**, and **PBDTSetComment**. For complete information on how to use and manipulate the desktop database, refer to the Finder Interface chapter of *Inside Macintosh*, Volume VI.

▶ Reading Comments

Listing 9-8 shows the source code for a ReadComment routine you can call to retrieve and display the user comment for a specific file from the desktop database. The comment can be up to 200 characters long. This routine uses the **PBDTGetPath** routine to obtain the desktop database's reference number, which must be passed to **PBDTGetComment** in order to retrieve the actual comment.

Listing 9-8. Reading user comments from the desktop database

```
/* Retrieve the comment that's stored in the desktop database for */
/* the user-selected file.*/

void ReadComment( void )
{
    StandardFileReply  reply;
    OSErr        myError;
    DTPBRec      theDTRecord;
    char         theComment[201] = "Room for 200 chars & length byte";

    StandardGetFile( 0L, -1, 0L, &reply );

    if ( reply.sfGood ) {
        theDTRecord.ioCompletion = 0L;
        theDTRecord.ioNamePtr = 0L;
        theDTRecord.ioVRefNum = reply.sfFile.vRefNum;

        myError = PBDTGetPath( &theDTRecord );
        if (myError == noErr) {
            theDTRecord.ioNamePtr = reply.sfFile.name;
            theDTRecord.ioDirID = reply.sfFile.parID;

            /* leave room for length byte at the beginning */
            theDTRecord.ioDTBuffer = theComment + 1;

            myError = PBDTGetComment( &theDTRecord, false );
```

Listing 9-8. Reading user comments from the desktop database (continued)

```
            if (myError == noErr) {
                /* put in length byte */
                theComment[0] = theDTRecord.ioDTActCount;
                /* draw the string in the message window */
                PrintString( theComment );
            }
        }
    }
}
```

The function prototype for **PBDTGetPath** is as follows:

```
pascal OSErr PBDTGetPath( DTPBPtr paramBlock );
```

The parameter you pass to **PBDTGetPath** is a pointer to a DTPBRec record which is used to provide data to, and return results from, this routine. There are 25 parameters in DTPBRec, but you only need to be concerned about a few of them for retrieving and setting comments. The parameters you will be most interested in for the **PBDTGetPath** routine are as follows:

ioNamePtr—A pointer to the name of the volume whose desktop database reference number you're trying to determine. If this field is 0L, **PBDTGetPath** identifies the volume by the ioVRefNum.

ioVRefNum—Contains the reference number for the volume containing the file whose comment you want to obtain or set. The desktop database for this volume contains the comment for the file.

ioDTRefNum—Contains the desktop database reference number. You need this reference number to use most other desktop database routines.

The function prototype for **PBDTGetComment** is the following:

```
pascal OSErr PBDTGetComment( DTPBPtr paramBlock,
                             Boolean async );
```

The Boolean tells the system whether this call is to be made synchronously (false) or asynchronously (true). When called synchronously, the routine does not return until it is finished. When called asynchronously,

PBDTGetComment returns immediately, retrieves the comments while the calling application continues running, then calls a completion routine (supplied as a pointer in the `ioCompletion` field of the parameter block) when it's done.

`paramBlock` is a pointer to the same `DTPBRec` used by **PBDTGetPath**. The parameters in that record of interest to the **PBDTGetComment** routine are the following:

`ioNamePtr`—A pointer to the name of the file whose comment you are trying to retrieve.

`ioVRefNum`—The reference number for the volume on which the file resides.

`ioCompletion`—Contains a pointer the completion routine if you call **PBDTGetComment** asynchronously. For synchronous calls (the usual case), set this field to `0L`.

`ioDirID`—Contains the directory ID for the folder containing the file whose comment in which you are seeking.

`ioDTBuffer`—A pointer to a buffer that will hold the comment after the call to **PBDGetComment**; the buffer must be 200 characters long since that's the maximum size for a comment. (When using **PBDSetComment**, you store the comment in this buffer before making the call.)

`ioDTActCount`—The length of the comment, in bytes.

`ioDTRefNum`—The desktop database reference number for the volume containing the file in which you are interested.

You can call the `ReadComment` routine from the `DoTest` procedure in the Skeleton program, so that you can try it out by selecting the Test item in the Special menu. To simplify the example, **StandardGetFile** is called to select the file whose comment you want to retrieve. In an actual application, the file would already be known and this step could be eliminated.

▶ Saving Comments

Adding a comment to a file is almost as easy as reading the comment— see the sample code for the `SaveComment` routine in Listing 9-9. Such a comment would be visible at the Finder level (so the user could see it without opening the file). In addition, the application itself could display the comment at an appropriate time—perhaps when the file is being loaded. Remember that the comment will be lost if the user rebuilds the desktop database, so don't include essential information in the comment unless you are able to recreate it.

Listing 9-9. Source for recording a file's comment in the desktop database

```
/* Set the comment that's stored in the desktop database for */
/* the user-selected file.*/

void SaveComment( void ) {
    StandardFileReply    reply;
    OSErr                myError;
    DTPBRec    theDTRecord;
    char theComment[201] = "This is a demand letter template.";

    StandardGetFile( 0L, -1, 0L, &reply );

    if ( reply.sfGood ) {

        theDTRecord.ioCompletion = 0L;
        theDTRecord.ioNamePtr = 0L;
        theDTRecord.ioVRefNum = reply.sfFile.vRefNum;

        myError = PBDTGetPath( &theDTRecord );
        if (myError == noErr) {
            theDTRecord.ioNamePtr = reply.sfFile.name;
            theDTRecord.ioDirID = reply.sfFile.parID;
            theDTRecord.ioDTReqCount = 33; /* # of chars */
            theDTRecord.ioDTBuffer = theComment;

            myError = PBDTSetComment( &theDTRecord, false );
        }
    }
}
```

The function prototype for the **PBDTSetComment** routine used in Listing 9-9 is as follows:

```
pascal OSErr PBDTSetComment( DTPBPtr paramBlock,
                             Boolean async );
```

The two input parameters have the same meanings as they do in the **PBDTGetComment** routine.

Figure 9-12 shows what a custom save file dialog that allows the user to specify a file comment might look like. See Chapter 2 for information on how you can create such a custom dialog.

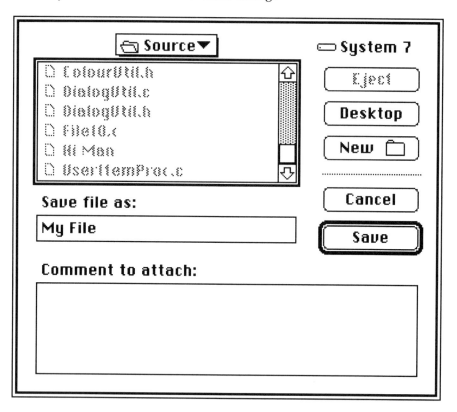

Figure 9-12. Custom Save File Dialog for attaching user comment to files

▶ Summary

In this chapter, we told you about several new System 7 features that improve the interaction between the Finder and your application and its documents, demonstrated what you have to do to take advantage of these new features, and presented several examples along the way. By following the tips and techniques discussed in this chapter, your application and its documents will look their best and fit seamlessly with the System 7 Finder.

Appendix A

A Rez Primer

Each of the two basic techniques for creating Macintosh resources has its own set of advantages and disadvantages.

The first technique is to use a tool, such as ResEdit or Resorcerer, that allows resources to be created and edited visually by direct manipulation. This technique is fine for resources that have a visual component, but cannot be used to create a source document that describes precisely how to recreate the resources.

The second technique is to define resources in a readable source-code form that can be compiled to create the actual resources. This technique can be awkward or inappropriate for defining complex images, such as icons and pictures, but it does provide an exact description of the resources. You can then compile this description to automatically recreate the resources when you need them.

The standard resource description language for the Macintosh is called Rez. Under Macintosh Programmer's Workshop (MPW), Rez is also the name of the tool for converting text descriptions of resources into actual resources, so the name is often used to refer to the *resource compiler*. Under THINK C and THINK Pascal, this tool is called SARez (for *standalone Rez*) and runs as a separate application. The resource examples in this book are all presented as lines of Rez source code so that you can easily reproduce them.

Key Point ▶

Creating certain resources with a visual component—such as alerts, icons, and menus—by typing in text descriptions is often cumbersome, so you may prefer to create them with ResEdit. You can later decompile such a resource into Rez source code using the resource decompiler called DeRez (under MPW) or SADeRez (under THINK). Once you get used to Rez, however, you will probably define most of your resources with it.

Some of the important features of Rez are discussed in this appendix. For a complete description, see the reference manuals that come with THINK C (or THINK Pascal or Macintosh Programmer's Workshop).

▶ Rez Templates

Unlike traditional compilers, Rez creates only data structures. It does not generate any machine-executable code. The syntax for Rez is similar to that of a typical C compiler. If you can read C code, you can read Rez code as well.

Templates for standard resource types are available in the interface folder for SARez. You use statements like `#include "Types.r"` to refer Rez to standard resource templates when compiling. Templates are available in other files for resources used by the Help Manager (BalloonTypes.r), Communications Toolbox (CTBTypes.r), the Installer (InstallerTypes.r), and the System (SysTypes.r).

Take a few minutes to open `Types.r` and browse through it to get a feel for what Rez templates look like. Understanding how a template is constructed makes it easier to create a resource from that template.

Listing A-1. Template for a 'STR ' resource

```
type 'STR ' {
        pstring;                /* pascal string */
};
```

Listing A-1 shows the template from `Types.r` that defines the structure of a 'STR ' resource (a simple string resource). The keyword `type` tells Rez that the information following this keyword defines a template of a specific type—in this case, 'STR '. The left brace starts the definition of this resource type and the right brace closes it. The trailing semicolon notifies Rez that the type definition is complete.

The `pstring` between the braces is the data type for the only data element in this resource—a Pascal string (a string of characters preceded by a length byte). The Rez language supports several other data types, including `integer`, `longint`, `boolean`, `point`, `rect`, and `cstring`.

▶ Rez Comments

Programming languages always allow comments in source files, and Rez is no different. In this respect Rez is more like C++ than C, since it supports both the `//` and `/* */` style comments. A pair of slashes (`//`) means Rez treats the rest of that line, and only that line, as a comment. A slash followed immediately by an asterisk (`/*`) starts the other style of comment. To end such a comment, Rez expects an asterisk followed by a slash (`*/`). This second form can be as long as you like and can span multiple lines. Where space is critical for formatting in the various listings throughout this book, the shorter double-slash style is used.

▶ Rez Resource Definitions

You specify resources in Rez using a template as a guide, since templates simplify working with Rez and provide a convenient type-checking mechanism. The description for each resource starts with the keyword `resource`, followed by the resource type (which tells Rez which template to use), and, in parentheses, the resource ID, resource name, and attributes for that resource. The resource name and attributes are optional, but the type and ID are mandatory. This information is followed by an opening brace (marking the beginning of the resource's contents), the contents of the resource, and a closing brace followed by a semicolon. Listing A-2 shows a simple resource definition.

Listing A-2. Rez source for a `STR ` resource

```
resource 'STR ' (131, "TAB help", purgeable) {
    "Rent this space."
};
```

The resource defined in Listing A-2, after compilation with SARez or Rez, will be of type `'STR '`, have an ID of 131, carry the name TAB help, and have its purgeable attribute set. This is a simple string resource, and the string it represents is Rent this space.

Like C, Rez supports the `#define` command for associating symbolic names with constants—making Rez sources much easier to read. Resources that include the IDs of other resources in them (such as menu bar resources), are harder to read and maintain if the IDs inside the resource definition are hard-coded. Using a well-named constant simplifies life considerably. Using a constant for the ID of the ʻSTR ʻ resource presented in Listing A-2, for example, makes it easier to guess how the application uses the string (see Listing A-3).

Listing A-3. Rez source for a ʻSTR ʻ resource, using a symbolic constant

```
#define rTabStopHelpMessage      131
resource 'STR ' (rTabStopHelpMessage, "TAB help", purgeable) {
   "Rent this space."
};
```

Some resource templates contain multiple items. A comma separates each item within the text describing the resource. A simple example is a ʻSTR#ʼ resource (a list of strings). Listing A-4 shows the Rez source for a ʻSTR#ʼ resource containing three strings; each string is separated by a comma.

Listing A-4. Rez source for a ʻSTR#ʼ resource with three strings

```
#define rDynamicBalloonContents 131
resource 'STR#' (rDynamicBalloonContents, "dynamic help", purgeable) {
   {
      "Tune in tomorrow to find out what this does.",   // string 1
      "Slide this dohickey to adjust the florple.",     // string 2
      "Click this button to activate "                  // string 3
        "the intercerebral telelink.",    // still string 3
   }
};
```

Key Point ▶

If the commas had been left out, Rez would have considered all of the text to be one long string. This feature makes it easier to manually format long strings—just close the quotes on the current line and reopen them on the next line and do not terminate the first line with a comma. The third string in Listing A-4 takes advantage of this feature since that string is too long to fit cleanly on one line. Formatting is optional in Rez, but like any language it's much easier to read well-formatted code.

▶ Symbolic Constants

Not all constants are created using #define; some templates have imbedded constants that have meaning only within that resource's template. Balloon Help resources (see Chapter 8) are a complex example of this. A simpler example is shown in Listing A-5, where development, alpha, beta, final, and release are defined as symbolic constants for the value of the third byte of a 'vers' resource. Instead of specifying the hex number when creating a resource of this type, you can use the constants (which makes our sources much easier to read and maintain). Listing A-6 presents a sample resource created using the template from Listing A-5 and shows how the constants are used when creating a resource from a template.

Listing A-5. Template for a 'vers' resource

```
type 'vers' {
     hex byte;                            /* Major revision in BCD*/
     hex byte;                            /* Minor revision in BCD*/
     hex byte    development = 0x20,  /* Release stage */
                 alpha = 0x40,
                 beta = 0x60,
                 final = 0x80, /* or */ release = 0x80;
     hex byte;                            /* Non-final release # */
     integer     Region;              /* Region code */
     pstring;                         /* Short version number */
     pstring;                         /* Long version number */
};
```

Listing A-6. Resource created using 'vers' template from Listing A-5

```
resource 'vers' (1, purgeable) {
     0x1,                              /* Major revision in BCD*/
     0x00,                             /* Minor revision in BCD*/
     beta,                             /* Release stage */
     0x9,                              /* Non-final release # */
     verUS,                            /* Region code */
     "v.1.0B9",                        /* Short version number */
     "v.1.0B9, © 1991 Gary Little"     /* Long version number */
};
```

▶ Resource Type Coercion

Some custom resource types you may define use the same internal representation as a standard resource type. For example, signature resources are identical to 'STR ' resources in that they are made up of a single Pascal string. Rather than create a custom template for your signature resource, you can just tell Rez to treat your signature resource as though it were a 'STR ' resource. Do this by specifying the `type` keyword, followed by your custom resource type ('SKel' in this case), the word *as*, and the type it should be treated like ('STR ' in this case). Listing A-7 shows you how to do this.

Listing A-7. Example of Rez type substitution

```
// treat this resource as though it were of type 'STR '
type 'SKel' as 'STR ';
resource 'SKel' (0, "App's Signature") {
    "Skeleton, v.1.0, © Copyright 1991 Gary Little"
```

Appendix B

The 'SIZE' Resource

For versions of the Macintosh operating system prior to System 7, MultiFinder is an optional desktop environment. The user can also choose to use Finder, which allows only one application to run at a time. Under System 7, however, MultiFinder is always present, although it's now referred to as Finder.

Applications that are MultiFinder-aware need to communicate their level of awareness to MultiFinder (or the System 7 Finder) through a special resource, known as a 'SIZE' resource, attached to the application itself. The System 7 Finder inspects the 'SIZE' resource to determine the level of awareness; it also determines the application's ability to deal with certain new System 7 features, such as stationery pad documents and high-level events.

A 'SIZE' resource contains one flag word (16 single-bit flags) and two long words containing Finder partition size information; the ID of the original 'SIZE' resource is always -1. If the user changes the settings of the Preferred Partition field or the localAndRemoteHLEvents flag from the Finder, a 'SIZE' (ID 0) resource is created which the system refers to instead.

The structure of a 'SIZE' resource is shown in Listing B-1 as a Rez template. The flag settings for the most common types of System 7 applications are highlighted in boldface.

Listing B-1. The Rez template for a 'SIZE' resource. The most important flags are in bold.

```
type 'SIZE' {
    boolean     reserved;                   // so don't use it!
    boolean     ignoreSuspendResumeEvents,// app can suspend and resume
                acceptSuspendResumeEvents;
    boolean     reserved;                   // private, keep out
    boolean     cannotBackground,           // does something if in background
                canBackground;
    boolean     needsActivateOnFGSwitch,    // app will activate own stuff
                doesActivateOnFGSwitch;
    boolean     backgroundAndForeground,    // not a background-only application
                onlyBackground;
    boolean     dontGetFrontClicks,         // ignore click that activates
                getFrontClicks;
    boolean     ignoreAppDiedEvents,        // don't say if sublaunched app died
                acceptAppDiedEvents;
/* the next five bits are new for System 7 */
    boolean     not32BitCompatible,         // copes with 32-bit addressing
                is32BitCompatible;
    boolean     notHighLevelEventAware,     // sends/accepts high level events
                isHighLevelEventAware;
    boolean     onlyLocalHLEvents,          // sends/accepts events over network
                localAndRemoteHLEvents;
    boolean     notStationeryAware,         // handles stationery pads properly
                isStationeryAware;
    boolean     dontUseTextEditServices,    // uses TextEdit inline text stuff
                useTextEditServices;
/* the last three bits are reserved */
    boolean     reserved;                   // no trespassing
    boolean     reserved;                   // off limits
    boolean     reserved;                   // yeah, what he said
/* preferred and minimum memory partition settings */
    unsigned longint;                       // preferred partition size
    unsigned longint;                       // minimum partition size
};
```

The purpose of each entry in the 'SIZE' resource is as follows:

acceptSuspendResumeEvents—Indicates that the application knows how to react properly to suspend and resume events. If you write System 7 applications properly, you should always set this flag to acceptSuspendResumeEvents. See Chapter 3 for more information on suspend and resume events.

canBackground—Indicates that the application is able to perform some activities in the background. To avoid stealing processor time need-lessly, set this flag to canBackground only if your application has something useful to do in the background; otherwise, set it to cannotBackground. See Chapter 3 for a discussion of background processing under the System 7 Finder.

doesActivateOnFGSwitch—Indicates that the application correctly handles switches into or out of the foreground. Applications with this flag set to doesActivateOnFGSwitch should treat a suspend event as a deactivate event (by hiding scroll bars, dimming controls, and so on) and should treat a resume event as an activate event. This flag should be set to doesActivateOnFGSwitch for all well-written System 7 applications.

backgroundAndForeground—Indicates that the application, like most applications, can run in the background or foreground. If your application operates only in the background (and thus doesn't directly interact with the user), set this flag to onlyBackground.

dontGetFrontClicks—Tells the operating system not to let the application see the click used to bring a background application to the foreground. This flag is usually set to dontGetFrontClicks (so the click is absorbed by the operating system) to prevent a user's click from also performing an action within the application as it is brought to the foreground. If you want clicks to be passed through, as the Finder does, for example, set this flag to getFrontClicks.

ignoreAppDiedEvents—Set by most applications. However, if your application launches other applications and wants to be notified via an Apple event when the other application crashes or quits, set this flag to acceptAppDiedEvents.

is32BitCompatible—Indicates that the application uses 32-bit addressing and is otherwise *32-bit clean*. Ensure that all applications you write are 32-bit clean by not directly manipulating flag bits that are stored in the upper 8 bits of addresses when the 24-bit Memory Manager is in effect. If System 7 is running with the 32-bit Memory Manager active and the user tries to launch an application that has this flag set to not32BitCompatible, the Finder displays a warning dialog.

isHighLevelEventAware—Indicates that the application is able to handle high-level events it may receive when calling **WaitNextEvent**. All System 7-specific applications should be able to handle high-level events, so they will set this flag to isHighLevelEventAware.

localAndRemoteHLEvents—Indicates that the application is willing to accept high level events that originate from another computer on the network. Users can toggle this flag using the Sharing... command in the Finder's File menu if the isHighLevelEventAware flag is set and

Program Linking is turned on (use the Sharing Setup control panel to turn Program Linking on and off). Figure B-1 shows the Finder window that gives users direct control over this flag. Toggling this flag via the Sharing window creates a 'SIZE' resource with an ID of 0. The Finder uses the settings in this 'SIZE' resource instead of the 'SIZE'(ID -1) resource settings, which contains the original "factory" settings.

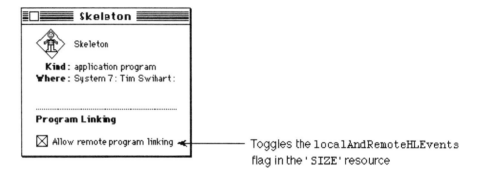

Figure B-1. The Finder's Sharing... window allows users to toggle the state of the localAndRemoteHLEvents flag

isStationeryAware—Indicates that the application understands the concept of a stationery pad file. If this flag is set to notStationeryAware and the user double-clicks on a stationery pad file, the Finder presents a dialog box advising that a copy of the file will be made and passed to the application instead. Proper handling of stationery pad files is covered in Chapter 2.

useTextEditServices—Indicates that the application uses TextEdit's inline text services. The inline text services TextEdit provides allow non-Roman script system users to enter two-byte characters directly into a TextEdit field instead of into a special conversion window. See *Inside Macintosh,*Volume VI, for more information on TextEdit's inline text services.

Preferred Partition—The first unsigned longint in a 'SIZE' resource, known as either the *preferred partition size* or the *current size*; tells the Finder how much memory the application would like to have when it is launched. The user can change this value by entering a new value in the *Current Size* field of the Finder's Get Info window for the application. The Finder stores the new value in the 'SIZE' (ID 0) resource, which overrides the value stored in the 'SIZE' (ID -1) resource.

Minimum Partition—The second unsigned longint, known as the *minimum partition size* or the *suggested size*; tells the Finder the minimum amount of memory in which the application is willing to run. If the Finder is unable to allocate this much memory, it will not launch the application.

Appendix C
Support for Macintosh
Programmers

Important to the success of any Macintosh development project are support and service organizations that can help solve your programming problems, teach you new programming techniques, or keep you informed on developments of interest to programmers. This appendix provides you with information on many such organizations that specialize in Macintosh issues.

▶ Services for Developers from Apple

For complete information on the various programs that Apple offers to Macintosh developers, contact Apple's developer hotline at:

Apple Computer, Inc.
20525 Mariani Avenue, MS: 75-2C
Cupertino, CA 94014
Attn: Developer Hotline
Telephone: 408/974-4897
AppleLink: DEVHOTLINE

▶ Developer Associations

BMUG—BMUG is a large, national user group that caters to Macintosh users and programmers. It publishes a variety of useful material, including an excellent (and very large) newsletter, public-domain software on CD-ROM, and books. For membership information, contact:

> BMUG
> 1442A Walnut Street, #62
> Berkeley, CA 94704
> Telephone: 415/849-9114

MacApp Developers Association—The MacApp Developers Association (MADA) is for developers interested in using Apple's object-oriented application framework, MacApp. MADA publishes an excellent technical journal, *FrameWorks*, and holds an annual developers' conference. For membership information, contact:

> MacApp Developers Association
> P.O. Box 23
> Everett, WA 98206
> Telephone: 206/252-6946
> AppleLink: MADA

MacTechGroup of the Boston Computer Society—The Boston Computer Society (BCS) is another large, national user group that supports Macintosh developers through its MacTechGroup special interest group. The MacTechGroup has a large library of public-domain material for programmers and publishes a newsletter. For membership information, contact:

> The Boston Computer Society
> 48 Grove Street
> Somerville, MA 02144
> Telephone: 617/625-7080

SPLAsh—SPLAsh is an association for programmers who use Symantec's THINK C and THINK Pascal languages. For more information, contact:

SPLAsh
1678 Shattuck Avenue, #302
Berkeley, CA 94709
Telephone: 415/527-0122
AppleLink: SPLASH

▶ Training Courses

The following organizations offer classroom-style technical training courses for Macintosh developers:

Apple Computer, Inc.
20525 Mariani Avenue, MS: 75-6U
Cupertino, CA 95014-6299
Attn: Developer University
Telephone: 408/974-6215
AppleLink: DEVUNIV

Bear River Institute, Inc.
P.O. Box 1900
Berkeley, CA 94701
Telephone: 415/644-0555
AppleLink: D1939

▶ Electronic Information Services

An excellent source of support for Macintosh developers are national electronic information services, most of which have specific forums for discussing Macintosh development issues. The three most popular are America Online, CompuServe, and GEnie:

America Online—America Online has a lot of material useful to Macintosh programmers. To get on to America Online, you need to buy a starter kit from any convenient source. The starter kit includes the software you need to run to access America Online; you can't access it from a general-purpose communications program. Call 800/227-6364 for more information about America Online.

CompuServe—CompuServe's forum for Macintosh developers is called MACDEV. To join CompuServe, buy a starter kit at your favorite computer store and follow the instructions that come with it. You can call 800/848-3199 for more information. Once you've logged on to CompuServe, you can go to MACDEV by typing GO MACDEV (followed by Return) at the system prompt.

GEnie—GEnie's forum for Macintosh developers is called MACPRO. To join GEnie, place a modem call to 800/638-8369 at 300, 1200, or 2400 baud (half duplex). (For voice information, call 800/638-9636.) When you connect, type HHH and wait for the U#= prompt; when you see it, type XTX99496,GENIE followed by Return and GEnie will guide you through the rest of the sign-up process. Once you're a member of GEnie, you can access MACPRO by typing MACPRO at the prompt for the opening menu on the system.

▶ Acquiring Apple Development Tools

Most of Apple's development tools are available only by mail order from Apple's Apple Programmers and Developers Association (APDA) group. APDA also carries a great number of popular tools from third-party vendors. For information, contact:

APDA
Apple Computer, Inc.
20525 Mariani Avenue, MS: 33-G
Cupertino, CA 95014-6299
Telephone: 800/282-2732 (U.S.A.)
Telephone: 800/637-0029 (Canada)
Telephone: 408/562-3910 (international)
AppleLink: APDA

Appendix D

Bibliography for Macintosh Programmers

This appendix contains lists of useful books and magazines for Macintosh programmers.

► Encyclopedic References

Apple Computer, Inc. *Designing Cards and Drivers for the Macintosh Family, Second Edition*. Reading, Mass.: Addison-Wesley, 1990. This book explains how to write drivers and firmware for a peripheral device attached to a Macintosh through a processor direct slot or a NuBus slot.

Apple Computer, Inc. *Guide to the Macintosh Family Hardware, Second Edition*. Reading, Mass.: Addison-Wesley, 1990. This book contains comprehensive information on all Macintosh computers up to the Macintosh IIfx. (Information on each model introduced since then is generally available from the Apple Programmers and Developers Association.)

Apple Computer, Inc. *Inside Macintosh*, Volumes I, II, and III. Reading, Mass.: Addison-Wesley, 1985. *Inside Macintosh* is the definitive reference to the Macintosh toolbox and Macintosh system software. You cannot survive without it if you are writing software for the Macintosh.

Apple Computer, Inc. *Inside Macintosh*, Volume IV. Reading, Mass.: Addison-Wesley, 1986. This volume covers extensions made to the Macintosh toolbox to support the Macintosh Plus.

Apple Computer, Inc. *Inside Macintosh*, Volume V. Reading, Mass.: Addison-Wesley, 1988. This volume covers extensions made to the Macintosh toolbox to support the Macintosh SE and Macintosh II computers.

Apple Computer, Inc. *Inside Macintosh*, Volume VI. Reading, Mass.: Addison-Wesley, 1991. This volume is a comprehensive reference to programming for System 7.

Apple Computer, Inc. *Inside the Macintosh Communications Toolbox*. Reading, Mass.: Addison-Wesley, 1991. This book is the definitive reference to System 7's Communications Toolbox.

▶ Tutorials

Chernicoff, Stephen. *Macintosh Revealed, Volume One: Unlocking the Toolbox, Second Edition*. Indianapolis: Hayden, 1988. This great book deserves to be in every programmer's library. It covers the most important toolbox concepts and explains them in understandable terms.

Chernicoff, Stephen. *Macintosh Revealed, Volume Two: Programming With the Toolbox, Second Edition*. Indianapolis: Hayden, 1987. This book is a tutorial on some of the most common toolbox managers on the Macintosh.

Huxham, Fred A.; Burnard, David; and Takatsuka, Jim. *Using the Macintosh Toolbox With C, Second Edition*. Alameda, Calif.: Sybex, 1989. This book shows how to use the C programming language to access many of the most common Macintosh toolbox routines.

Mark, Dave, and Reed, Cartwright. *Macintosh C Programming Primer, Volume I: Inside the Toolbox Using THINK C*. Reading, Mass.: Addison-Wesley, 1989. This is an excellent introduction to toolbox programming. Examples are given in the THINK C language.

Mark, Dave, and Reed, Cartwright. *Macintosh Pascal Programming Primer, Volume I: Inside the Toolbox Using THINK Pascal*. Reading, Mass.: Addison-Wesley, 1990. This book is the THINK Pascal adaptation of the previous book.

Mark, Dave. *Macintosh C Programming Primer, Volume II: Mastering the Toolbox Using THINK C*. Reading, Mass.: Addison-Wesley, 1990. This book maintains the spirit of Volume I and explains how to use more toolbox managers, notably Color QuickDraw and TextEdit. It also contains an introduction to object-oriented programming.

▶ Debugging and Resource Editing

Alley, Peter, and Strange, Carolyn. *ResEdit Complete*. Reading, Mass.: Addison-Wesley, 1991. This book is chock full of all sorts of interesting information on how to use ResEdit effectively. It comes with the ResEdit software.

Apple Computer, Inc. *MacsBug Reference and Debugging Guide*. Reading, Mass.: Addison-Wesley, 1991. This is Apple's official reference for the MacsBug debugger. It also contains a great deal of useful information on how to debug Macintosh applications. Editions of the book are available with and without the MacsBug software.

Apple Computer, Inc. *ResEdit Reference for ResEdit version 2.1*. Reading, Mass.: Addison-Wesley, 1991. This is Apple's official reference for the ResEdit resource editor. Editions of the book are available with and without the ResEdit software.

Knaster, Scott. *How to Write Macintosh Software*. Indianapolis: Hayden, 1988. This book is an invaluable source of debugging information for Macintosh programmers. Get it if you really want to know what's going on underneath the hood of the Macintosh.

Knaster, Scott. *Macintosh Programming Secrets*. Reading, Mass.: Addison-Wesley, 1988. This follow-up to *How to Write Macintosh Software* is not quite as generally useful, but it contains all sorts of interesting information about the inner workings of various toolbox managers.

▶ Advanced Programming

Chernicoff, Stephen. *Macintosh Revealed, Volume Four: Expanding the Toolbox*. Indianapolis: Hayden, 1990. This latest volume in the *Macintosh Revealed* series covers such topics as MultiFinder, programming in color, and styled TextEdit.

Chernicoff, Stephen. *Macintosh Revealed, Volume Three: Mastering the Toolbox*. Indianapolis: Hayden, 1989. This book covers toolbox customization techniques, device drivers, the Print Manager, the Sound Manager, and how to write desk accessories.

▶ Specific Languages and Environments

Andrews, Mark. *Programmer's Guide to MPW, Volume I*. Reading, Mass.: Addison-Wesley, 1991. This book is indispensable if you're programming in the Macintosh Programmer's Workshop environment. It provides a great deal of tutorial material that you won't find in Apple's MPW documentation.

Weston, Dan. *Elements of C++ Macintosh Programming*. Reading, Mass.: Addison-Wesley, 1990. This is currently the only book that teaches the C++ programming language from the point of view of a Macintosh programmer.

Wilson, Dave; Rosenstein, Larry; and Shafer, Dan. *Programming with MacApp*. Reading, Mass.: Addison-Wesley, 1990. MacApp is Apple's object-oriented application framework. This book carefully explains how to write applications with MacApp and provides examples in the MPW Object Pascal language.

_____ . C++ *Programming with MacApp*. Reading, Mass.: Addison-Wesley, 1990. This book is similar to the previous book except that the programming examples are in the MPW C++ language.

▶ Magazines

develop, Apple Computer, Inc., 20525 Mariani Avenue, MS: 33-G, Cupertino, CA 95014 (telephone: 408/282-2732). This journal for programmers is published by Apple, and comes out four times per year.

MacTutor, 1250 North Lakeview, #0, Anaheim, CA 92807 (telephone: 714/777-1255). *MacTutor* has been an invaluable monthly source of Macintosh programming material since 1984. The *MacTutor* people also sell *Best of MacTutor* books which are collections of articles that have appeared in back issues of *MacTutor*.

Index

Titles in the Macintosh Inside Out Series

▶ **Extending the Macintosh® Toolbox**
Programming Menus, Windows, Dialogs, and More
John C. May and Judy B. Whittle
A complete guide to programming the Macintosh interface.
352 pages, $24.95, paperback, order #57722

▶ **Programming QuickDraw™**
Includes Color QuickDraw and 32-Bit QuickDraw
David A. Surovell, Fred M. Hall, and Konstantin Othmer
The first in-depth reference to the Macintosh graphics system.
352 pages, $24.95, paperback, order #57019

▶ **Programming for System 7**
Gary Little and Tim Swihart
A complete programmer's handbook to the newest version of the Macintosh system software.
400 pages, $26.95, paperback, order #56770

▶ **Programming with AppleTalk®**
Michael Peirce
An accessible guide to creating applications that run with AppleTalk.
352 pages, $24.95, paperback, order #57780

▶ **The A/UX® 2.0 Handbook**
Jan L. Harrington
A complete and up-to-date introduction to UNIX on the Macintosh.
448 pages, $26.95, paperback, order #56784

▶ **System 7 Revealed**
Anthony Meadow
A first look inside the important new Macintosh system software from Apple.
368 pages, $22.95, paperback, order #55040

▶ **ResEdit™ Complete**
Peter Alley and Carolyn Strange
Contains the popular ResEdit software and complete information on how to use it.
576 pages, $29.95, book/disk, order #55075

▶ **The Complete Book of HyperTalk® 2**
Dan Shafer
Practical guide to HyperTalk 2.0 commands, operators, and functions.
480 pages, $24.95, paperback, order #57082

▶ **Programming the LaserWriter®**
David A. Holzgang
Now Macintosh programmers can unlock the full power of the LaserWriter.
480 pages, $24.95, paperback, order #57068

▶ **Debugging Macintosh® Software with MacsBug**
Includes MacsBug 6.2
Konstantin Othmer and Jim Straus
Everything a programmer needs to start debugging Macintosh software.
576 pages, $34.95, book/disk, order #57049

▶ **Developing Object-Oriented Software for the Macintosh®**
Analysis, Design, and Programming
Neal Goldstein and Jeff Alger
An in-depth look at object-oriented programming on the Macintosh.
352 pages, $24.95, paperback, order #57065

▶ **Writing Localizable Software for the Macintosh®**
Daniel R. Carter
A step-by-step guide which opens up international markets to Macintosh software developers.
352 pages, $24.95, paperback, order #57013

▶ **Programmer's Guide to MPW®, Volume I**
Exploring the Macintosh® Programmer's Workshop
Mark Andrews
Essential guide and reference to the standard Macintosh software development system, MPW.
608 pages, $26.95, paperback, order #57011

▶ **Elements of C++ Macintosh® Programming**
Dan Weston
Teaches the basic elements of C++ programming, concentrating on object-oriented style and syntax.
512 pages, $22.95, paperback, order #55025

▶ **Programming with MacApp®**
David A. Wilson, Larry S. Rosenstein, and Dan Shafer
Hands-on tutorial on everything you need to know about MacApp.
576 pages, $24.95, paperback, order #09784
576 pages, $34.95, book/disk, order #55062

▶ **C++ Programming with MacApp®**
David A. Wilson, Larry S. Rosenstein, and Dan Shafer
Learn the secrets to unlocking the power of MacApp and C++.
624 pages, $24.95, paperback, order #57020
624 pages, $34.95, book/disk, order #57021

Order Number	Quantity	Price	Total
————	———	——	———
————	———	——	———
————	———	——	———
————	———	——	———

Name _____

Address _____

_____

City/State/Zip _____

Signature (required)_____

___Visa   ___MasterCard   ___AmEx

Account # _____ Exp. Date _____

TOTAL ORDER ———

Shipping and state sales tax will be added automatically.

Credit card orders only please.

Offer good in USA only. Prices and availability subject to change without notice.

Addison-Wesley Publishing Company
Order Department
Route 128
Reading, MA 01867
To order by phone, call (617) 944-3700

Programming for System 7 *The Disk*

All the programs and routines listed in this book are available on disk, in source code form, directly from the authors. The disk also includes several Communications Toolbox tools that have been licensed for redistribution from Apple Computer, Inc.

To order the disk, simply clip or photocopy this entire page and complete the coupon below. Enclose a check or money order for $20.00 in U.S. funds made payable to Gary Little. (California residents add applicable state sales tax.)

Mail to:

Gary Little
3304 Plateau Drive
Belmont, CA 94002

— —

Please send me a copy of the *Programming for System 7* disk. I am enclosing the amount of $20.00 in U.S. funds, plus applicable California state sales tax.

Your Name:

_____

Address:

_____

City: _____ State: _____ Zip Code: _____

Country: _____